Investing in Gold & Silver

by Paul Mladjenovic

A Wiley Brand

Investing in Gold & Silver For Dummies®

Contents at a Glance

Table of Contents

Introduction

The world economy and financial markets were hit with shock waves in 2020 that had lasting impacts and opened the door to many issues, challenges, and problems that we're all facing now. One of the changes is that this profound year catapulted the prospects of gold and silver. Both have embarked on what is possibly their greatest bull market. This means historic potential gains for those who are positioned for them — hopefully, you, my reader! The public may catch on, but usually, they're late. As you read this book, you have the chance to profit before the crowds come and witness the tail end of what is coming now.

During 2019–2020, I told my clients and students that precious metals are (and will be) a necessary part of a healthy and growing investment portfolio. I don't tell people that gold and silver are great considerations because I'm the author of this book; I wrote this book because I thought that 2020–2022 would be a great time for those two timeless metals. The time is now, and the place to be is in gold and silver (and investments related to them such as stocks, exchange-traded funds, and other vehicles).

About This Book

Investing in Gold and Silver For Dummies comes at the right time and place for both me and you. As I write this, during the opening rounds of what may become a great bull market (cool!), there's plenty of information to share with you on these enduring metals that have been a store of value for thousands of years yet still are as fresh and as vital as today's varied events and headlines.

Nearly anything (or almost everything) a beginner or intermediate investor needs to know about gold and silver is inside this book. At the very least, I also include those analysts and experts who I think know more than I do so that you have what you need at your fingertips (or your screen) to make knowledgeable decisions with gold and silver. As with all *For Dummies* guides, you won't have to read this book from start to finish like so many other books. If the only thing you're interested in is how to buy gold or what you need to know about investing in silver, the information is here, easily found, and ready to be read and comprehended in minutes.

A quick note: Sidebars (shaded boxes of text) dig into the details of a given topic, but they aren't crucial to understanding it. Feel free to read them or skip them. You can pass over the text accompanied by the Technical Stuff icon, too. The text marked with this icon gives some interesting but nonessential information about investing in gold and silver.

One last thing: Within this book, you may note that some web addresses break across two lines of text. If you're reading this book in print and want to visit one of these web pages, simply key in the web address exactly as it's noted in the text, pretending as though the line break doesn't exist. If you're reading this as an e-book, you've got it easy — just click the web address to be taken directly to the web page.

Foolish Assumptions

Dear reader, I make a few assumptions about you. No, you're not a dummy, but you want more information on the topic of investing in gold and silver. You have some very basic knowledge about investing, and you understand that diversification means considering investments beyond merely stocks or bonds. You also understand that inflation and other pressing financial concerns and risks are problems of modern life and that investing in gold and silver as a diversifying strategy is a good consideration for both long-term investors and speculators in the turbulent and uncertain 2020–2022 period.

Icons Used in This Book

I include some handy icons that you may notice in the margin of this book. They point you to certain types of information, so be sure you know which is which.

I include some text that tips you off into certain directions — this icon makes sure you notice. These aren't shady tips of the "Psssst, Mac, have I got a tip for you" variety; they're joyfully more like "Holy smoke — such a great tip!"

Although I'd like for you to remember everything I say, I do have two kids and realize that's a losing battle. However, if you see this icon, be sure to ingrain this info on your brain.

WARNING

Just like I want you to remember everything I say in this book, I'd love for you to *do* everything I say, but again, having two teenage kids, I can calculate the rate of return on that. But to truly stay away from pitfalls that can cause you serious financial harm, you should heed any warnings you see associated with this icon.

TECHNICAL STUFF

Just like any expert, I do have nuggets of knowledge that only participants on game shows like *Jeopardy* and/or my uncle from Bratislava could love. But I guarantee that after discovering the value of gold and silver and how they could enhance your portfolio, you could fall in love with some of this technical stuff, too. However, if you prefer, you can skip the info associated with this icon. This is *the only* icon that points you to info that you can skip if you choose to.

Beyond the Book

In addition to the material in the print or e-book you're reading right now, this product comes with some access-anywhere goodies on the web. Check out the free Cheat Sheet for interesting statistics about gold and silver investments and questions to ask a dealer before you buy physical gold and silver. To get this Cheat Sheet, simply go to www.dummies.com and search for "*Investing in Gold and Silver For Dummies* Cheat Sheet" in the Search box.

Where to Go from Here

At this point . . . browse! Check out the detailed table of contents and go straight to those chapters that pique your interest. This isn't a novel that you need to read from start to finish. It's like opening your fridge and pulling out what interests you. (If you're totally new to gold and silver investing, though, why not start with Chapter 1?)

As you watch the precious metals markets become more popular (for many good reasons), come back to this book and discover more information; you'll be pointed in the right direction for more and better ways to profit from gold and silver. Good luck!

1
Getting Started with Gold and Silver

Chapter **1**

Exploring the World of Gold and Silver

Chaos. Mayhem. Crashes. Massive unemployment. Scandals and collapse. And that was only last week! The world throws plenty at us, and we must do what we can to get by. As they say, we can't control the world, but we can control our response to it.

As a "Raving Capitalist" (I'm not kidding; that's my website, too), I believe that building wealth and financial security is a two-pronged approach where you build your prosperity using both passive wealth-building strategies (having your money work for you such as with stocks, mutual funds, and options) and also active wealth-building (such as starting a home-based business in your spare time). You are your own greatest asset, so you can do plenty of things to assure greater financial security.

Given that, I'm delighted that you have this book in your hands. As part of your wealth-building approach, I want you to seriously consider adding some gold and silver, especially when you take a full, realistic view of what's going on in our society, economy, and financial markets.

Yes, there's ugliness out there. You and I can't make the world pretty, but we can add some attractive positions in our assets so we can sleep better. Those positions start with some gold and silver. In this chapter, I briefly explain the benefits of gold and silver in today's world and give you some actions to take before you jump into investing.

Considering Gold and Silver for Your Situation

In the modern age, most investors keep their investments in either paper or digital form, and each of them has a risk that hard assets such as physical gold and silver don't have. Yes, we're talking about gold and silver that you can hold in your hand and in your safekeeping and looks something like Figure 1-1, which shows gold and silver bars. (As you find out in Chapters 9 and 10, gold and silver also come in bullion and numismatic coins and commemoratives.)

FIGURE 1-1:
Unlike most other investments, you can hold gold and silver bars for safekeeping.

Content: © Konstantin Inozemtcev/123RF.COM

In the following sections, I take stock of current global financial issues (pun intended) and explain how gold and silver can help your investment portfolio.

REMEMBER

Before you invest in gold and silver, you need to realistically assess yourself and your financial status (assets, debt, career, and so on), and you need to ask yourself, "Am I adequately prepared for what is happening now and what will likely come my way tomorrow?" I have some suggestions you can start with later in this chapter.

Assessing the world's financial issues

As I write this in August 2020, the world and financial markets look so radically different from what they looked like back in January 2020. I thought that the world had many problems and challenges that were percolating and financial bombs whose fuses were lit, but the game changed for the worse. Those events and conditions are part of the reason that gold and silver are a necessity in many portfolios.

Here is a short list of global issues and problems to be aware of:

>> Unemployment is up. In January 2020, unemployment was at a 50-year low, but six months later, with 50-plus millions of lost jobs due to the COVID-19 pandemic and government lockdown, unemployment is at a multi-decade high. Although unemployment is coming down, there are still millions of jobs that may not come back.

>> Because of job losses, more than 5 million folks are behind on their mortgage or rent. This will cause problems with debt, home sales, and more.

>> Government debt is exploding. Federal and state/local debt is skyrocketing. This may lead to high inflation.

>> Due to the government lockdown, hundreds of thousands of businesses were temporarily shut down for months, but a huge swath of those may never reopen.

>> Pensions and Social Security are dangerously underfunded by trillions. If the federal government bails these out by printing trillions, that can also cause high and punitive inflation.

Before I ruin your day, I'll cease adding more items to that list (there was more, you ask?!), but diversification and financial planning are urgently needed before the next crash in the stock market or the next leg of the economic downturn. Keep reading to see how gold and silver fit into this plan.

Knowing how gold and silver can help you

There are many solid, reasonable, profitable reasons to own gold and silver, and all those reasons are spread across this chapter. If you want a neat list of reasons, check out Chapter 18. But here I mention the top reasons that consumers and investors should take a hard look:

>> **Diversification:** Having stocks, mutual funds, and cash aren't enough to achieve true financial safety. Gold and silver are true diversification that complements your paper and digital assets and investment vehicles (Chapters 2 and 3 flesh this point out).

>> **Safe haven:** Gold and silver (although more with gold) are considered a safe haven asset, meaning that in times of economic decline and uncertainty, investors move to these "safe haven" assets, typically precious metals and cash (the U.S. dollar). But the dollar (and other currencies) are now at risk (see the next point). That leaves . . . gold and silver!

>> **A guard against inflation:** For 2020–2030, currencies are in danger of being overproduced in an attempt to resolve economic and financial crises unleashed due to the pandemic of 2020. This means . . . inflation! Gold and silver excel during inflationary times.

Taking Action Before You Invest in Gold and Silver

I know what you're thinking: "Holy smoke! I'm so glad I'm reading this book!" So what should you do next? The following sections describe steps to take before you dive into the world of gold and silver investing. (You should be doing these anyway, and given recent market chaos and volatility, you should do them today.)

Reviewing your portfolio

You should understand what's in your portfolio and why it's there. If you're talking about stocks that are part of your foundational, long-term positions, they should be quality stocks where the company is profitable, has a good balance sheet, and has products/services that are a necessity in the economy.

REMEMBER

In recent years, I've told my clients and students (I teach about investing and speculating across the nation) to make sure that at least 80 percent of their investment stock portfolio is tied to "human need." Those companies should be (profitably) selling goods and services that the public will keep buying no matter how good or bad the economy is. Think of things such as food, water, beverages, and utilities.

TIP

To find out more about prudent stock picking, check out the latest edition of my book *Stock Investing For Dummies* (Wiley). In this edition, I share what to look for when you're choosing quality stocks, and I also give you the "heads-up" on what I see coming for 2020–2030, so you can be a step ahead of the crowd.

Boosting your cash position

REMEMBER

Although cash can lose long-time value during inflationary times, here I'm talking about its short-term value. Everyone should have (during bad times) a minimum of three to six months' worth of gross living expenses sitting in their savings account for unexpected events, such as losing their job, money for big-ticket necessities, and so on.

In other words, if your gross monthly expenses are $3,000, then you should have a minimum of $9,000 (three months' worth of gross living expenses) to $18,000 (six months' worth). This is cushion money, or emergency funds.

Using your talents in your spare time

I'm one of the few certified financial planners (CFP) who recommends to his clients and students that they should have (or start) a part-time, home-based business in their spare time to be diversified in their active wealth-building pursuits. The primary reason is to generate income and be diversified from their job. During the COVID-19 pandemic and government lockdown of 2020, nearly 50 million people lost their jobs between March and June 2020. These are folks who didn't see this catastrophe only a few months earlier.

My point is that if all your active wealth-building income (100 percent) is coming from a single job, *that means you are not diversified.*

TIP

A home-based business gives you the ability to generate extra income in your spare time. It also means tax benefits and the ability to turbocharge your ability to save and invest for retirement. With your own business, you can qualify to have more generous retirement accounts (such as a SEP-IRA). To get more details about launching a home-based business, check out my book *Micro-Entrepreneurship For Dummies* (Wiley).

Doing your research on gold and silver

Yes, I realize that some of the preceding points aren't about gold and silver, but they're part of a sensible plan with both your passive and active wealth-building, and you can see that gold and silver play a crucial part in the passive wealth-building portion.

Look, many investors and financial advisors are ignoring or avoiding gold and silver, and that will be to their detriment. Educate yourself on the pros and cons of all the major investment categories (covered in Parts 2 and 3 of this book) so that you know what can work for your financial security and what can't.

REMEMBER

Gold and silver can be useful and versatile components of your overall portfolio, but keep your perspective on them. They're merely tools for your financial security during a time they're useful. The time will come again that they won't shine, but that is on the other side of today's brewing storms. Meanwhile, discover their benefits and how they can complement today's (hopefully) weatherproof portfolio.

Chapter 2

Understanding Gold and Silver's Greatest Benefit

A s a certified financial planner (CFP) who teaches and consults on investing, I eat, sleep, and think about diversification all the time (it's not as fun as it sounds!) because it's always seen as a positive move for investors. Most financial advisors believe in diversification, but I take it to a level that many don't. When financial advisors talk about diversification, it's predominantly about "paper assets" such as stocks, bonds, exchange-traded funds (ETFs), mutual funds, and so on.

Yes, those advisors may also cover "hard assets" such as traditional real estate property and conventional assets such as personal holdings (jewelry, collectibles, and so on), but I'm an advocate for including hard assets such as gold and silver in the investor's portfolio. And here's the primary reason why.

REMEMBER

Where possible, investors should have a variety of investment vehicles in their portfolio for obvious reasons. Diversification helps minimize risk as well as increase the chances of seeing your overall portfolio grow, and the time has come for investors to diversify with precious metals because the economic and financial environment for precious metals is better than ever. Gold and silver are an important part of your portfolio because they're the only major assets on the financial landscape without counterparty risk. The bottom line is that gold and silver — hard assets used since the dawn of civilization — offer a unique quality of endurable value that paper assets don't have.

REMEMBER

All paper assets have counterparty risk, so what is it really? Here is the essence of this risk: A paper (or digital) investment asset only has value given the promise or performance of the counterparty involved. If the counterparty fails to perform, it will mean the decline of the value of the asset to the point that the asset can be worthless.

Because each class of paper assets has a different counterparty risk, I flesh out this foundational point in this chapter, and you'll do an "Ooooh . . . I see what you mean!" (Flip to Chapter 4 for more information on other kinds of investment risks.)

Looking at Counterparty Risk in Today's Investments

Having all your money in a variety of paper assets may be diversified, and many (most?) financial advisors may be confident that you're properly diversified, but an issue occurs, which is getting more and more pronounced during the 2020s.

Maybe the best way I can illustrate the problem with having "all your eggs in the paper-asset basket" is to use the old reliable example of the *Titanic* (don't roll your eyes!). If you were onboard the *Titanic* and you owned a luxury compartment at midlevel, a warehousing unit on the bottom level, and a gorgeous unit with a stunning view of the ocean on the top deck, then you'd be "in like flint" versus that schlub who occupies the unit with no view and the size of a phone booth on level 15.

But if the ship sinks, the great equalizer is that both of you lose. With a "100 percent paper-assets boat," it'd be good to have as part of your setup a "life boat" that doesn't rely on the sinking ship. It has the power to float no matter what happens to the paper-assets ship.

The year 2020 is a major, consequential year that reminds us that our paper-assets ship is surrounded by icebergs, and a life boat is a huge plus. ("But Paul, what if your life boat hits an iceberg?" Because you ruined my great example, switch that to a helicopter so I can move on. Sheesh!)

In the following sections, I explain the counterparty risk with paper investments and how investing in gold and silver can help balance that risk.

Stocks

When you buy stock, you're really buying (or participating in) the performance of a company or, more to the point, a company's executive management. If the company behaves poorly or in a substandard fashion, then the company won't succeed. This cuts to the heart of the matter: A successful company is profitable.

Profit is the lifeblood of the company, and I could easily make the case that profit is the lifeblood of a successful economy. Without profit, the company fails. If it continues to lose money, its losses will grow and it will ultimately go out of business and end up in bankruptcy. Given that, the stock will go to zero.

TECHNICAL STUFF

In the history of the stock market, thousands of companies went out of business and we witnessed their stock go to zero. Some famous examples are Enron and Bear Stearns, and you can find many others. The Dow Jones Industrial Average (DJIA) has been the most watched stock market barometer for more than a century, and it lists 30 of the largest and most successful companies in the world. Yet the 30 stocks within the DJIA aren't the same 30 stocks that were first listed in the original average. In fact, only one stock remains (General Electric). The rest either went out of business or were taken over by other companies.

Yes, stocks can fluctuate and can go up or down given the daily interaction of a huge group of buyers and sellers, but if the company's management team and the overall company itself ceases to perform profitably, then the stock will suffer.

REMEMBER

A stock will be only as valuable as the performance of the stock's counterparty: the company's performance. Keep in mind that although mining stocks may have counterparty risk (as any other stock), you can mitigate the risk by focusing on the stock's fundamentals (profit, market, and so on), so check out Chapter 7 for more details.

Bonds

In times of stock market mayhem and economic uncertainty, many investors tend to flock to bonds. Whether corporate bonds, municipal bonds, or what's considered the safest category — U.S. Treasury Bonds — bonds are considered a safer bet than stocks during periods of economic difficulty such as a recession.

All things being equal, that's generally true, especially in conventional times as has been the case in recent decades. But 2020–2030 isn't a conventional time. Regardless, a bond is a perfect example of counterparty risk. A bond is essentially an asset for the bond buyer (basically the creditor), but on the other side of this, it's a debt that must be satisfied by the debtor. Given this, a bond's value is only as good as the promise or performance of the payer of the bond. The payer of the bond (a company, municipality, state, or sovereign government) is the counterparty.

Many times throughout history, bonds went to zero because the counterparty defaulted on the legal obligation to pay back any interest plus principal. But now we're in unconventional times with epic amounts of trillion-dollar, unsustainable debt. During 2020–2030, you *will* see defaults. Corporate and municipal entities will default and/or pay creditors (such as investors) only a tiny fraction of what's due. Bonds are paper assets entering a uniquely hazardous time in history.

REMEMBER

Gold and silver that you own and hold in your possession aren't someone else's liability or promise to pay. There's no counterparty that needs to perform so that gold and silver retain their value. Gold and silver have their own, intrinsic value — no matter what's going on in the world or across the financial and economic landscape. That has been true for thousands of years. For more details on buying and owning physical gold and silver, check out Chapter 9 (on bullion coins) and Chapter 10 (for numismatic and collectible coins).

ETFs and mutual funds

In the world of paper assets, ETFs and mutual funds are great, and a neat feature is that diversification is present to some extent in most of these vehicles. I love ETFs and mutual funds, I own them, and they're indeed appropriate for many folks.

However, ETFs and mutual funds are only as good as the assets they own. If they own successful investments, the fund will do well; if they own failing investments, then the fund will definitely not do well. If a mutual fund, for example, has stocks and bonds, then these investments have counterparty risk. So do ETFs and mutual funds have counterparty risk? Yes!

I think that investing in gold and silver ETFs that guarantee ownership of physical bullion is as safe as you can get within the boundaries of a portfolio held at a brokerage account (whether a regular or retirement account). You still need to be aware of the counterparty risk of the issuer, but it does have greater safety when compared to alternative ETFs. For more details, check out Chapter 8.

Keep in mind that inverse and leveraged ETFs have financial and market risks, but they can be a good way to speculate in gold and silver in the event of a precious metals bull market. Read up on the details of these aggressive vehicles in Chapter 11.

Cash and bank investments

Typically, if you have a savings account, checking account, certificates of deposit, and other bank instruments, these don't have market risk. In other words, they're not usually traded in some marketplace and subject to fluctuation, and they don't go up or down as you normally see, such as in the stock market. You know that if you put, say, $1,000 in a bank savings account in January, you could reasonably expect that money (plus some interest) to be there in December (unless you gave access to that relative who goes on spending binges).

WARNING

U.S. banks are considered among the safest banks in the global financial arena, but don't assume 100 percent safety at all times. When times are extraordinarily difficult, the safety of your funds can be an issue. Bank safety was a major issue during the Great Depression, and as you read this, U.S. banks have entered times that may again be considered difficult, so stay alert. If you suspect that your bank has issues, you can find out about the bank's safety from sites such as www.fdic.gov.

Cash — whether it's in your pocket, your sock drawer, that crevice in your couch, or any bank or credit union account — is subject to inflation risk. Inflation risk is a form of counterparty risk.

WARNING

Inflation means that more dollars (or whatever the currency is) are being over-produced so that more dollars are chasing the same basket or goods or services (or, as in the case of bubbles, chasing assets). When more and more dollars are produced, and these dollars head into the purchase of something, that "something" will see its price rise. Monetary inflation (problem) leads to price inflation (symptom).

So, where is the counterparty risk? Monetary inflation comes from the management of the currency; it doesn't "just happen." It's a direct result of the performance of those in charge of the currency. The "managers" of the currency are the folks at the central bank charged with the creation and management of the currency (also referred to as the "money supply"). Those who manage the currency are said to be conducting "monetary policy." Ultimately, the central bank will generally follow the edicts of the political leaders, and seriously, what political leaders are immune to the idea of inflating the currency? It's like creating money out of thin air.

It will happen when they want to be popular with the electorate and spend, spend, spend. This is why we have trillions in national debt. This is how entire countries bankrupt themselves. This is why hyperinflation has commonly dotted history's landscape.

REMEMBER

A currency is only as good as the performance of the counterparty, the issuer (the federal government). If the currency is mismanaged (overproduced!), the currency loses value (perceived or otherwise) and (as history shows) often goes to zero (becomes worthless).

Real estate

I hate to burst your bubble, but real estate is loaded with counterparty risk, too, even though it's a hard asset. What if the renter doesn't pay? What if the area has problems and no one wants to live there and whoever is there is leaving? What if the managers of that area (such as a municipal government) malfunction and the area becomes very unattractive due to crime and other social ills? What would happen to the value of your property?

Whether an area "goes bad" or worse, there's chaos or war, these are real events happening right now across the globe. If you still aren't sure about counterparty risk with real estate, then I can't help you, but a trip to a neighborhood next to Chernobyl may.

Futures and options

Okay, do I really have to convince you of the risks of these vehicles? Futures and options are speculative vehicles that come with their own set of risks. They certainly have counterparty risk but also market risks to be aware of. I suggest you find out more in Chapter 12 (futures) and Chapter 13 (options).

Bitcoin and other cryptocurrencies

Cryptocurrencies are the new kids on the block, and many are touting some of their benefits, especially compared to conventional currencies. Bitcoin, for example, tries to maintain its digital scarcity, which can be an advantage in maintaining its value, especially because regular currencies are being overproduced as I discuss in the earlier section "Cash and bank investments."

The problem with these are risks associated with electronic hacking and . . . wait for it . . . electricity. Electronic hacking means that someone with enough technical prowess can get into your digital stash of cryptocurrency and take it. There have been cases of folks seeing their accounts go to zero. Also, these currencies are totally reliant on electricity, which makes them worthless during a blackout.

Given this, cryptocurrencies may not technically have a strict counterparty risk (such as a currency, stock, or bond) because there isn't a specified, identifiable counterparty (such as a government agency or corporate entity). The risks are more attached to digital piracy and associated risks such as electricity.

Knowing That Gold and Silver Have Risks, Too

Keep in mind that no investment or asset is without risk, as you find out in Chapter 4. Everything has risk. Life itself is risky. Getting out of bed is risky. Heck, I got out of the bed on the wrong side this morning, but my bed is next to a wall (I moved it away from the stairwell).

WARNING

Gold and silver certainly have advantages (from a risk point of view) when compared to many assets, paper or otherwise. But gold and silver have risks, too. Here are the two major ones:

>> **Theft:** If you own physical gold and silver, it can be taken from you, so find out about safekeeping ideas. Resources in Appendix A can help.

>> **Government seizure:** This can be an issue given the type of government it is or if the times are risky. During the Great Depression, gold ownership by private citizens was banned as Franklin D. Roosevelt's administration implemented gold confiscation. Also, governments that are communist or socialist commonly seize private property (it's called "nationalizing" or "socializing").

REMEMBER

The bottom line is that the prudent investor learns about the benefits and risks of as many common investments as possible and applies reasonable strategies of diversification. Yes, have a diversified mix of stocks, cash, mutual funds, and so on, along with some gold and silver. For investment approaches and strategies with gold and silver for your situation, head over to Chapter 3.

Chapter 3

Adding Gold and Silver to Your Portfolio Mix

I n Chapter 2, I give you a big reason why gold and silver deserve a spot in your personal portfolio: They lack counterparty risk. In good times and bad, gold and silver can deserve a modest or relatively small spot (but definitely some type of presence). But for 2020–2030, given how perilous these times will be for many traditional investments, gold and silver (and/or related investments) may deserve a more prominent presence.

In this chapter, I principally answer two basic issues: How much gold and silver you should consider, and what to do in various approaches such as investing and speculating. After all, a conservative investor should approach gold and silver differently from an aggressive investor or a more daring speculator. Fortunately, gold- and silver-related vehicles are varied, and some vehicles could be a good fit for you.

TIP

Long ago, the question was gold, and the answer amounted to yes or no. Well, that's the good thing about today's world. The choices are now varied and something can be right for you. I devote a chapter to every distinct related investment vehicle. Check out Parts 2 and 3 for more information.

Defining Saving, Investing, Trading, and Speculating

Before you dig into the rest of this chapter, make sure you understand the crucial differences between the following terms because each is distinctly different, and I make an excruciating effort in using these terms appropriately.

Saving

REMEMBER

The classical, economic definition of saving is "income that has not been spent," but the modern definition is "money set aside in a savings account (regardless of the interest rate) for a 'rainy day' or emergency." Everyone should have a savings account with money that is safe and accessible just in case you encounter an unexpected interruption in your cash flow. In fact, you should have at least three months' worth of gross living expenses sitting blandly in a savings account or money market fund.

Although precious metals in the right venue is appropriate for most people, including savers, you need to have cash savings in addition to your precious metals investments. A good example of an appropriate venue in precious metals for savers is buying physical gold and/or silver bullion coins as a long-term holding (see Chapter 9).

Investing

This term refers to the act of buying an asset that fits an investor's profile and goals, and that is meant to be held long term (in years). The asset will always run into ups and downs, but as long as the asset you're holding is trending upward (a bull market), you'll be okay.

Investing in precious metals may not be for everyone, but it's an appropriate consideration for many investment portfolios. The common stock of large or midsize mining companies is a good example of an appropriate vehicle for investors. (See Chapter 7 for details.) Another great vehicle for investors is exchange-traded funds (ETFs) and mutual funds (covered in Chapter 8).

Trading

WARNING

Trading is truly short term in nature and is meant for those with steady nerves and a quick trigger finger. Many "trading systems" are out there, and this activity requires extensive knowledge of market behavior along with discipline and a definitive plan. The money employed should be considered risk capital and not money intended for an emergency fund, rent, or retirement.

The gold and silver venue for traders could be mining stocks (see Chapter 7), but more likely it would be futures and/or options because they're faster-moving markets. Get more information on futures in Chapter 12 and options in Chapter 13.

Speculating

Speculating can be likened to "financial gambling." Speculating means that you're making an educated guess about the direction of a particular asset's price move. You're looking for big price moves to generate a large profit as quickly as possible, but you also understand that it can be very risky and volatile. Your appetite for greater potential profit coupled with increased risk is similar to the trader (see the previous section), but your time frame is different. Speculating can be either short term or long term.

Your gold and silver venue of choice could be stocks, but more likely, the stocks would be of mining companies (called junior mining stocks or exploratory companies) that are typically smaller companies with greater price potential (see Chapter 7). Speculating is also done in leveraged and inverse ETFs (covered in Chapter 11).

For shorter-term speculating, my main preference is long-dated options on stocks, futures, or ETFs. If you think that a stock, ETF, or futures contract is going up in the short term, then use call options. If you think their price will decline or crash in the short term, then consider put options. Both types of options are covered in Chapter 13.

TECHNICAL STUFF

The year 2020 was a great speculating year. My clients and I made plenty of money with call options on gold and silver vehicles while we also bought put options on stocks, and both produced fantastic gains.

TIP

For more information on successful approaches to aggressive speculating in stocks and ETFs and for details on advanced options strategies, consider my book *High-Level Investing For Dummies* (Wiley).

Building Your Financial Profile

Your approach to gold and silver will be dictated by what type of participant you plan on being (conservative, aggressive, and so forth) and what goals you have (long term, short term, or intermediate term). Some approaches with gold and silver are great for, say, retirement while others are more short term to fund near-term projects like adding to savings or for a down payment on a real estate purchase. Spend plenty of time analyzing your personal style, your needs, and your goals.

For the conservative investor

A conservative investor seeks quality investments (such as stocks with good fundamentals and undervalued assets such as silver) and holds them for the long term. Conservative investors generally avoid short-term speculating and trading, and they avoid assets that are not undervalued and that offer features such as paying dividends. They also participate in a market where there are favorable trends (such as increasing demand for the product/service offered) so that the stock or asset has steady price appreciation going forward.

The conservative investor should consider a long-term approach with quality vehicles and quality stocks (meaning profitable and financially strong companies). The best vehicles would be some mix of the following:

>> Direct physical bullion (see Chapter 9)

>> Major mining stocks (see Chapter 7)

>> Physical gold and silver ETFs (see Chapter 8)

>> Major mining stock ETFs

>> Gold and silver mutual funds (see Chapter 8)

TIP

You don't need to get all of those, of course, just choose one or more as you judge your preferences and goals.

For the growth investor

Growth investors hope to add assets or stocks/ETFs that have strong potential in the near to long term to rise in value (strong price appreciation). They see growth as the primary concern, and income (such as dividends) is either a minor or unimportant consideration.

For those who prefer choices that have greater growth potential while tolerating more risk, the range of choices are

>> Major mining stocks (as a foundational choice; see Chapter 7)

>> Junior mining stocks

>> Junior mining stock ETFs (see Chapter 8)

>> Mining stock leveraged ETFs (but not a huge amount; see Chapter 11)

For the speculator

A speculator seeks rapid price appreciation in the near term (over weeks or months) and accepts the possibility that volatility and (hopefully) temporary price declines may occur on the path to high potential gains.

Speculators want to get set up for outsized gains, so they've done their homework and are aware of greater risks. Here are their range of choices:

>> Junior mining stocks (see Chapter 7)

>> Junior mining stocks leveraged ETFs (see Chapter 11)

>> Long-dated call and put options (see Chapter 13)

For the trader

Traders are looking for gains within days or weeks typically, so they want to play volatility and don't mind seeking short-term profits, say, being bullish on an asset this week and cashing in quickly for a profit and playing the other side (bearish) if they feel the same asset is ready to decline in price the following weeks. My associate Charlie puts it nicely: "While I play the 'tides,' typical traders play the 'ripples.'"

Traders gravitate to the following choices:

>> Stocks (some play stocks directly; see Chapter 7)

>> Futures (see Chapter 12)

>> Options on stocks/ETFs (see Chapter 13)

>> Options on futures

Of the choices, the most common are options because they're lower-cost vehicles and offer plenty of upside and downside volatility in the short term.

TIP

When it comes to stock speculating and trading, it pays to read the exploits of those who truly mastered the craft. One of the greats in the history of financial markets is Jesse Livermore. In the late 1920s, he speculated on a stock market crash (which famously occurred in late 1929), and he made $100 million on that speculation — an astounding amount at that time. His thoughts on trading can be found in the book *Reminiscences of a Stock Market Operator* by Edwin Lefèvre (Wiley).

Making Other Portfolio Considerations

Often, the choices in your portfolio aren't always 100 percent "yes or no" when it comes to making the move to purchase (or sell) an asset or investment. As you find out in this section, there can be alternate, modified ways to proceed as every investor or speculator can have different circumstances, preferences, and so on.

Deciding on a percentage to put in metals

The percentage to invest in precious metals is actually a personal choice, and no hard and fast formula exists for choosing how much gold and/or silver you should buy or what percentage it should be. Plenty of expert folks have an opinion on the matter, and they're included in Appendix A.

Part of the reason for this is that every situation is different. A senior citizen in her 80s will require much less exposure to gold and silver than someone in her 30s. Someone with positions that may get harmed by inflation will need some significant exposure to gold and silver. Check out the earlier section "Building Your Financial Profile" to see whether a particular approach appeals to you. You can also refer to the later sidebar "The Permanent Portfolio" for a technique from investment advisor Harry Browne.

Choosing gold, silver, or both

When knowledgeable people describe the difference between gold and silver, I like this comparison: Gold is like a jumbo airliner, while silver is like a jet fighter. Gold is that steady large vehicle, while silver can be quick and nimble. Either or both is fine. Many experts on the topic will give different answers like "have X percent in gold and Z percent in silver." I think they both have different properties found in their related vehicles such as stocks, ETFs, and futures, but in the physical form, I am agnostic.

TIP

Go half and half if you aren't sure. I personally prefer a greater percentage in silver. You may be thinking of both in investment terms, but also consider both in terms of barter. In the worst-case scenario (such as hyperinflation), gold and silver will be very tradable. Gold would be great for large purchases while silver would be great for common, everyday transactions. I think a good consideration is a third in gold and two-thirds in silver, but take into account your own personal circumstances.

Investing for income

Although most investors do gold and silver for appreciation such as long-term or short-term capital gains, there are ways to gain steady income from gold and silver. The most obvious are

>> Dividend income from major mining stocks (see Chapter 7)

>> Writing covered calls on stocks/ETFs

>> Writing puts on stocks/ETFs

TIP

If you're holding a mining stock that just had a great rally, that could be a good time to write a covered call on it and generate option income. Many folks have been able to generate up to 5 to 10 percent income just by being proficient on doing covered calls. Find out more in Chapter 13.

THE PERMANENT PORTFOLIO

In early 2006, Harry Browne died. I thought it was a great loss to the investment and political world. (He ran for president on the Libertarian platform in 1996 and 2000.) His claim to fame is that he was very successful in anticipating the extreme market condition of the 1970s and profiting from it. He wrote several bestselling investment books, and my favorite aspect of his writings was his insights on practical economics, which can be very useful when making investment decisions.

One of the last books he wrote was a short book that was a concise, true gem of financial wisdom called *Fail-Safe Investing: Lifelong Financial Security in 30 Minutes* (St. Martin's Griffin). In it, he detailed a model portfolio that was easily constructed by the average investor, and it had performed very well in a variety of economic conditions. It consisted of 25 percent each of cash, stocks, bonds, and . . . gold. He suggested that you rebalance it each year to keep the 25 percent allocation.

In other words, if one asset class performed very well and ended up being much higher than 25 percent at the end of the year, then you'd sell a portion of that part of your portfolio and distribute that amount to other parts so that at the start of the following year, you were at 25 percent in each. You would then repeat that process at the end of that subsequent year.

In any given year, one (or more) of the categories would perform well. Of course, performance of different parts of the portfolio changed as the economic conditions changed year in and year out.

Mr. Browne constructed this portfolio because he was keenly aware of the dangers of inflation, recession, and other systemic problems that occur because of political and government mismanagement (such as through inflation, taxes, and regulation). He recognized that gold, meanwhile, was not easily produced and manipulated by the government.

When you do your research online for the Permanent Portfolio, you'll see that other investors did their variation on it. You should consider doing your own variation, but the Permanent Portfolio is a great starting point as you develop an approach that works for your personal needs.

Chapter **4**

Recognizing the Risks

T
he saying goes "no guts, no glory," and in the world of money and finance, the equivalent is "no risk, no really cool gains." Risk is part of the world of building and maintaining wealth and seeking financial security. So risk is something you should be aware of so you can minimize your exposure to it while you try to maximize your gains (and income).

In my financial seminars, I spend a lot of time talking about risk because it obviously needs to be dealt with but also because it's very entwined in the deepest desires of most investors — increasing return. It goes without saying (so I'll write it down) that the age-old equation in the world of investing is risk versus return. This equation states that if you want a greater return on your investment, you have to tolerate greater risk. If you don't want greater risk, you have to tolerate a lower rate of return.

The world is full of pitfalls, and precious metals are no different, but keep in mind that precious metals can excel when your other investments don't. Precious metals guard or hedge against risks that can hurt conventional stocks, bonds, or other fixed-rate vehicles.

Here are some of the risks against which precious metals excel:

» **Purchasing power risk:** As inflation rears its ugly head, this results in higher prices.

» **Currency crisis:** As nations increase their money supply, the long-term result is usually a crisis or even collapse of the currency.

>> **Geopolitical risk:** This can range from war to terrorism to international strife.

>> **Systemic financial risks:** This is when a crisis occurs due to problems with vehicles such as derivatives.

>> **Counterparty risk:** Gold and silver, for example, don't have counterparty risk, unlike most "paper assets" (such as stocks, bonds, and currencies). I cover this very important point in depth in Chapter 2.

In this chapter, you find out about types of investment risks in the world of precious metals, discover how to minimize your risk when you invest in gold and silver, and get tips on balancing risk versus return.

THE VALUE OF GOLD IN RECENT HISTORY

A good example of the value of, say, gold or silver is when we discuss inflation risk. Throughout history, when inflation raged in an economy (such as Venezuela from 2015 to 2020 or Yugoslavia during 1993–1994), gold and silver held their value while currencies were rapidly losing their value in terms of buying goods and services. Those citizens were able to trade using gold and silver to exchange with goods and services and get that same basket of goods and services when, in terms of the currency, the price was skyrocketing.

Take Zimbabwe during its hyperinflation in 2006–2007. A roll of toilet paper skyrocketed to a price of $145,750. Meanwhile, that same roll of toilet paper was selling for $0.69 in the U.S., and a single ounce of gold could have literally bought a truckload of toilet paper (I guess that gives an entrepreneur a great opportunity to sell toilet paper at a nice profit in Zimbabwe).

In the 1950s, you could have bought a nice man's wool suit for about $30. However, that same equivalent suit would cost you about $1,000 in 2020. In that case, an ounce of gold in each case would have helped you acquire that same suit with money to spare (in case you also want to buy a pallet of toilet paper!).

At the time of writing this book, the Federal Reserve had printed nearly $10 trillion in dollars in an attempt to mitigate the financial and economic crisis stemming from the global pandemic hitting the U.S. economy in spring 2020. Given that, the risks of inflation increased, which, in turn, give gold and stock investors another reason to add those shiny metals to their portfolio.

Exploring Different Kinds of Risks

Before I make you paranoid about risk, keep in mind that it's ubiquitous and just a normal part not only in building wealth but also in living life. Heck, just getting out of bed in the morning could pose a problem. Here are the various types of risks you face when you invest in gold and silver (now that you're out of bed).

Physical risks

By *physical risks*, I don't mean that you may hurt your back from picking up precious metals (heavy metal is a different animal altogether). It just means that if you have gold in physical form, you have to understand that having it has risks, as does owning any valuable property. You have to keep it in safekeeping. For some, that means keeping your physical metals (such as gold, silver, and platinum) possessions in a safe-deposit box at the bank. For others, it means keeping them in a secure hiding place at home. For still others, it means getting storage with vendors such as bullion dealers.

You have to decide. Gold as a physical holding means you have to be concerned about the risk of loss or theft. Then there's the relative risk — what if your relative finds out? Removing some risk always means common sense. After all, if gold hits $3,000 an ounce, I don't think you should be boasting about your investing skills at the local bar.

Market risks

REMEMBER

Market risks may be the most prevalent risks associated with gold. What is market risk? It's the fact that whenever you buy an asset (physical, common stock, and so on), its price is subject to the ups and downs of the marketplace. In gold, as in many investments, the price can fluctuate and can do so very significantly. What if you buy today, but tomorrow there are more sellers than buyers in the gold market? Then obviously, the price of gold would go down. The essence of market risk in commodities such as precious metals is supply and demand.

Another element of market risk can occur when you're involved in a "thinly traded market." In other words, there may not be that many buyers and sellers involved. This is also called *liquidity risk*. This can happen, for example, in futures (covered in Chapter 12). Although futures are usually a liquid market (an adequate pool of buyers and sellers), there may be some aspects of it when it may not be that liquid. Say that you want to sell a futures contract that you recently bought that isn't an actively traded contract. What if there are no buyers when you want to sell? Your order to sell through the broker may sit there for a long time. The sale price of the contract would drop, and you would lose some gain or even end up with a loss. Be sure to communicate with the broker regarding how active that particular market is.

Another example is the market risk of mining stocks. The stock of mining companies certainly can go up and down like most any other publicly traded stock. Stock investors can sell stock when they see or expect problems with the company. If, for example, you're considering a gold mining company, the risk to consider is more than just the fact that it's gold and the commensurate market risks with gold itself. It's also about the company. Is management doing a good job? Is the company profitable? Are sales increasing? How about their earnings? Do they have too much debt? And so on. Mining stocks are covered in Chapter 7.

Futures exchange risks

What the heck is *exchange risk?* That sounds odd! Well, it's not a reference to currency exchange; it's a reference to the risks that could occur at the exchanges where futures and options are traded. When futures (see Chapter 12) and options (see Chapter 13) are transacted at an exchange, such as at the Chicago Board of Trade (CBOT) or the New York Mercantile Exchange (NYMEX), they are done so under the rules and regulations of the exchange. The exchange can either purposely or accidentally encourage market outcomes by changing the rules and regulations on an ongoing basis.

A real-life example happened in the spring of 2011 with silver futures at the NYMEX. Silver rallied to $49.85 (pennies away from matching its all-time high), and the exchange, in an effort to dampen what seemed like frenzied buying, aggressively raised the margin requirements on silver futures contracts to try to quell overspeculation. When normally you could put down 10 percent to speculate on a futures contract, the new amount would be raised to, say, 12 or 15 percent or possibly more. When you require people to put more funds in for the ability to speculate, then of course you'll diminish that activity. If the margin requirements are raised too high, that will result in more selling. More selling results in prices dropping.

 The exchanges want an orderly market, and they may change regulations or adjust requirements to encourage or exact an outcome. Sometimes that outcome may result either purposely or accidentally in a negative way for you. Here are the several events that may happen at an exchange:

WARNING

>> **Margin requirements may change.** I give an example earlier in this section, and this is the most common event that an exchange could enact.

>> **"Liquidation only" can happen.** Although rare, this means that the exchange may temporarily restrict the buying side, and only selling can occur, thus forcing the price down. This occurred with silver in 1980 when it hit its then all-time high of $50.

>> **Trading is halted.** Another rare event, the exchange may temporarily halt trading in a particular futures contract.

Political risks

Political risk is probably one of the biggest dangers that investors and speculators don't see coming. It's the one that comes out of the blue and blindsides your portfolio. What is political risk? *Political* is a reference to politicians who, in turn, run government. As far as you and I are concerned, *political risk* and *governmental risk* can be synonymous. In other words, politicians are Dr. Frankenstein, while government is Frankenstein's monster. The bottom line is that political risk means that the government can change laws and regulations in a way that can harm your investment or financial strategy. This can happen in your own country or by another country.

Consider what happened in the 1930s right here in the United States. In 1934, Franklin D. Roosevelt (FDR) and Congress passed the Gold Reserve Act, which made gold ownership illegal. Had you bought gold in prior years to preserve your wealth in the midst of the Great Depression, well, you were now out of luck. FDR then issued a presidential order fixing the price of gold at $35 an ounce, which stuck for decades to come. FDR didn't want private citizens to have an alternative outside of the official paper currency.

Fast-forward to current times. Political risk is alive and well (unfortunately). In many countries, such as China and Venezuela, the government nationalized (taking private property by force) properties by foreign companies — among them, mining companies. Had you owned stock in these mining companies, you would have seen the share prices drop. Sometimes the share prices drop at the mere threat of government action. In 2005, for example, the Venezuelan government mentioned that it may take property owned by the Toronto-based gold mining company Crystallex International. Its share price fell by a whopping 50 percent in a single day. Venezuela's dictator Hugo Chavez did increase taxes on many foreign companies while nationalizing some industries.

That's the problem with political risk. As an investor or speculator, you can do all your homework and make a great decision with your portfolio backed up by great research and unflinching economic logic and still lose money because of a government action that could have been unforeseen.

WARNING

An ounce of prevention is worth a pound of cure. It's best to stay away from investments (such as mining companies) that are too exposed to risk in a politically unstable or unfriendly nation. There are still plenty of precious metals opportunities in politically friendly environments such as the United States, Canada, Australia, and Mexico (at least until the next election!).

The risk of fraud

The risk of fraud is as real in precious metals as in every other human endeavor. It's tough enough trying to make a buck when the market seems honest. But you must understand that as a market becomes popular or "hot," it also becomes a target for scam artists. Fraud can materialize in a variety of ways, but I think that it can be safely categorized into three segments: scams, misrepresentations, and market manipulation.

» **Scams:** Those events that the consumer organizations always warn about. The image is conjured up about those boiler-room operations where a slick con artist calls up a little old lady in Pasadena and talks to her about riches to be made in gold and silver if she could crack open her piggy bank and send off a nice money order chunk of her savings. This is certainly a real risk, and it becomes more apparent when the source of potential fraud is popular. When internet auctions became a hot consumer area, there were more internet auction–related scams. When the real estate market became red-hot in 2005, there were more real estate scams. When precious metals become the "bubble du jour," then you'll need to be wary of scammers here as well.

» **Misrepresentations:** I put this as a separate topic from scams because it can be a different animal. Basically, the point is that you may put your money into a venue and you may not be getting what you think you're buying. A good example is what the respected silver analyst Ted Butler warned about regarding silver certificates. There have been millions of silver certificates issued in recent decades, but there's the real possibility that there isn't any real silver backing them up. In other words, there are purchasers of silver certificates who believed that they could convert their paper into actual silver in due time but, in fact, won't be able to. That sounds like a misrepresentation to me.

» **Market manipulation:** Early in 2020, the financial media reported a serious matter regarding naked short selling among smaller stocks. Short selling can send a stock's price plummeting. Some large brokers and their clients have been caught illegally profiting through a manipulative technique called *naked short selling*. This was an especially egregious activity with the stock of smaller mining companies. In naked short selling, the perpetrator can sell massive quantities of stock essentially created out of thin air to force the price of the stock to come crashing down. Imagine if you owned shares of a small mining company, and you saw the share price plummet by 40 or 50 percent or more for no apparent reason.

Minimizing Your Risk

First of all, don't forget that including precious metals (to whatever extent) in your portfolio minimizes risk because precious metals such as gold and silver have historically helped investors in times of economic uncertainty and political and financial tensions in the world at large. The long-term picture for precious metals should continue to bear this out. But as this chapter points out, nothing is without risk. Precious metals do carry risks, and you can minimize your risks with the help of the following sections.

REMEMBER

Risk (or the lack of it) isn't just where you put your money; it's also how you go about doing it. 'Nuff said.

Gaining knowledge

The more you understand how markets work, the better decisions you'll make and the more you'll minimize risk in your financial situation. I remember getting into options on silver futures some years ago. It was early 2004, silver was rising very well, and my account was performing superbly. I thought to myself, "Gee! What a genius I am!" Then along came April 2004. Silver plummeted by nearly 40 percent. I thought to myself, "Gee! What a moron I am!" In retrospect, it worked out just fine, and I made some great profits, but I was sweating bullets that spring. Seeing the value of your "investment" drop by 40 percent can make you freak out. I would have jumped out the window, but I'm on the first floor. The point is that I learned that precious metals futures and options could have very wide and scary price swings. That is the nature of the market.

REMEMBER

In fact, it isn't uncommon for precious metals to "correct" by 20 to 30 percent or even more at least once a year (I've come to learn that a "correction" seems awfully incorrect at the time). The terms *correct* or *correction* mean that a market came back down after going up too far and/or too fast. Don't confuse a market "correcting" with a market experiencing a *bear market* — a long-term falling or decreasing market. The correction is a temporary pullback in the price of the asset that is in a long-term *bull market,* or rising market. In other words, the difference between a correction and a bear market is the same difference as fainting and dropping dead. In the former, you recover and get back on track. The point is that gaining knowledge about your market helps you understand moments such as the difference between a correction and a bear market.

Being disciplined

When markets go up and down, it can be difficult to stay disciplined. Markets can't be controlled by individual investors, but they can and should exercise self-control. People can let their emotions overrule their thinking and do the wrong things when they ought to do the opposite. It happens especially in fast-moving markets.

My client (I'll call him Bob) had put $2,000 in a commodities brokerage account. Under my guidance, he purchased some options (see Chapter 13) on silver futures. Within a few weeks, the value shrank to $900. Imagine that: He was down 55 percent. Of course, he was very concerned (wouldn't you be?), and we discussed the situation. I told him to stay the course because my research told me that the underlying asset (silver) was in a bull market and that this price drop was a temporary condition. In addition, the options that he purchased had two full years to go before they expired. This is an example of what happens in the marketplace; no matter how solid your research and logic, the market can go against you. If your research and logic were sound, then the odds would swing back in your favor in due course. He decided not to panic and stay the course.

For Bob, the discipline paid off. The $2,000 he speculated with became $4,000 a few months later as the silver market rebounded. Those options were finally cashed in for $5,000 about 12 months after the initial purchase for a gain of 150 percent. To this day, the account is still growing because we stayed disciplined and bought (and cashed in) at points that made sense. Bob could have panicked when it was at $900, cashed out, and jumped out the nearest window, but thankfully he stayed disciplined and reaped some excellent profits.

REMEMBER

When you are in fast-moving markets, have a plan in place regarding how much you will put at risk, when you plan to get in, and under what conditions and price points you'll take profits (or losses). Chapter 14 has some strategies to help you.

Having patience

Everyone wants to get rich quick. Who wouldn't like to make a fast buck? Well, people that reach for the fast gains end up with fast losses. But if they invested in quality assets (stocks of solid, profitable companies, for example), the gains can materialize over a longer period of time. Had you bought quality stocks just before the crash of 2008 or, more recently, the ugly crash during the pandemic crisis of spring 2020, your positions looked ugly in the short term. But in due course, if you chose wisely, those stocks would have risen, and you'd see the hoped-for gains.

REMEMBER

In a nutshell, I think impatience has been the greatest "personal" problem among investors in this decade. I'm not just saying this for long-term investors; it also goes for traders and speculators. Very often, that investment or speculative position you underwent may go down or sideways for what seems like forever. Sooner or later, if you chose wisely, others notice it, too, and the payoff can then be swift and impressive. Flip to Chapter 14 for tactics to help you in the short and long term.

Using diversification

The advice to use *diversification* is probably the oldest investment advice (right after "don't loan money to your relatives"). Diversification in precious metals can mean several things. It could mean spacing out your money among different metals (some precious metals and some base metals). It could mean spreading your money among different classes of investment vehicles (a mix of gold and silver mining stocks along with a precious metals mutual fund). For speculators, it may mean deploying strategies that could benefit in up or down markets (such as using an option combination like the long straddle; see Chapter 13).

You can even diversify when you're speculating on a single vehicle. In 2019, most of my clients with commodities accounts were overwhelmingly in silver futures options. It is indeed a high-risk approach, but it paid off very well. Silver that year ended up 45 percent, and most of the silver futures options were up in triple digit percentages (sweet!). But where possible, the options strategies involved a diversified mix of strike prices, time frames, and some *hedging*. All hedging means is that you do something in the account that could do well if the market goes against you. Hedging is covered in greater detail in Chapter 14.

Since this book covers the world of precious metals, I can cover diversification in this area, but it's important to understand that this singular area should be only a single slice of your total financial picture. You need to address other areas of your situation such as

» Money in savings

» Reducing and managing liabilities (such as debt and taxes)

» Money in conventional investments such as stocks and bonds

» Real estate and other tangible assets

» Insurance and other risk management tools and strategies

» Pension matters and retirement security

It's not a complete list, but it's important to point out that whatever you do in precious metals, it doesn't happen in a vacuum. Hopefully you've looked at your entire financial picture and the economic/political landscape and you've discovered that the best way to protect and grow your wealth in these times is by diversifying into precious metals!

REMEMBER

Diversification can be accomplished in two ways:

>> You can add precious metals into your portfolio to gain benefits that may not be there with other, more traditional investments

>> You can be diversified inside the precious metals portion of your portfolio by having both physical metal (such as gold and/or silver bullion coins; see Chapter 9) and paper investments (such as mining stocks and precious metals exchange-traded funds [ETFs], covered in Chapters 7 and 8, respectively).

Keeping some risk management tools in your arsenal

TIP

Risk isn't like the weather ("Everyone talks about it, but nobody does anything about it!"). It's something that you can manage and profit from. Here are some proven strategies:

>> **Buy the dips.** If you bought what you think is a great stock at $10 per share and a correction sends it down to $8, don't just crawl under a rock and wait it out; if possible, buy some more. Why not? If it's truly a great stock and your research and logic tell you it's still a solid investment, buy some more. Ultimately, time will pass, and the odds are good that when that stock goes to $12 or $15 or more, you'll end up saying, "Gee whiz! I could have had it at $8!" No guts, no glory.

>> **Keep cash on the sidelines.** This goes in tandem with the preceding point. Have some money sitting somewhere safe, liquid and earning interest waiting for an opportunity. I tell my students that if they're ready to take the plunge with, say, $10,000, don't invest everything in one shot. Invest half now and stagger the rest in over a few weeks or a few months. Opportunities go hand in hand with risks, so do the Boy Scouts thing and be prepared.

>> **Use stop-loss orders.** If you have a brokerage account and it's a major firm with a full-featured website, it has some excellent risk management tools available for you. The most commonly used tool for keeping your portfolio's value intact is the stop-loss order. If you bought a stock at $10, then put a

stop-loss order in at, say, $9, or 10 percent below the purchase price. That way, if the stock goes up, there is no limit to the upside, but if the stock goes down and hits $9, a sell order is triggered and you get out. You minimize loss. A stop-loss order can be activated for a single trading day or for an extended period of time (referred to as a GTC order, or "good 'til canceled" order). Stop-loss orders are a common feature in a stock brokerage account, but it may not be in a commodities brokerage account. Find out more about brokerage accounts in Chapter 16.

>> **Use put options.** Put options are a great way to protect your investment during corrections or bear markets. They can be used as "insurance" to protect gains or the original principal. The put option is also used as a speculative vehicle to make money as well, but it's included in this chapter as a risk management tool. It's covered in detail in Chapter 13.

Weighing Risk against Return with the 10 Percent Rule

I realize that after reading an entire chapter on risk, you may think it's a terrible concept; however, some things in this world thrive on risk. The world can be an uncertain place, and many potential events and entities out there have no problem with raining some bad news on the U.S. economy in general (and your portfolio in particular). When those types of risks become evident, precious metals revert to their historical role as a safe haven. Without risk, how can you grow your money faster? It's a necessary part of your success, and in many cases, it's the reason for your success.

TIP

To offset some of the risk potential that is inherent in any place you put your money, use a very simple criteria. The most you should have in any single vehicle is 10 percent of your money. Easy! Yes, you could make it more precise, more customized, and more complicated. Go ahead, but it's good to have a starting point and a simple strategy before you start to tweak and "optimize."

Table 4-1 is a neat summary of the major ways you can get involved in precious metals based on risk. Use it to leapfrog into your investment of choice or, more appropriately, where to get more details.

TABLE 4-1　　　**Risk Levels of Precious Metals Investments**

Type/Category	Relative Risk Level	Most Common Direct Type of Risk	Chapter with Details
Physical			
Bullion coins and bars	Low	Market, physical	9
Numismatic and collectible coins	Medium	Fraud, physical	10
Paper			
Major mining companies	Low-medium	Market, political	7
Midsize mining companies	Medium-high	Market, political	7
Junior mining companies	High	Market, political	7
Mutual funds	Low	Market, political	8
Exchange-traded funds (ETFs)	Low-medium	Market, political	8
Leveraged ETFs	High	Market	11
Futures	Highest	Market, exchange	12
Options: covered call writing	Low	Market	13
Options: buying calls and puts	High	Market	13
Digital			
Precious metals cryptocurrencies	Medium-high	Market	13

2

Spanning the Gold and Silver Landscape

Find out why gold and silver are so important for almost any investor's (or speculator's) portfolio — physical metal in your hand!

Are mining stocks a good idea for your portfolio? If you're not sure about direct investments in stocks, figure out whether mutual funds make sense instead.

Discover how good exchange-traded funds (ETFs) are for today's portfolios.

Chapter 5

Investing in Gold

"**G**oing for the gold," "good as gold," and many other familiar phrases mentioning gold have been around for what seems like forever, but for good reason. Few things conjure up thoughts of wealth and affluence the way gold does. I don't recall any pirate in a B movie shouting, "Aargh! There's zinc buried on that island, mateys!" On the other hand, gold . . . now we're talking.

Gold is an element found on the standard periodic table of the chemical elements. Gold is listed there with the symbol AU and the atomic number 79 (don't worry, the quiz has been canceled). The most malleable and ductile of the metals, you could actually take a single ounce of gold and essentially stretch it out into 300 square feet (no, I don't know why you would do it, but it sounds impressive). Gold is a good conductor of heat and electricity (and probably thieves as well). Because it's generally resistant to rust and corrosion, gold quickly became an ideal material to fashion into jewelry, coins, and, therefore, money. The desirability of gold now became ensured.

However, as you read this book, every major society is inflating its currency at record rates, which is good news for gold and silver aficionados. In this chapter, I highlight the important reasons gold is (or should be) an essential part of the modern portfolio and how it has stacked up against other investments and common economic conditions.

Comparing Gold to Other Investment Assets

Gold is a finite element (literally — it's the symbol AU on the table of elements) and has all the necessary qualities needed as money. It's durable, portable, and divisible. It's malleable enough to turn into coinage. It doesn't decay or tarnish and is indestructible. In ancient times, it became an ideal medium of exchange and a store of value ever since. In short, it's nearly an ideal form of money especially when compared to other forms of money (such as paper and digital currencies). When you juxtapose gold against modern world currencies, such as the U.S. dollar, the euro, the British pound, and the Japanese yen, you come away with some compelling points.

Figure 5-1 provides a snapshot of gold's price performance since the beginning of this century (as of the first trading day in January 2000).

Gold – London PM Fix 2000 – present

FIGURE 5-1: Gold's price performance since the beginning of this century.

Gold began in early 2000 at a price of $288, and when you measure its performance with the price in mid-2020 (June 30, 2020) — $1,817.50 — you get a 531 percent total gain (sweet!). But how well did gold do against other conventional investment assets? Take a look in the following sections.

Gold versus the financial world in general

So how did gold stack up versus the titans of the financial world? See Table 5-1.

TABLE 5-1   **Gold's "Tale of the Tape"**

Asset	Price Jan. 2, 2000	Price June 30, 2020	Total Gain/Loss Dollar Amount $	Total Gain/ Loss Percentage %
Gold	$288.05	$1,817.50	$1,529.45	530.97%
Silver	$5.29	$18.58	$13.29	251.22%
Dow Jones Industrial Average (stocks)	$11,501.85	$25,812.88	$14,311.03	124.42%
Nasdaq (Stocks)	$4,186.19	$10,063.67	$5,877.48	140.40%
S&P 500 (Stocks)	$1,455.22	$3,100.29	$1,645.07	113.05%
Average Savings acct*	$100	$120.50	$20.50	20.5%
Inflation**	$1.00	$1.53	$0.53 more	53%

* Assuming a savings account balance of $100 for comparison purposes.

** Inflation rate for the sake of comparison. What would $1.00 buy in January 2000, and what would it cost to buy that same item in June 2020? (source: www.bls.gov/data/inflation_calculator.htm)

Well, well, well. Table 5-1 speaks volumes about the past 20-plus years. How many people knew that gold — a dead rock — outpaced the stock market so dramatically?! Time to break it down:

>> Gold crushed it! Generating a gain of more than 530 percent is awesome — who would have thunk it? It beat everything by a country mile.

>> Our companion metal, silver, came in second place with a 251 percent gain — not too shabby! (Chapter 6 has the full scoop on silver.)

>> Next comes the primary stock indexes. Nasdaq came in at 140 percent, then the Dow Jones (DJIA) at 124 percent, with the S&P 500 index coming up at 113 percent.

>> The savings account is there for those folks too skittish at investing and playing the safe route. But safety often means that you settle for a much lower return. In this case, you're getting an average of 1 percent per year, ending up with 20.5 percent. And it didn't beat inflation.

>> Inflation — our yardstick and the nemesis of savers everywhere — was up 53 percent for the same time frame.

The amazing thing is that the general public barely noticed the blistering performance of gold (and silver, too) during that time frame. The question is, how high can gold go once the general public starts to participate?

Gold versus stocks versus currencies

You see in the prior section how gold was the 800-pound gorilla in the battle royale versus other mainstream investment vehicles, but it's important to measure gold versus its primary competitors such as stocks and currencies. In this, you're comparing "apples to apples."

When you're comparing gold to stocks, for example, I don't advocate that you should be 100 percent in one or another. I could put on my "stock hat" and make a strong case for stocks in some economic conditions (such as the 1980s), and I could put on my "gold hat" and make the case that gold is superior in other conditions (such as 2020–2025).

REMEMBER

The bottom line is I think both stocks and gold are important and needed in your portfolio. The only thing is that you rebalance the percentages of your portfolio between regular stocks and gold-related investments. You keep more in stocks when times are good for stocks and more in gold when times are good for gold. But always have something in gold (say 2 to 5 percent of your investable assets at a minimum), even when it's not doing as well because it excels as a hedge and a backup form of "portfolio insurance." Sometimes you don't see the market crash or financial crisis coming, and afterward, you'll be glad you were diversified and had some gold and/or silver on hand.

WARNING

Gold plays an important role as money and as a hedge against the issues of government-issued money, which is also referred to as fiat money. As I write this book, all the major currencies — the U.S. dollar, the euro, the British pound, the yuan, the Japanese yen, and other currencies — are losing their value (depreciating) slowly but surely. Some currencies are rapidly losing their value, such as those in Venezuela, Zimbabwe, and Argentina (more to come!). The main reason currencies lose their value is because they can easily be overproduced by the country's central bank and typically at the behest of the country's political leaders.

Because paper currencies are easily inflated, each unit of currency (dollar, euro, yen, and so on) loses value — not so for gold. As the data from the World Gold Council (WGC) confirms, the mining of gold typically adds about 2 percent to the above-ground global supplies of gold. It's very difficult to extract it from the earth, which is part of the reason gold can retain its value versus central bank–issued currencies. You can use this chapter to find out how gold stacks up as a tangible investment amidst all the investment choices available today.

Part of what makes "money" retain value is scarcity. If it ceases to be scarce and easily created (usually leading to overcreating it), then this leads to its diminishing value. Some gold experts even make it a big point of their speeches that a paper/digital currency will always revert to its intrinsic value, which is "zero." Gold, meanwhile, outlived every currency in the past two millennia and likely will do so in this millennium. As I write this (August 2020), we're in the early stages of a precious metals bull market.

Understanding the Gold Market

For investors and speculators, you must get familiar with two general areas when it comes to gold. The first is the gold market, which consists of demand and supply. This relationship is important with gold, of course, but demand and supply is *extremely* important in virtually all matters tied to other markets and financial sectors because many of these sectors are inexorably tied to gold. (The second area is understanding what markets and assets are tied to gold and silver, such as currencies and government economic policies.)

Gold demand

Who is buying gold, and why? Is demand trending up or not? The more gold that is bought, the more pressure there is on gold's price to rise, especially if supply isn't keeping up with demand. For 2019, according to the World Gold Council (WGC), global demand was at a total of 4,389.70 metric tons, down 1 percent from 2018 but still trending upward historically. The following sections cover different types of gold demand.

TIP

The WGC has a treasure trove of gold data, news, and information for gold investors of any stripe. Renowned experts write in their blogs with timely commentaries and help make sense of what's moving and influencing gold and gold-related investments. Its main site is www.gold.org, and it has a wealth of information at its "Gold Hub" (www.gold.org/goldhub).

Jewelry demand

The largest buying comes from the worldwide jewelry sector (consumer demand). In 2019, the WGC reported that jewelry-related sales for gold was 2,122.6 metric tons, which was down 6 percent from 2018. This drop was due to gold's rising price in the second half of 2019.

In terms of who has done the buying, China and India are the primary drivers of consumer demand.

Central bank demand

The second area of demand is from central banks that buy gold as a store of value and to diversify their asset and currency reserves. This category of demand hit an all-time high of 667.7 tons.

What I find interesting about central banks is that they have a love/hate relationship with gold. On the one hand, they hate (perhaps *dislike* is a better word) gold because it's a competitor to the currency they issue. When the public buys gold, it's an admission that the currency isn't attractive in terms of holding its value.

But many central bankers do realize that ultimately gold wins over currencies . . . sooner or later. In this case, the smart(er) central bankers prefer to have gold in their corner to boost their currency. Maybe not always officially but indirectly. If gold can make the central bank of that country strong(er), that in turn boosts confidence in that particular currency. The great tendency has been historically that the East (principally China, India, and other countries) have been, on balance, greater buyers of gold than their Western counterparts. Given the history and endurance of gold, central banks in the West, especially Western Europe and the U.S. central bank, the Federal Reserve, will see the wisdom and become net buyers, too.

ETF and investment demand

The third area of demand (1,273.4 tons) is investment demand, ranging from buying from gold-backed exchange-traded funds (ETFs; see Chapter 8) and from coins and bars sold (see Chapters 9 and 10). This area rose significantly in late 2019 due to gold's price increase. Total buying rose to 401 tons, which nearly offset the decline in jewelry sales.

The reason cited for why ETFs and other investment sources increased their gold holdings was low/negative interest rates, and geopolitical uncertainty fueled this growth, while the gold price rally also attracted momentum-driven inflows. By the end of 2019, gold-backed ETFs were holding a record amount of physical gold at 2,885.5 tons.

Technology demand

Lastly (and making up the remaining quantity of sales) is global technology sales because gold is increasingly used for circuitry and electronics tied to the technology industry. In 2019, this area of gold demand hit 326 tons.

Gold supply

In 2019, the WGC reports that the gold supply went up 2 percent to a total of 4,776 tons. The primary source was from mining, which was at 3,463.7 tons — marginally lower than 2018 but the first annual decline in ten years. Extracting gold from the ground is getting more difficult, and that is a positive sign for investors and speculators. Why? Because a decline in gold supply will put pressure on the price of gold to go up if gold demand continues to be stable or increasing.

The remaining supply came from recycling. In 2019, recycling sharply increased by 11 percent as the public took advantage of gold's rise and sold their gold holdings such as jewelry and other consumer items with gold content. Because 2020 was a good year for gold's price rise, I suspect that recycling will be strong because gold's price rise occurred in an economic backdrop that was dreadful as thousands of businesses closed and unemployment hit record highs due to the pandemic and subsequent government lockdown procedures across the globe.

Going Over Gold's Recent Bull and Bear Markets

In the modern age, gold has gone through periods of popularity when its price has risen (bull markets) and when it was unloved and its price was flatlining or going down (as with bear markets). Each of these bull and bear markets essentially coincided with how the rest of the world was doing, and this bore an inverse relationship.

REMEMBER

As you find out in the following sections, when the world was generally doing well, and there was minimal conflict and financial instability, there was little demand for gold as an investment alternative or hedge. The opposite was generally true. When the world was experiencing difficulties, especially with economics and financial matters (usually coupled with geopolitical conflict), then gold was popular and its rising price reflected that.

TIP

With commodities and precious metals, demand and supply are key fundamental drivers of the asset's price, so stay tuned with that data. For gold and silver, I provide those resources throughout this book and in Appendix A.

The 1970s bull market

During the second half of the 1970s, gold soared as the world was struggling with financial crises and geopolitical conflicts. Inflation in the United States, for example, was hitting double-digit levels and trying to come out of the recession of 1974–1976 with its companion stock bear market (the Dow Jones Industrial Average had fallen more than 40 percent in that bear market). So investors fled to a reliable safe haven: gold.

Gold was under $200 in the middle of the decade, and it peaked at $850 on January 21, 1980. But new policies brought on by a new president marked the end of this gold bull market.

The 1980s bear market

After Ronald Reagan won the presidency in 1980 in a landslide, he retained as Federal Reserve chairman Paul Volker, who held (fortunately) an austere guidance with the money supply and allowed interest rates to be at a high and painful level (as high as 21 percent at one point), and this austere approach broke the inflationary spiral. The country experienced a recession in 1981, but it was worth it. Coupled with historic tax cuts, the economy rebounded, and the stock market had a strong decade.

The public's appetite for safe-haven assets declined, which in turn sent gold into an extended bear market. Nimble investors rebalanced their portfolios. They decreased (or removed entirely) their gold-related stocks and assets and switched to assets that would excel with a stronger economy such as stocks.

The 1990s range-bound market

During 1990–1999, gold essentially traded sideways and ended the decade on a bearish note. It started the decade at a hair under $400 per ounce and ended the decade at about $290 per ounce. Although gold had some rallies and corrections along the way and still offered profitable opportunities for both investors and speculators, the 1990s were generally a lackluster time for gold.

Despite this unspectacular activity, the mining industry did well. It successfuly found strong gold deposits in its exploratory activities, and the majors were profitable as they increased the quantity and sales of gold despite the lower market price.

The bull and bear markets of 2000–2008

Now we fast-forward to the 21st century. Stocks started the millennium at unsustainable highs. You may recall the "internet bubble" and the "tech stock bubble." These deflated on their own, but the next whammy was the terrorist events on September 11, 2001, which sent the markets reeling downward. The public's appetite for safety returned, and a gold bull market during 2000–2008 saw gold's price go from $288 (January 2000) to breach the $1,000 level in March 2008 for a gain of 247 percent. It trended lower for 2008 in a modest and relatively brief bear market that lasted mere months (versus years in prior bear markets).

The 2008 financial crisis could, of course, be a whole book all by itself. The stock market and other paper assets (such as mortgages) had a historic crisis and crash. Virtually every major asset was down for the year except the U.S. dollar and gold:

>> The U.S. dollar was the world's reserve currency, and it became a safe haven of sorts. Because paper assets and the world's other currencies declined sharply, investors across the globe fled to financial safety.

>> Gold started the year at $857 (January 2, 2008) and ended the year at $883.60 for a modest percentage gain of about 3 percent.

Maybe 3 percent doesn't sound great, but it's spectacular when you compare it to the broad wreckage of most major investment assets that year. A good example is the hammering of major stocks in the Dow Jones (DJIA) that year. The DJIA started the year at 13,043 and ended 2008 at 8,776 — a brutal decline of 33 percent. Also, gold's kid brother — I'm talking about silver — had a rough 2008. It was in the far corner sobbing quietly with a loss for the year at 25.6 percent. However, silver's story gets better, and that narrative is in Chapter 6.

The bull market and bear market of 2008–2018

Fortunately, the shiny seeds of a bull market are usually planted in the muddy dirt of a grim bear market (poetic — you can quote me). Stocks got on the comeback trail in 2009, but gold was ready to roar again, too. The end of 2008 marked the beginning of gold's second bull market for this millennium. After wallowing under $1,000 during much of the second half of 2008, it got its footing during 2009.

REMEMBER

Very often when an asset is moving sideways and/or slightly declining, it's typically called "consolidating," which is essentially building a base or launchpad for the next move up. Sometimes consolidating is done in a few weeks; sometimes it's much longer, perhaps months or years. But if demand and supply is strong or somewhat favorable, the upmove — bull market — eventually returns. And usually it potentially means new highs.

This was the case for gold in 2009. Gold languished under $1,000 during much of the first half of 2009; it came close to cracking the $1,000 level twice but failed. The $1,000 level was "resistance" (a technical analysis term explained in Chapter 15), and gold didn't finally crack it until September 2009. At that point, the $1,000 level became "support." Usually, once you soundly break resistance, it can become your new support as the asset keeps moving upward.

With corrections along the way (common with most bull market moves), gold zigzagged its way to a new all-time high. On September 6, 2011, gold hit $1,911.60. For gold, this was a brief visit above the $1,900 level, and its second bull market ended before a long, multiyear bear market and consolidating pattern ending in early 2019.

REMEMBER

Bull markets are long moves punctuated with corrections along the way. A correction is usually a 5 to 10 percent move, although it could be deeper but not more than 20 percent because that's considered technically a bear market. A bear market is a long move downward punctuated by brief rallies along the way. I tell readers in my book *Stock Investing For Dummies* (Wiley) that if you choose wisely (using fundamental analysis), it will zigzag upward. If you don't choose wisely, it will zigzag downward.

Making the Case for Gold Today

Welcome back to your current time — uh, the present! And welcome to what is possibly the third and best bull market for gold. I say that because the scale of factors is much greater now than before and certainly greater than the prior two bull markets discussed earlier in this chapter.

As of early 2019, the bull market was taking hold. Gold's price started at $1,282 and then traded sideways in the $1,250 to $1,350 channel for much of the first half, but the bull market started in earnest by summer. Gold ended 2019 at $1,520 with a solid gain of 18.5 percent. And it was just getting started!

For 2020, gold was one of the top performers given how chaotic and problematic the year was. With stocks both crashing and rallying while the economy was hammered by the global pandemic and strict government lockdown, gold soared from $1,520 to new heights in August 2020 with a gain of 28 percent, with a third of the year still to go!

News flash! For the first time *ever*, gold hit $2,000 per ounce on August 4, 2020. It went on to hit an all-time high of $2,089.20 as of August 7, 2020 (gold futures, intra-day high). As I write this, the price took a break and pulled back below $2,000.

In the 1970s, there were aggregate dollar moves of assets and markets in the millions; in the 1980s and 1990s, it was billions. By the first decade in this millennium, we were talking about trillions, and now, circa 2020–2021, we are in the tens of trillions. The world is now facing many trillion-dollar problems, and gold is better situated than ever for getting through the storm — multiple storms.

In the sixth edition of *Stock Investing For Dummies* (Wiley), I detail ten challenges and pitfalls during 2020–2030 for stock investors. I could have easily placed that information in this book and titled it "Ten opportunities for gold investors and speculators." Here are some of those challenges that face not only stock investors but the world at large:

» Trillion-dollar pension shortfalls

» Bond and debt bubbles

» Social security shortfalls

» Currency crises

TIP

Read the full list at www.dummies.com/personal-finance/investing/stocks-trading/10-investing-pitfalls-and-challenges-for-2020-2030 and view them as solid reasons gold will do well. Between favorable demand and supply factors coupled with the trillion-dollar issues with paper assets (bond bubble, debt defaults, and so on) and conventional currencies (such as inflation), you have a perfect storm for much higher gold prices. Get some gold for yourself soon.

Chapter **6**

Surveying Silver

For the 2020–2022 time frame (give or take a few months), silver is both my favorite investment and my favorite speculation. It's a lot more than being a pretty metal (which it is). I just think that when you take into consideration all the factors involved, you have the ingredients of what could be historic gains.

In the modern era of precious metals markets (starting circa 1971), silver in two prior bull markets had reached the fabled $50 level and then pulled back. I think that this current unfolding bull market has the power to break that $50 glass ceiling and that silver can reach an all-time high.

This is what I glean from all the market and global data and research for both silver and other markets that have an indirect (yet impactful) effect such as currencies, bonds, and government spending. The bottom line is that I like silver — because of the green ($)!

Silver's future profit potential is truly its silver lining (you were expecting that line, am I right?). In 2020, few things have as sterling and shiny a future as silver. This chapter gives you some insights into its potential as a wealth-building work-horse in your portfolio.

Comparing Silver and Gold

Gold (the subject of Chapter 5) has been the king of the hill in the world of precious metals and man-made currencies since the dawn of civilization, but it's good to see how silver stacks up against its heavyweight buddy. The following sections compare silver's similarities to and differences with gold.

Silver's similarities to gold

REMEMBER

Silver is similar to gold in the following ways:

>> It's been an accepted form of money since ancient times.

>> It isn't man-made; it must be mined (not easy!).

>> It doesn't have the risks of paper assets and man-made currencies.

>> Total global supply, both aboveground and underground (still unmined), is limited in its totality. Both ultimately have a finite supply.

>> The underground (unmined) quantity of both metals may not be completely measurable at this point, but in the future, there will be a point when no more can be found or extracted.

Those are the primary similarities to gold that have benefited silver throughout history, but as they say in the infomercials: Wait! There's more!

Silver's unique qualities

REMEMBER

As great as gold is, silver has qualities and uses that give it a unique advantage and provide strong appeal to win a place in your investment and asset portfolio. Here are the main differences:

>> **Silver's myriad of industrial uses:** Few raw materials on the planet are as useful and as versatile and as widely used as silver. More on this important aspect of silver appears later in this chapter.

>> **Silver in the age of pandemic worries:** Centuries ago, folks used to put a silver dollar in water to avoid sickness, and its qualities are needed now more than ever. Silver is a natural biocide (it kills germs), and it's being used in greater quantities in healthcare and related fields. Given the 2020 global pandemic, that demand will only continue and likely increase.

>> **Silver mining as a by-product:** There are very few pure silver mines. Some exceptions are in Mexico. But overwhelmingly, silver is mined only as a by-product of mining other metals, such as base metals (copper, zinc, and so on). Base metals mining is an activity sensitively tied to economic activity. When the economy is doing well, then demand for base metals increases as we construct more buildings, factories, and so on.

Because these require base metals, the mining is necessary and the mining companies extract more silver because they're extracting more base metals. The opposite is generally true, too; when the economy is shrinking or stalling, demand for base metals tends to diminish, and subsequently, fewer base metals are mined. This, in turn, means less silver is mined and less silver makes its way to aboveground supplies.

>> **Silver's shrinking aboveground supply:** Gold's supply continuously is increased, year after year. Meanwhile, silver's supply is dwindling. Now when I say dwindling, I don't mean that it's disappearing; to be precise, I mean that its *usable* supply is dwindling. Take an ounce of silver, for example. It can be melted down and used in very tiny amounts and likely find its way into a few hundred smartphones. Ultimately, these smartphones will end up in landfills, but the silver won't be reclaimable (at least not in an economically feasible way).

Given this, silver as a usable asset shrinks in supply, and that will continue as a condition because uses for silver keep growing.

Digging into the Silver Market

For the coming decade, the silver supply has the potential of getting into a massive deficit that bodes well for silver investors and speculators. As demand continues to grow and accelerate due to technology and healthcare needs, this will put great pressure on the world's ability to find adequate supplies. All the supplies of gold ever found (by and large) are still available aboveground in some form or another. Silver, however, is a different animal in that it does get used up, and supply will ultimately not keep up with growing demand. Who knows how high the price of silver could go in five or ten years?

TIP

The more you know about silver and its market, the better your investing will be. Demand and supply are a major reason for price movements, of course, and you should be aware. Visit the Silver Institute (www.silverinstitute.org), which maintains and provides a wealth of useful information about the silver market.

Silver demand

Who is buying silver and why? It's time to see what demand is about for silver, given current market data and what's reasonably expected in the near future. Looking at the most recent complete year (2019), demand was 963.4 million ounces, according to the Silver Institute. This demand for silver comes from several places, as you find out in the following sections.

Manufacturing demand

Roughly half of the 2019 annual amount, 475.4 million ounces, are for industrial uses. In the past, the primary engine of industrial usage for silver was photography. As traditional photography went the way of the rotary phone and throwing rice at a wedding, silver's true strength and versatility came forward. There are thousands of industrial applications for silver. As a matter of fact, out of all the commodities in use in our economy, only petroleum is used in more different ways.

TECHNICAL STUFF

David Morgan of the Morgan Report (www.themorganreport.com) made the point that there are more patents filed at the U.S. Patent Office with silver (as a key ingredient or component) than with all other metals combined. See the nearby sidebar for more information on silver's many uses.

The largest use of silver comes from industrial demand (such as technology, healthcare, jewelry, silverware, and so on) followed by investment demand (such as bullion coins). Although photography has gotten all the attention in recent years, of the three major categories, it's the smallest. Industrial demand for silver makes up 43 percent of total demand, and this area is also the fastest *growing* area of silver demand. The industrial portion of the market is growing at about 2 percent per year.

It's important to understand that in almost all instances, the amount of silver used in a cellphone, laptop computer, or microwave oven is so small that it can't be recovered. For all practical purposes, the silver used in these applications is lost and unrecoverable. This type of demand is called *price-inelastic* by economists. The small amount of silver used makes it an insignificant factor in the price of the product. The amount of silver used in the manufacture of a battery, an automobile, a computer, or a cellphone is insignificant when compared to the price of labor and other materials. A doubling in the price of silver wouldn't affect, for example, what Honda uses in making an automobile. Because the price of silver has such a small relationship to the cost of the finished product, there is really no substitute. If the price of silver went to more than $100 per ounce, for example, the only possible substitute for silver would be palladium or platinum, both costing much more than $100 per ounce.

Investment demand

The next area of demand is from the world of investing with an annual amount of 215.8 million ounces. The biggest purchaser in this category is exchange-traded funds (ETFs; see Chapter 8). Also included here but to a much lesser extent is bullion dealers and other investment-related purchasers (see Chapters 9 and 10).

Jewelry demand

The third largest category at 187.5 million ounces is jewelry. Considering how much the missus buys on the home front, I am surprised this category isn't larger. India is the largest buyer in this category.

Silverware and photography

Lastly, the remaining small categories are silverware (54.3 million ounces) and photography (30.5 million ounces). Photography tells you how new technology can radically change the situation. This was once the leading category.

Silver supply

The annual supply of silver for 2019 was 978.1 million ounces, which means that for this particular year there was enough supply to meet the annual demand (supply exceeded demand by 14.7 million ounces). This supply mostly came from mining and recycling.

Then 797.8 million ounces came from global silver mining production. The largest source was Mexico, with Peru and China coming second and third. The U.S. was tenth.

For 2020, mining production will likely decline due to temporary mine closures because of the COVID-19 pandemic that hit the world in the spring. This shrinkage in supply may have been a contributing factor in silver's rise during midyear.

TIP

Given the great demand for silver, it's a good idea to bone up on mining stocks (check out Chapter 7 for details).

The second area for silver supply was recycling and reclamation at 169.4 million ounces, and finally 11 million ounces from miscellaneous sources.

SORTING THROUGH SILVER'S MANY USES

The multiple uses for silver started growing almost exponentially as industry figured out that silver's unique properties made it an ideal component in a broad array of products. Here is a partial list:

- Bactericide
- Batteries
- Bearings
- Brazing and soldering
- Catalysts
- Clothing (lining to kill bacteria)
- Coins
- Computer components
- Electrical
- Electronics
- Electroplating
- Healthcare
- Jewelry and silverware
- Medical applications
- Mirrors and coatings
- Nanotechnology
- Photography
- Plasma screens
- Solar energy
- Super conductivity
- Surgical instruments
- Washing machines
- Water purification

Yes, it's a partial list, and it keeps growing.

Future drivers of silver

As you can figure out, silver isn't a static asset; it's quite dynamic. New uses emerge regularly, and being among the first to find out gives you a profitable edge before the pack finds outs. Many of the resources provided in this chapter and in Appendix A will keep you ahead of the curve.

A good example is the latest projection of silver usage in solar energy that I just picked up as I researched for the latest data to include in this chapter. An industry report was recently issued that photovoltaic cells and other solar technology will consume 888 million ounces of silver during 2020–2030. Just this one use means an amount that's over 50 million ounces more than all silver mine production from 2019!

REMEMBER

This is a recipe for investment success — positioning yourself in an asset that is (and will) experience tremendous demand while supply can't keep up.

Starting with Silver's Modern History in the 1970s

I won't go to ancient times to provide the backdrop to silver's price, but I will start at what may seem like an odd year: 1971. This was a tipping point year for both gold and silver because it essentially launched the modern gold and silver market.

This is a historic year as the federal government severed the dollar's last connection to the price of gold (August 15, 1971) that was present since the mid-1940s with the Bretton Woods accord. This essentially allowed the limitless production of dollars and unleashed the modern era of inflation.

Before, the gold standard did place a break or limit to the quantity of dollars created, but now all constraints to increasing the supply of dollars were gone. Just before that fateful date, silver was under $1.80 per ounce, and gold was under $43 per ounce. From 1934 to 1968, gold's price was fixed at $35. Then the transition to a market-based price started.

TECHNICAL
STUFF

Gold rose from less than $45 in 1971 to about $200 in the middle of the decade. At that time, the dollar started to be created at greater quantities by the Federal Reserve, inflation rose to double digits during the latter years of the 1970s, and gold hit $850 in January 1980. Anyone who bought gold at or less than $45 and rode it to $850 would have achieved a mind-boggling rise during that time frame of approximately 1,788 percent. But how about silver?

Silver's price ranged from $1.30 to nearly $1.80 during 1971. Anyone who backed up the truck and bought a load of it could have, by the end of the decade, uh, bought a new truck (and a new house, too!). Silver hit $50 by January 1980. That rocket-ship ride was a moon shot at 2,677 percent.

The 1980s and 1990s were unspectacular times for silver, so I'll spare you the blow-by-blow of that time frame, but then things get interesting and profitable in the next millennium. Keep reading.

Picking Apart Silver's Performance during 2000–2020

Fast-forward to our century (welcome back!) and we see that silver (along with gold) experienced two bull markets, and we're likely in the third one as of the 2020–2022 time frame.

To get a snapshot of silver's performance for January 2000 to 2020, look at Figure 6-1.

Silver – London PM Fix 2000 – present

© John Wiley & Sons, Inc.

FIGURE 6-1: Silver's performance for January 2000 to 2020.

Figure 6-1 indicates the first bull market was from 2000 to early 2008, as silver went from about $5 to $21 in March 2008. The second bull market started late 2008–early 2009 and ended in May 2011 when silver peaked near $50 ($45.83) before it tumbled into an extended bear market starting in mid-2011 and lasting eight years into 2019.

I take a closer look at silver's performance in the following sections.

The first silver bull market (2000–2008)

Silver started off the millennium around $5 an ounce, and although it had a slow climb upward, there was still good money to be made. The silver mining stocks (see Chapter 7) were a good example. Many were available at single digits and had a great ride up with silver. A good example was the stock Silver Wheaton (now called Wheaton Precious Metals with its new stock symbol WPM). Investors could have picked it up for less than $2 during 2000–2002. I initially got in at $3.25, and it hit a high near $40 in early 2008.

The run for silver itself was great. When it hit $21 an ounce in March 2008, the ride was a gain of 320 percent for those who got in at $5. But the silver market was interrupted by a timely crash. Silver had a rough year in 2008 in roller-coaster fashion. Yes, it soared during the first half but crashed with the stock market, oil, and other vehicles during the second half.

Silver started 2008 at $15.16 then peaked at $21.18 (March 2008). It traded sideways until August 2008 when the massacre began. Its plunge hit bottom at $8.78 (October 2008) before it limped across the finish line at year's end at 11.27.

Silver lost 25 percent that year, but it wasn't finished yet with its upmoves.

The bull market of 2009–2011 and the bear market of 2011–2018

The end of 2008 and early 2009 marked silver's last extended period when its price was in single digits (less than $10). Silver consolidated and this became a firm launchpad for its second bull market.

The bull market lasted about 2½ years starting the end of 2008 and culminating in its peak of nearly $50 by May 2011. The interesting thing is that during this 2½-year stretch, silver had an amazing 23 corrections (as reported by Jeff Clark of www.goldsilver.com). Each correction was 5 to 10 percent. This meant that speculators and short-term traders could have made some nice small profits along the way as silver zigzagged its way to its second trip to $50.

For investors who merely bought at under $10 and rode it up with a buy-and-hold approach, they would have made a handsome 455 percent — not too shabby!

For the 2011–2018 time frame, silver was basically trading sideways in the high teens as it built a base for its next bull market starting in 2019. As it languished in low prices ($14–$21 range), I think of the adage that the cure for low prices is . . . low prices. This means that the price is low given the value and potential demand, which becomes the setup for the next rally in higher prices.

TIP

For those who are short-term speculators and who want to profit from the mini-rallies and corrections in a given bull (or even bear market), be sure to use technical analysis and watch indicators such as the Relative Strength Index for conditions of "overbought" and "oversold," and also watch for moving averages. Find out more about technical analysis in Chapter 15. Make sure also to use limit orders, stop-loss orders, and trailing stops for easier purchase and sell transactions. More about these stock brokerage orders are in Chapter 16.

Long-term investors should use stock brokerage orders, too, but also keep in mind the fundamentals of a stock, which are very important for long-term investing time frames. I cover fundamentals extensively in my book *Stock Investing For Dummies* (Wiley), but you can find a good overview for mining stock fundamentals in Chapter 7.

Silver versus the financial world in 2020 and beyond

So how did silver stack up against gold and other titans of the financial world? In Chapter 5, I show silver's performance during 2000–2020 so you can readily see that it was in second place with a percentage gain of 251 percent. I guess that means it got the "silver" medal (am I clever or what?!).

There's no need to replicate Chapter 5's information here, so I take the short-term approach and focus on the first seven months of 2020 (I'm writing this in August). Check out Table 6-1 comparing silver with the rest of the financial world.

Would you look at that — silver isn't the second banana it was from Chapter 5's table. Here, it was the top performer in what has been an incredible year. Gold came in a strong second place (no gold medal in this short-term round). Here are some further thoughts on this snapshot of data:

>> The worst performer for this 2020 time frame (again, only seven months) was crude oil. Because of the pandemic and the government lockdown that shut down economic activity from February to July 2020, this, in turn, sent oil plummeting because demand plummeted drastically.

TABLE 6-1   **Silver's "Tale of the Tape" in the First Part of 2020**

Asset	Open Price Jan. 3, 2020	Closing Price July 31, 2020	Total Gain/Loss Dollar Amount $	Total Gain/ Loss Percentage %
Silver	$18.28	$24.22	$5.94	32.49%
Gold	$1,520.85	$1,985.90	$465.05	30.58%
Crude Oil	$61.52	$40.27	–$21.25	–34.54%
Dow Jones Industrial Average (stocks)	$28,638.97	$26,428.32	–$2,210.65	–7.72%
Nasdaq (Stocks)	$9,039.46	$10,745.28	$1,705.82	18.87%
S&P 500 (Stocks)	$3,244.67	$3,271.12	$26.45	0.82%
Average Savings acct.*	$100	$100.56	56 cents	0.56%

Assuming a savings account balance of $100 and assuming an annual interest rate of 1% for comparison purposes.

>> For stocks, the numbers don't adequately convey what an incredible roller-coaster ride this time frame was. Virtually across the board, mainstream stocks were down approximately 30 to 40 percent during February to April. The Federal Reserve swung into action and had trillions of dollars (artificial demand) push (or reinflate) stocks in a herculean rescue mission. What would have happened with stocks if the Fed didn't perform this outsized rescue mission?

>> You didn't have losses in your average savings account, which is why you settle for paltry returns.

What are some lessons for investors? Diversification is the obvious lesson. Stocks and the economy were heading in dangerous, overheated territory even before February 2020. Stocks were getting overbought before the pandemic, so red flags for investors and speculators were already present.

REMEMBER

The remark from some experts that the stock market was "a bubble looking for a pin" proved a correct observation. Gold and silver did well this year due to fundamentals (such as supply and demand). Fundamentals is the foundational information that should be guiding investors' long-term decisions. For gold and silver, 2020 showed the investment world that they have the fundamentals amidst the wreckage to do well and to earn a spot in a well-diversified portfolio, especially because problems with the rest of the financial world will persist and may get much worse for 2021–2022.

REMEMBER

For silver, when you focus on the demand-and-supply fundamentals coupled with what's going on in the rest of the world, it can become a compelling case for what may be silver's greatest bull market in this century. In my estimation, I believe that the third time is the charm and that silver has the drivers in place now to eventually break through the $50 level to an all-time high.

Resources for Informed Silver Investors

Key analysts in the industry see silver's potential to be in triple digits. Your best approach is to keep informed so that you can be appropriately positioned to capitalize on the potential gains. The resources in this section can help you stay informed.

TIP

Here are three great sources of data on the silver market that you should be regularly reviewing:

>> Silver Institute (www.silverinstitute.org)

>> Kitco Silver (www.kitcosilver.com)

>> CPM Group (www.cpmgroup.com)

TIP

And here are some of the top analysts who cover silver:

>> Ted Butler (www.butlerresearch.com)

>> David Morgan (www.themorganreport.com)

>> Doug Casey (www.internationalman.com)

>> Jay Taylor (www.miningstocks.com)

There are more great resources in Appendix A — now go forth and profit!

Chapter **7**

Making the Most of Mining Stocks

I love stock investing, even during insane periods such as 2020–2021. I could write a whole book about it — oh, wait, actually, I did: *Stock Investing For Dummies*, published by Wiley. But here I get to do a chapter and be focused on a specific industry: gold and silver mining. In this chapter, I give you my favorite points about stocks (any kind, actually) and the specific numbers and features that are particularly important for mining stocks.

Mining stocks are an excellent consideration during a gold and silver bull market. They can offer great profit potential, and as long as you understand the risks going in, you'll be good to go. Some types of mining stocks are indeed a good consideration for investors, but many are more appropriate as speculative opportunities. In this chapter, you discover the difference.

Examining the Essentials of Stock Investing

When it comes to stock investing, there's something for everyone. But if you're going to choose good stocks, you have to ignore "what everyone is doing." In this section, I cover the main aspects of stock investing; I get to mining stocks specifically later in this chapter.

REMEMBER

When you're buying stock, you're actually buying a tiny percentage of ownership in a particular company. Your stock will be more (or less) valuable based on how well that company is doing, and this is as evident with companies in the gold and silver mining industry as anywhere else. Read this entire chapter before you buy your first share of that company.

The whole point of stocks is to choose one that has the greatest chance of having a rising share value. We all want to buy a $3 stock and sell it later for $257 per share or better. But how would you proceed to accomplish such a feat? What would make a stock rise so much? If the company does well, ultimately, the price of the stock attached to it will rise. If the company does poorly, ultimately, the stock will go down. Why would the stock go up (or down)?

REMEMBER

Always keep in mind that the real force that moves the price of the stock up or down is the marketplace. The marketplace is composed of buyers and sellers that are individuals and organizations. If there are more buyers (versus sellers) of a stock, then the stock price will go up. If there are more sellers (than buyers), then the stock price will go down. The buying and selling goes on in stock exchanges such as the New York Stock Exchange (NYSE; www.nyse.com) and places that aren't technically exchanges such as Nasdaq (www.nasdaq.com). For you to conduct your stock transactions, you need a stock brokerage account (stock brokerage accounts are covered in Chapter 16).

Why does anyone buy a stock? Of course, we can say the obvious: that you buy a stock because you think that the stock's price will go up and you can sell it later at a profit (capital gain). So the primary reason the public buys a stock is for gain. The second reason to buy a stock is for income (dividends). Ultimately, the stock and its performance will be based on the company's performance as measured by sales and profits. It seems like a pretty logical process: Find a company with strong prospects and potential success, and the stock attached to it will rise and, you'll profit. Not so fast!

Sometimes you'll see Company A doing well and being profitable, yet the stock's price goes down. Or you may see Company B doing poorly and losing money, yet its stock rises. It makes you scratch your head. What gives? I can boil down to one word why anyone buys a stock: expectation. When you see the stock of a profitable company go down, it's obvious that there were more sellers than buyers, but why? The answer is that stocks don't go up and down because of how well (or how poorly) a company is doing presently; they go up or down because of what buyers or sellers *expect* will happen with that company in the near future.

Understand that the behavior of a stock in the short term is irrational; the stock's price will behave in ways that are seemingly crazy and illogical. However, the performance of the company and the performance of the stock over the *longer term* do become a logical relationship. In the long term, solid, profitable companies have rising stock prices while poorly run, unprofitable companies have declining stock prices. The lesson to investors is that trying to make short-term profits in their stock investing approach is a gamble (it's speculating), while making money is easier when you're patient and focused on the longer term. Sooner or later, the market figures it out. Good companies whose share prices have gone down in the short term become a buying opportunity. Bad companies whose share prices have gone up in the short term give you the opportunity to unload the shares.

The bottom line is to not worry about the short-term gyrations of the stock. Instead, focus your time and effort in finding companies that are strong, are well positioned in the right industries, and have solid fundamentals (good products or services, growing industry, rising sales, increasing profits, and so on). The following sections focus on some of those fundamentals.

A profitable company

What insightful advice: Choose a company that's profitable! Well, this point isn't as obvious as it sounds. Many companies have been unprofitable and their stock rose dramatically. There's nothing wrong in buying the stock of a company that's losing money. But if you do that, you're not investing; you're speculating. Investing means that you're putting your money into assets (stock, bonds, gold, and so on) that have provable value and that you understand how the investment works and that it's appropriate for you and your financial objectives.

Speculating is a different animal altogether. Speculating is a form of financial gambling. Now that may be too extreme a definition because speculating is a bit more complicated than tossing some dice at a casino table. However, the essence of the transaction is an educated guess. In speculating, the payoff could be big and fast. However, the potential loss could be equally big and fast. You should speculate with only a relatively small portion of your total finances. I personally enjoy speculating, and I do a lot of it, but I still keep the bulk of my money in more stable, predictable venues such as conservative stocks and cash.

Back to profitability. Profit is important. Actually, profit is the *most* important part of the company's total financial picture. Profit is the lifeblood of the company; profit is the engine of growth for innovation, jobs, and so on; and I'll take it a step further: Profit is the lifeblood of a successful economy. You show me an economy where profit is abolished, and I'll show you an economy that either has collapsed or will collapse. It's true for the company as well. How do you find out about the company's profitability?

The profit is also expressed as net earnings, net gain, and net income. It's the end result in the company's income statement (sales less expenses equals net profit or net loss), which can be found in a number of places. The income statement (also called the P&L statement, or profit-and-loss statement) can be found in the company's annual report or website. In addition, it's part of the financial statements that are made available at other venues such as at the Securities and Exchange Commission (go to www.sec.gov and use the agency's EDGAR database to locate any public company's public filings) and many financial websites such as Market-Watch (www.marketwatch.com).

TIP

As a general rule, investors should look at how profitable the company has been in the most recent three consecutive years. You want to see consistent profits, and it's preferable that the profits are at least 10 percent (or more) higher than the year before. In addition, you want to see rising sales in conjunction with those rising profits. Total sales should be consistently rising year-over-year (again, I like to use an easy benchmark like 10 percent or more).

A growing industry

Ever heard the expression "a rising tide lifts all boats"? Well, before you go buy a yacht, think over what that really means for your stock portfolio. Having tracked the stock market over the past few decades, I've seen it over and over again. I've seen the stocks of mediocre companies go up because they're in a strong and growing industry. And of course, I've seen the reverse. Picking a stock doesn't happen in a vacuum. Understanding and being aware of that company's industry and the overall economic environment is critical to stock-picking success.

Sometimes I think that the industry and overall economy matter more than the company itself. I have avoided good companies because I expected their industry to experience tough times. I also had no problem buying shares of average or below-average companies that were in hot industries. You'll also find out that figuring out the general direction of the industry is easier than for the individual company.

For gold and silver stocks, mining companies are really a leveraged play on the price of gold and/or silver. If those metals' prices keep rising, then the fortunes of the company will rise significantly, and the share price can soar. Find out more about mining companies later in this chapter.

A healthy balance sheet

Another thing to look at when you're evaluating fundamentals is the company's balance sheet. It's simply a snapshot at a point in time showing what the company owns and what it owes. It's expressed as assets minus liabilities equals share-holders' equity (or net assets or net worth). A company's financial statements aren't that difficult to figure out because there's a lot of similarity to your financial picture. You personally have a budget and you need to track your income and expenses (just like a corporate income statement). You track what you own and what you owe (again, just like a corporate balance sheet).

REMEMBER

Look for a few things that are key to the company's financial health:

>> **Is the company's net worth growing every year?** Each year should be at least 10 percent higher than the year before (preferably more).

>> **Are assets increasing?** The more it owns, the better.

>> **Are its debts stable, low, and/or decreasing?** The less it owes, the better.

Yes, there's always more to know, but if you get the major numbers right, you'll be almost home free. How do you get those major numbers? You need to take a close look at an intimate relationship. No, don't go peering into your neighbor's window — I mean the company's numbers! I'm talking about ratios that help you analyze a company's finances to get a clear picture of the company's financial health. Here are some ratios that are critical for your analysis:

>> **Price-to-earnings (PE) ratio:** This is based on a per-share basis. You divide the price of a share price by the net earnings per share. The PE ratio estab-lishes a connection between the share price and the company's bottom line. All things being equal, a relatively low PE ratio (under 15) is considered safer than a relatively high PE (over 30). Large, stable companies tend to have low PE ratios. Small, speculative companies tend to have very high PE ratios (some are over 100, sometimes way over!), which indicates greater risk. Companies with no PE ratio are the riskiest. (They have a share price but have no earnings or have losses, therefore no PE ratio.)

>> **Debt-to-asset (DA) ratio:** This ratio puts the company's total debt (or total liabilities) and total assets in perspective. For example, a company with total debt of $1 million and total assets of $2 million has a 0.50 DA ratio. In other words, the company has 50 cents of total debt for every dollar of assets. A DA ratio of 0.50 or less is desirable. A DA higher than 1.0 indicates a debt load that's too high, and it could cause the company problems, especially if the economy is slowing down.

>> **Comparative year ratios:** This is simple. You compare the important line items of one year to the prior year. If total sales this year are $15 million and last year they were $10 million, your sales are 50 percent higher. You do the same calculation with net earnings and with the important numbers on the balance sheet (such as the net equity).

TIP

There are excellent websites with information for beginners looking for explanations regarding ratios and other financial terms. Check out Yahoo! Finance at www.finance.yahoo.com and the extensive glossary at www.investopedia.com. For more details on choosing stocks, check out my book *Stock Investing For Dummies*, which is published by Wiley and can be found at www.dummies.com.

Knowing What to Look for When You Evaluate Mining Stocks

The points about stock investing fundamentals earlier in this chapter are indeed a mini crash course in stock investing ("Paul, don't use the word *crash* in a stock investing chapter!"). Setting aside the basics of stocks in general, it's time to take a closer look at the heart and soul of this chapter, the mining stocks. The following sections provide pointers on what to look for in mining stocks and companies.

Value that isn't cheaper than dirt

Why do you buy the stock of a gold mining company? How about a silver mining stock? Or any stock of any company involved primarily or exclusively in natural resources? It's what they have. It pays for you to find out about their properties and their provable reserves. It can tell you whether the stock's price is undervalued or overvalued.

Here's an example: I know of one silver mining company that was recently priced at $37 per share. Yet the company has in provable reserves more than 1 billion ounces of silver in its properties. With silver at $13 an ounce, it means that its total silver reserves are valued at $13 billion. When you divide the company's total shares into that number, the company would be worth more than $200 a share on a silver-per-share basis. If you can buy a stock for $37 that is actually worth at least $200, then you have an undervalued stock.

Always find out the total value of the metal/mineral reserves because that will give you a strong idea of the company's potential worth, especially in a bull market. The details on the company's reserves are typically at the company's website and in its annual report. If the company is on Nasdaq or the NYSE, the data will be in the company's 10-K report that can be found at the SEC's website, www.sec.gov.

Management that you can dig

The management team of a mining company should be loaded with mining professionals with at least a decade or more of industry experience. This is information that is usually readily available at the company website or industry Who's Who directories. They should have had successful top-management positions with prominent, recognizable mining companies in their career. Professionals that lead midsize companies and/or have developed a track record of successful mining projects/properties are also desirable.

Politics: Not in my backyard

Where the company's mining properties are located (the political jurisdiction) is very important. On the global scene, a lot of mining is being done in countries that have an unfriendly or hostile political climate. Many mining firms were victimized by socialist or authoritarian governments that changed the rules on them. Some of these dictators imposed draconian steps such as arbitrarily raising taxes to exorbitant levels or just outright confiscating the mining company's property (a practice referred to as nationalizing). This can be dangerous for the mining company and, of course, the shareholders as well. There are companies that have seen their stock fall by 50 percent or more in a single day!

Investors need to keep informed about the politics involved. They need to ask what countries are risky and whether the company has much exposure there. Political risk is very real, but investors and speculators can add a measure of safety by making sure that they invest in companies that predominantly (or exclusively) are in mining-friendly jurisdictions such as the United States, Canada, Australia, Mexico, and a few other countries. More about political risks is in Chapter 4.

Distinguishing Different Types of Mining Stocks

The world of mining stocks is very varied. Some choices are conservative as well as aggressive. Some are appropriate for the stodgy investor as well as for the firebrand speculator. You just need to know the difference.

REMEMBER

At the crux of a mining company's success is the property to be mined and how productive that property is. A company will refer either to a property's resources or to its reserves. There is a crucial difference:

>> When a property has resources, that means it may have metals/minerals in the ground, but it isn't confirmed about the quality and quantity.

>> Reserves is a higher standard. Extensive and reliable testing took place, and the company is assured of the quantity and quality of the metals/minerals in the property. The bottom line here is you want to be sure the company has reserves.

When you're researching the company, here are the types of properties that are most desirable:

>> **Producing properties:** Properties with high-grade deposits are being mined and the metal is extracted and sold.

>> **Development properties:** This property has proven and extractable reserves verified by a reliable feasibility study.

>> **Predevelopment properties:** Preliminary drilling indicates it has reserves and is ready for a feasibility study.

WARNING

Any other type of property is purely speculative. If it's referred to as dormant, dead, or speculative, then you're better off leaving it to a man named Jed Clampett and just moving. However, note that the locations of these properties are very important, so read the earlier section "Politics: Not in my backyard."

REMEMBER

Diversifying is more than just buying a bunch of different stocks. In the world of precious metals, it's more than just a bunch of different mining stocks. It also means understanding yourself and your goals and being aware of the different kinds of mining stocks. You'll read about the three basic categories of stocks in the following sections. From an investor's point of view, you can reasonably assume that the first category (the majors) is conservative, the second is growth (the mid-tier, development companies), and the third is speculative (exploratory companies). Depending on the amount you're willing to invest/speculate with, consider

5 to 15 companies across the categories. If you're conservative, then by all means have more of your choices tipped in favor of the majors and the development companies. If you put 100 percent of your portfolio money into mining, then you're getting too speculative, so it's a safer idea to have a large portion of your money elsewhere, such as energy, consumer staples, and so on.

The majors

Among mining stocks, this is the safest bet. This top tier is the most appropriate category for conservative investors considering precious metals for their stock portfolios. Besides the fact that they're large companies, they're producing companies. This means that the metals/minerals are already being extracted from producing properties and being sold.

Some examples of large gold mining companies that are producers are Newmont Goldcorp (NEM), Yamana Gold (AUY), AngloGold Ashanti (AU), Freeport McMo-Ran (FCX), and Barrick Gold (GOLD). Although they're referred to as gold mining companies, they do mine in the course of their business other metals/minerals that are found in the same mines.

There are fewer primary silver producers, but among the major ones are Pan American Silver (PAAS), Apex Mining (SIL), and Coeur D'Alene Mines (CDE).

TIP

The large producers are listed on the major stock exchanges, and you can find them and other mining companies at the stock exchange's website and do a keyword search. In addition, websites such as Yahoo! Finance (https://finance. yahoo.com) have great stock screening tools that let you find stocks by industry, size (such as market capitalization), and keyword.

Midtier mining companies

This category is also referred to as midsize or midtier companies. They may very well have producing properties, but they're primarily developers. They may even do some exploratory activity. Some mature into producing companies. Some examples include Harmony Gold (HMY), Agnico Eagle Mines (AEM), and Seabridge (SA). They may operate properties that have proven reserves that they're ready to take into the production phase.

This middle category is appropriate for growth-oriented investors. It can be aggressive but not as speculative as the lower tier of small miners.

Junior miners, eureka! Exploratory companies

This is the category for those looking for the home run. The problem is that you get a lot of strikeouts, too. In this category, you have the smaller companies that are drilling and exploring on properties that may or may not prove to be valuable. This becomes the crapshoot for those who want to speculate. It's important to look for companies (and management) that have a proven record for successful projects, as I explain earlier in this chapter.

TIP

Unless you have the contacts and the time to do exhaustive research (like visiting the companies and their properties), it's best to get the guidance of experts who extensively cover this corner of the mining world. Some names that come to mind are Rick Rule, Jay Taylor, Doug Casey, David Morgan, and Lawrence Roulston. These individuals have newsletters and websites; they're listed in Appendix A, and some are spotlighted at the end of this chapter.

TIP

Junior mining stocks may be speculative, but because they are generally inexpensive (most are under $10 per share and many are less than $5 per share), it isn't a bad idea to buy 3 to 10 different juniors. Just know that although some will lose money and be a "strikeout," you may have a stock or two that could be "home runs." Be sure to only do so with risk capital (I have the phrase "play money," but you get the point).

Considering the Risks of Mining Stocks

Any company can run into problems. If you've followed the financials at all in recent years, you've got a good idea. Most companies go bankrupt for a variety of reasons, with the number one reason always being not having enough money. Among the surviving companies, you can run across lots of rough patches such as economic slowdowns, regulatory problems, too much debt, not enough sales, lawsuits, yadda yadda. This, you knew. But every industry or sector has unique negatives and positives as part of the territory.

WARNING

You know about the positive stuff about mining stocks (that's what drew you to begin with). But for the sake of completeness, here's a rundown of pitfalls in the mining industry:

>> Mineworkers strike

>> Inflationary production costs

>> Rising costs of raw materials and energy

- » Regulatory changes

- » Environmental problems (regulations, protestors, and so on)

- » Mining accidents

- » Political changes/upheaval (especially in unfriendly countries)

TIP

If you have a mining stock and you're concerned about its prospects or unsure about economic conditions facing your stock, consider making some defensive moves. Here are some considerations:

- » **Protective put:** This strategy means buying a put on your stock. It becomes a cheap form of insurance. Get more information on puts in Chapter 13.

- » **Stop-loss orders:** If your stock is at $20 per share, consider putting a stop-loss order at a price of, say, $15 and make it a GTC (good-till-canceled) order. If the stock rises, you can cancel your stop-loss order and replace it with a new stop-loss order at a higher price. More about brokerage orders is in Chapter 16.

Boosting Your Returns

Merely buying and holding mining stocks for future capital gain can be profitable, but with the help of the following sections, you can find ways to boost the profitability in your portfolio and squeeze more return on your investment.

Generating income

Until your mining stocks go through the roof because gold zoomed to $3,000 an ounce and the other metals hit nosebleed territory, you can do something to make more money on your portfolio. The following sections show you a few ways to do it.

Dividends

Normally, mining stocks aren't considered income stocks. An income stock refers to a stock that pays dividends greater than the average stock. Lately, this means a dividend yielding 3.5 percent or higher. Most mining stocks aren't income stocks, but there are some that issue regular dividends. Some of the large firms do provide a regular dividend, such as Newmont Mining (symbol NEM) and Wheaton Precious Metals (symbol WPM).

Also, just because the stock has a low dividend, that doesn't mean that it stays there. As company revenues grow, the dividend tends to grow as well. Studies have shown that dividends rise faster than the rate of inflation. That's another plus for long-term investors.

In addition, during the heyday of gold mining stocks (the late 1970s), many in fact issued dividends that very briefly qualified them as high-income stocks. Should gold and other precious metals hit new highs in the coming years (which is possible during 2021–2023), then it's very possible that some high dividends can be paid again. Stay tuned!

Writing covered calls

TIP

A very easy way to generate income from a portfolio of mining stocks is to write covered calls on your stocks. In fact, it's not difficult to safely generate income through this specific strategy of 10 to 20 percent. Imagine getting income that could be four or five (or more) times greater than a bond or certificate of deposit starting with a mining stock that issues no dividend! It's like being in the twilight zone. Aside from the usual risk of stock investing, covered call writing is virtually risk-free. To get more information regarding this income-generating approach, see Chapter 13.

Leveraging with warrants

Warrants can be an unusual security, and most investors aren't familiar with them. Technically, they trade like stocks (bought and sold like stocks), but essentially they work like options (covered in Chapter 13). So they warrant coverage here.

TIP

There are very few sources of information on warrants, but one that I like is Dudley Baker's website at `https://commonstockwarrants.com/precious-metals-warrants`. Discuss warrants with your financial advisor. I wouldn't be surprised if you end up educating him or her about the topic!

How warrants work

A warrant (or "stock warrant") is a financial vehicle that gives the investor the right, but not the obligation, to buy the underlying security (usually common stock) at a specific price during the life of the warrant. A warrant is a wasting asset, which means that it will expire on a specific date in the future. However, warrants usually have a long shelf life; freshly issued warrants could expire in as little as two years or as long as five years (or longer). You can say that a warrant can be a hybrid of both a stock and an option. Warrants can be private financial instruments, but of course, many are publicly traded.

The holder of a warrant (much like the holder or buyer of an option) can exercise the warrant to buy the underlying security, but what you can buy differs somewhat with the option. When you buy the typical option, a single option contract represents 100 shares of that particular stock (or exchange-traded fund). A two option contract means 200 shares, and so on. A warrant, on the other hand, isn't rigidly standardized the way publicly traded options are.

A typical warrant would have a ratio of one warrant to one share of stock. In other words, if you have 100 warrants of Groundhog Mining Co., this gives you the ability to purchase 100 shares of Groundhog Mining's stock. However, plenty of options aren't so cut-and-dry. There are warrants where the ratio is one warrant to two shares of stock or to one share of common stock and one share of preferred stock and so on. Check with the issuer of the warrant (in this case, Groundhog Mining) or the company's shareholder service department.

Where to find warrants

REMEMBER

Before you invest in warrants, get the full details. The most common place to find publicly traded warrants is Nasdaq's Over-The-Counter (OTC) small company market, and you can find information at the OTC Bulletin Board (OTCBB; www.otcbb.com). Don't invest in a warrant just because it's available. Instead, do your research on mining stocks, and then contact the company's shareholder service department and ask whether that particular company has or will issue warrants. Frequently, the details are available on the company's website.

Keep in mind that you can also find warrants at the New York Stock Exchange (NYSE; www.nyse.com) and Nasdaq (www.nasdaq.com), but your most successful searches for metals and mining-related warrants will most likely be at the OTCBB and some international exchanges. Some obvious ones will be in Canada, such as the Vancouver Stock Exchange (www.theexchangevancouver.com) and the Toronto Stock Exchange (www.tmx.com). Fortunately, many foreign stocks and warrants do trade on the OTCBB. At the OTCBB, you'll notice that foreign securities will be assigned a fifth letter in their symbol, the letter *f*, to signify a foreign security.

The risks of warrants

WARNING

Another thing that warrants attention is the risk. If the company's stock falls, then the warrant's price would fall, and it would likely fall more so. Keep in mind that a warrant (like an option) is a derivative. It's a fancy term that is essentially very simple. A derivative means that this particular financial vehicle or instrument derives its value from something else, the underlying asset.

A warrant or option on Groundhog Mining Co. would derive its value from the price and performance of Groundhog's common stock. Actually, when you think about it, its common stock is a derivative, too; it derives its value from the operations, assets, and profitability of the company itself. Stretching it a bit further, a gold mining company would derive its value from the value of the gold it owned or controlled. All right, I'll stop at this point before you derive a headache (aspirin is a derivative of tree bark). The bottom line is that you wouldn't analyze the warrant to understand its potential; you'd analyze the underlying asset (the company and the metals involved).

Lastly, the most important risk with warrants is the major risk that's also present with options; they can expire and be worthless. You must do something with them before they expire (such as sell them or acquire the underlying security). Fortunately, unlike most options, warrants do have a long shelf life, and that longer time frame does make them less speculative in comparison.

Checking out mining stock indexes

Indexes provide a great snapshot of the broad market or of a specific market, industry, or sector.

TIP If you want to invest or speculate on the indexes, you can do it through exchange-traded funds (ETFs) and/or through options. For investors, there are ETFs that closely mirror or track indexes. You can find more information on ETFs in Chapter 8. For speculators and experienced investors, consider options on the indexes (see Chapter 13 regarding the world of options). Further, there are options on ETFs as well. Man! Are there choices or what? This is cool stuff.

I cover the most widely followed indexes in the following list:

>> **PHLX Gold/Silver Sector Index (XAU):** This is a capitalization-weighted index created and maintained by the Philadelphia Stock Exchange (www.phlx.com). The XAU is the broadest index of the gold and silver mining sector.

>> **NYSE Arca Gold Bugs Index (HUI):** I like this name; gold bugs is a reference to those folks who are very enthusiastic about gold and its prospects. This index is called that because it includes only mining stocks that don't hedge. (Hedging is a practice by some mining companies that lock in a price for their gold for future delivery. This is great if gold goes sideways or goes down but a bad bet if gold goes up; you can't sell the gold at a higher price because you locked in the sale at a lower fixed price.) To be unhedged in gold production is to be very bullish in gold. The HUI is a modified equal dollar weighted index of companies involved in gold mining.

>> **NYSE Arca Gold Miners Index (GDM):** This index isn't as widely followed as the XAU or HUI, but it's an important index for precious metals investors. The GDM is a modified market capitalization weighted index comprised of publicly traded companies involved primarily in the mining for gold and silver. The index divisor was initially determined to yield a benchmark value of 500.00 starting in December 2002.

Spotlighting the Pros

What better way to end this chapter than with some insights from experts who have a long track record of mining stock success?

TIP

I'm just scratching the surface on my favorite gold and silver stock experts here, and I don't have space for every mining stock expert, but consider David Morgan (www.themorganreport.com) and Jay Taylor (www.miningstocks.com) as well. You can find more experts listed in Appendix A.

Rick Rule

Rick Rule is a veteran mining stock investor and analyst, and he's also the CEO of Sprott, Inc. (https://sprott.com), a billion-dollar investment firm that specializes in gold and silver investments (physical, stocks, and ETFs). In a nutshell, here are his main points about the gold/silver market and also on considering a mining stock. Four factors in today's global economy and financial markets make gold and silver very attractive:

>> Quantitative easing (QE) or money printing by the Federal Reserve

>> Excessive debt and deficits

>> Low interest rates

>> Gold and silver extremely under-owned

On mining stocks, Rick seeks the following four features:

>> Value

>> People and expertise

>> Developing pipeline of new mining projects

>> Provable reserves

Fortunately, Rick and the folks at Sprott do regular interviews regarding the industry and about the gold and silver market, and they make those videos and audios available at www.sprottmedia.com.

Doug Casey

For long-time observers and players in the gold and silver world, Doug Casey achieved legendary success. He (and his clients and readers) made a fortune during the precious metals bull market of the late 1970s, and he consistently succeeded in virtually every precious metals bull (and bear) market since.

When he analyzes mining companies to decide whether to invest, he uses a system using the "9 Ps":

>> **People:** Are they experienced, and do they have a successful track record of finding gold/silver deposits?

>> **Property:** Does the property have a strong geological presence of potential reserves?

>> **"Phinancing":** It's financing, but he has to get that P in. Does the company have the financial clout and/or access to financing so that the project (mining for gold/silver) can come to fruition?

>> **Paper:** This is a companion item to financing. Does the company have the ability to issue (or has it issued) shares to help with gaining capital?

>> **Promotion:** Does the company have the capability to communicate the benefits of this project to investors and analysts?

>> **Politics:** Is the project in a conducive regulatory and politically friendly jurisdiction?

>> **Push:** Is there something exciting about the project that can move investors to buy the stock now or in the near future?

>> **Pitfalls:** What are potential events that could affect the project (miners' strike, bad weather, earthquakes, and so on), and can you prepare?

>> **Price:** The price of the metal you're mining will affect success. If it's gold and gold's price is going up, that bodes well for the company and the stock price.

Of course, all nine points have more details for your review. To find out more about Doug Casey's research and greater mining stock insights, check out his main site at www.internationalman.com.

Chapter **8**

Examining Mutual Funds and ETFs

There was a great author who started off a book with "it was the best of times, it was the worst of times" or something like that. As I write this chapter, the conditions on the world scene could qualify as the worst of times depending on how you look at it. In 2020, we worry about a global pandemic, riots in cities, government budgets gone berserk, national debt skyrocketing, terrorism, inflation, market volatility, retirement, and so on. On the other hand, when it comes to the fantastic panorama of investing choices, techniques, and strategies available today, it can easily qualify as the best of times. This chapter offers a glimpse of the best of times (at least in investment vehicles).

As you find out here, you can invest, speculate, or otherwise participate in the world of precious metals in many ways. Mutual funds and exchange-traded funds (ETFs) are yet another way for investors and speculators to get involved. They're actually ideally suited for conservative investors but can also have features that traders and speculators find appealing.

Choosing Mutual Funds

For those of you who see the choices in precious metals or precious metals–related investments a little bit too dizzying, I don't blame you. The feeling's mutual. So why not a mutual fund? A mutual fund, as you find out in this section, is a great way to invest for many small investors and investors in general who are unsure about any specific investment.

REMEMBER

A mutual fund is basically a pool of money that's managed by an investment firm. This pool of money (the fund) is an accumulation of money from people like you and me and many other investors. The fund is managed by an investment firm with a particular investment objective in mind. That objective could be growth, income, preservation of capital, or some other objective. The investment firm will put this pool of money to use by buying a portfolio of securities such as stocks and bonds that the firm believes will meet the stated objective. The bottom line for the investor here is that you choose the fund, and you leave the task of choosing the investments in the fund to the investment firm.

The advantages of mutual funds

Mutual funds have endured in popularity since the 1960s and for some very good reasons. The number of mutual fund offerings when I first started in business in 1981 was fewer than 800. But between new mutual fund offerings and the sky-rocketing growth of exchange-traded funds (covered later in this chapter), the total number of funds now exceeds 15,000 choices, not including hedge funds (at first, I thought a hedge fund was something for landscapers). The point here is that there's a mutual fund for virtually any financial purpose, and investors can choose one that can truly pinpoint their need(s).

Fitting a specific need

With mutual funds, you can choose a fund that fits your needs, not vice versa (see Chapter 3 for more on determining your needs). If you want growth, you can choose a growth fund. From there, you have either aggressive growth or conservative growth. You don't have to fit your needs into a fund and hope that it works out. You can use a fund that comfortably fits into your personal situation. In the context of this book, mutual funds can fill in the need for those investors wanting a convenient way to include diversified exposure to gold and silver in their portfolio.

Diversification

Diversification is the perennial reason that every source in the universe points out as the advantage of mutual funds. You can choose mutual funds that invest in only stocks or only bonds, or some mix of the two. Then there are mutual funds that will invest in securities such as stocks in a given sector or industry. And yes, Virginia, there are mutual funds that specialize in the world of precious metals and related investments.

The financial commentators on TV are always crowing about diversification for investors to maintain a balance of both growth and safety. This is where mutual funds come into the picture. Because of this pool of money the mutual fund receives from all these investors, they have the financial clout to provide great diversification. This is especially true when you have a sector that could be more volatile and is uncertain and much harder for the average investor to choose winners from. The convenience of the mutual funds is that you pick the funds and let portfolio managers of that investment firm pick the winners for you. The great thing is they can choose a losing stock and little harm is done because their financial clout gives them the ability to buy 40 or 50 or more different stocks in the same portfolio.

Convenience and performance

Choosing an investment for your portfolio isn't easy. It can take considerable research and due diligence that's not only good but also appropriate. For investors who can't (or won't) do the necessary homework, mutual funds can be the answer. Of course, you still have to choose a fund, but it's not that difficult once you understand your investment objective and personal profile (see Chapter 3).

For precious metals investors who aren't sure about what to invest in and don't have the time or inclination to do the research and due diligence that is required of finding a good start to invest in, why not just choose a mutual fund? In a mutual fund, the professionals oversee the entire portfolio on a full-time basis and know what they make by sell and hold decisions on the securities every day.

Therefore, if you're the type of investor who just scratches his head when he thinks about buying gold (the physical or the paper), gold mining stocks, or precious metals futures, then you may want to consider a precious metals mutual fund. Would you have made some great money? Gold, silver, and other precious metals have done very well during 2000–2020 (even with some bear markets in that time frame). In fact, precious metals mutual funds were among the best performers during this time. Check out some of the highest-profile performers in Table 8-1.

TABLE 8-1 **Precious Metals High-Profile Performers, 2000–2020 (In Alphabetical Order)**

Fund Name	Securities Symbol	Investment Firm	Website
American Century Global Gold Fund	(ACGGX)	American Century	www.americancentury.com
Fidelity Select Gold Portfolio	(FSAGX)	Fidelity Selects	www.fidelity.com
First Eagle Gold Fund	(SGGDX)	First Eagle Investment Management	www.feim.com
Franklin Gold and Precious Metals Fund	(FKRCX)	Franklin Templeton	www.franklintempleton.com
Gabelli Gold Fund	(GOLDX)	Gabelli Funds	www.gabelli.com
Invesco Oppenheimer Gold and Special Minerals Fund	(OPGSX)	Invesco Funds	www.invesco.com
Midas Fund	(MIDSX)	Midas Funds	www.midasfunds.com
Tocqueville Gold Fund	(SGDLX)	Tocqueville Asset Management	www.Tocqueville.com
U.S. Global Investors Gold & Precious Metals Fund	(USERX)	U.S. Global Investors, Inc.	www.usfunds.com
USAA Precious Metals and Minerals Fund	(USAGX)	USAA Group	www.usaa.com
VanEck International Investors Gold Fund	(INIVX)	VanEck Funds	www.vaneck.com
Wells Fargo Precious Metals Fund	(EKWAX)	Wells Fargo Funds	www.wellsfargofunds.com

TIP

Please keep in mind that Table 8-1 presents a high-profile sample listing from more than 50 precious metals mutual funds available to investors today. Don't necessarily assume that they're a recommendation or the best performing; it's merely a sample of well-known, established funds. Continue your research at the mutual fund websites mentioned later in this chapter.

The downside of mutual funds

Keep in mind that investing in mutual funds is not all peaches and cream (unless you choose a food and beverage sector fund). Mutual funds do have their downside as well, as you find out in the following sections.

Relying on other decision makers

The professional management of the mutual funds is a double-edged sword. The good part is that you get the investment decisions of professionals. But the bad part is that you get the investment decisions of professionals. In other words, you may choose a mutual fund, but you generally can't make the decisions inside the fund and must rely on others.

I read an industry report some years ago that pointed out that the average age of the average mutual fund manager was under 35. Hmmm . . . I have socks older than that (just ask my wife). Usually that means that you have someone who hasn't had enough exposure to the markets and their ups and downs over an extensive period of time. During the stock market's 2000–2002 bear market, for example, many mutual funds lost money needlessly because the money managers who ran these funds graduated from college during an extensive bull market (the stock market's powerful rise during 1982–1999), so they were clueless about how to manage money in a bear market. The end result is that millions of investors, including mutual fund investors, lost trillions of dollars.

TIP

The word to the wise here is simple: Make sure you're choosing mutual funds that have been around a very long time and that have experienced both bull and bear markets (and that goes for their financial advisors, too!).

Fees and service charges

Another drawback to mutual funds is the various fees involved that investors are assessed through the mutual fund itself. Two types of fees to be aware of are management fees and marketing or sales fees:

>> Every mutual fund has management fees; obviously, you have to pay the people who manage the funds as well as pay for the expenses to maintain the fund, such as office, utilities, and research costs.

>> The marketing or sales fees are different matters because they get paid out to those who are actually marketing the fund. The marketing fees that you pay have no bearing on the performance of the fund, but they do have a bearing on the financial profitability of the fund. If, for example, you get into a mutual fund that has a 5 percent front-end loader and that year the mutual fund was up 10 percent, the real net gain to you as the investor is 5 percent.

REMEMBER

Please understand that I don't necessarily think of fees as a negative. After all, people should be paid for service, performance, and so on. I list them here just as a heads-up so that you understand the cost of investing. Some charge high fees; some charge reasonable fees. As an investor and consumer, you should be aware of all fees involved because they will ultimately have an impact on your investment return. The following sections run down the fees you should be aware of.

MANAGEMENT FEES

As I mention earlier, all mutual funds have management fees. These fees cover the operating expenses of the fund (research, office, utilities, and so on) and payment to the professionals running the fund. The amount of the management fee will be expressed as a percentage of the fund, and it will vary according to the mutual fund category.

Growth funds, for example, charge a higher management fee usually than, say, a money market fund. A growth fund could charge a management fee of 1.5 to 3 percent and possibly higher, while a money market fund would have a management of less than 1 percent and usually less than 0.5 percent.

Also, some investment firms (such as hedge funds) charge a performance fee, which is technically a management fee because it's directly tied to how well the fund is managed. Performance fees can vary widely, but most firms charge in the neighborhood of 10 to 20 percent.

WARNING

As a general rule, the more involved, complicated, and aggressive the portfolio, the greater the management fee. Always check the prospectus (which I discuss later in this chapter). The Securities and Exchange Commission (SEC) issues guidelines to make it clear to investors what the costs of investing are for that fund. A good place to check out is the SEC's educational site for investors at www.investor.gov/. It provides tips and guidance on mutual funds and other securities.

MARKETING FEE #1: THE FRONT-END LOAD

The second category of fees are the marketing and sales expenses, referred to as the load. This is paid to the people or organizations that are marketing the fund for the investment firm. Sometimes the load is paid in-house if the investment firm has its own sales force.

The first type of load is the front-end load. The load is typically expressed as a percentage of the investment amount. The front-end load is a fee that is paid in the beginning. If you invest $1,000 with a fund that has a 5 percent front-end load, then the initial value of your investment is $950 (5 percent of $1,000 is $50).

If the investment firm tells you the fund has gone up 15 percent, don't assume that your investment is now worth $1,150. Your net gain (after factoring in the 5 percent load) is really up only 9.25 percent because you have to remember that your investment started at $950. From $950, a 15 percent gain means that your investment is now at $1,092.50.

TIP

All fund fees are paid from the fund; no one will send you an invoice. If anyone calls you, you won't have to say the check is in the mail.

MARKETING FEE #2: THE BACK-END LOAD

The back-end load is a fee that may actually be good for you because it encourages long-term investing. It's a fee that's charged at the time you get out of the fund. It's also called a redemption fee or charge. Most back-end fees are staggered; the longer you're in the fund, the lower the fee is. Many funds actually wipe out the fee once you pass an extended time.

TIP

A typical back-end load may be structured as 5 percent if you're in the fund for less than a year, 3 percent if you're in one to three years, 1 percent if you're in three to five years, and 0 percent after five years. Again, double-check the prospectus for the specifics. (I cover the prospectus in more detail later in this chapter.)

MARKETING FEE #3: THE 12(B)-1 LOAD

The 12(b)-1 load (named after the section in the securities regulations that allow such a charge) is usually a small percentage that's charged every year for as long as you're in the fund.

Say that you're in a fund with a 1 percent 12(b)-1 load. If you're in that fund for a year, your charge would be 1 percent. If you're talking a $1,000 investment amount, then the charge would be $10. If you're in the fund for 5 years, then over that time span, you would have paid 1 percent per year or a cumulative amount of 5 percent. It may be a small fee, but it can erode the return on your investment if you happen to be in that fund for an extended period of time.

Questionable track records

How often do you see that mutual fund ad that raves, "The Fantabulous fund was up 47 percent last year" or "If you invested in our fund when it started ten years ago, today you could buy Rhode Island with enough change to fill your gas tank!" or "Our ultra-growth fund was up 97 percent just before breakfast." Well, some of it could be true, but more likely there was some tweaking of the numbers, and you also have to check the fund's premise for whatever performance was calculated. It's important to put any numbers in perspective.

For example, take the top-performing fund of 1979: a gold fund. The year 1979 was a hot year for gold as it rose through the late '70s and hit its high in January 1980. During the last five years of the 1970s, the U.S. Gold Services Fund soared over 1,000 percent. In 1980 and 1981, gold collapsed, and gold-related investments plummeted. Guess what? In 1982, that gold fund was still in the top 20 performing mutual funds, even though it was at the bottom of the heap for 1980 and 1981. How could that be? When you add up three ultra-fantastic years with one bad year and one horrible year, you still come up with a high, positive yearly average for those specific five years. Energy sector funds had a similar run because oil shot up during the late 1970s and collapsed during the early 1980s.

REMEMBER

The lesson is that you have to analyze track records in context and understand the effects of mega-trends. Both bull and bear markets tend to last years, so stay alert when trends stall, sputter, or change directions. For potential short-term moves in that market, technical analysis can be helpful (see Chapter 15), but long-term trends are detected with the market fundamentals that I cover throughout this book. And don't forget to do your research to uncover market trends using the resources and websites listed in Appendix A.

Keys to success with mutual funds

No, this isn't a book or a chapter on mutual funds per se, but there are things to watch for when you're looking at mutual funds in the metals and mining sector (and yes, some of these points apply no matter what kind of mutual fund you'll be investing in). The following sections give you some points to keep in mind.

Analyze yourself first before you analyze the fund

If you're conservative with your money and can't stomach risk and volatility, then spread your money over several funds that invest in larger, established companies. In the same way, the generic mutual fund realm has aggressive and conservative growth funds, the world of metals and mining also has aggressive and conservative choices. Mutual funds can buy the stock of, say, gold mining stocks that are large, major firms in the industry. Mutual funds can also buy the stock of smaller, more speculative mining companies. (Mining stocks are covered in Chapter 7. Find out more about the type of investor you are in Chapter 3.)

How you invest is as important as what you invest

A famous investing genius once proclaimed that stocks fluctuate. Man! I wish I'd said that! Anyway, investments, no matter how well-chosen, don't move in a straight line up — the same way bad investments don't go down in a straight line.

Single investments or portfolios or entire markets tend to either zigzag up or zig-zag down. Good investments that occasionally pull back (that's called a correction; don't ask me why) present you with a buying opportunity. Bad investments that occasionally go up (a bear market rally) give you a chance to cash out at a better price before they resume declining. Because the world of precious and base metals is in the midst of a long-term bull market, any pullback provides the opportunity to add to your position for further gains as the uptrend in the market unfolds. That is, if you agree with my prime contention in this book that we are indeed in the midst of a historic bull market for gold, silver, and other metals.

How would you profit on the upward zigzag of the market with a mutual fund? There are three ways:

>> **Reinvesting the distributions:** When you initially get into a mutual fund, you're asked (in the fund application) to decide what to do with the distributions. Distributions are what the portfolio generates, such as interest, dividends, and/or capital gains. Any and all income or capital gains generated should be totally reinvested. Numerous studies have shown that total reinvestment yields the greatest long-term gains (versus having the distributions sent to you or partially reinvested).

>> **Dollar-cost averaging:** On a regular basis or on pullbacks (or both), send in money to your fund. When the fund's shares are cheaper during those temporary corrections, you get a buying opportunity.

>> **Both!** Why not? If you're indeed bullish, then consider both total reinvestment of distributions and adding to your fund as opportunities present themselves.

The prospectus: Netting it out

REMEMBER

Yeah, I know. You'd rather wait for the movie. Fortunately, a mutual fund prospectus isn't that bad. Here's a quick way to get through it with relatively little pain. You got to read before you invest, right? As my uncle Yorgi would say, an ounce of prevention is worth a cheap suit or something like that, so read this before you dig in to the prospectus:

>> **What is the objective of the fund?** You'll usually find the fund's objective right on page 1. In a brief paragraph, you'll know immediately whether the objective is yours as well. If not, fuhgeddaboudit! If the objective is indeed your objective, read on.

>> **What does it cost to invest in that fund?** The prospectus should clearly spell out the fees and charges. The less you pay, the more you'll gain (all things being equal).

>> **What is the fund invested in, and what do they plan to invest in?** A snapshot of the portfolio usually accompanies the prospectus. Now you can see what's in the portfolio and how diversified it is.

>> **How has it done in the past?** What is the fund's record, and how well did it do not only last year but also over the past three and five years? If you're a long-term investor and the fund has a long history, check out how well it did over ten years.

>> **What services does the fund provide?** Ask how they can handle distributions and whether they can do things such as automatic transfer of money from your checking account for purposes of dollar-cost averaging.

Now, if you want to also ask them, "What's the capital of Bolivia?" well, that's up to you. Now, if you don't follow all these great tips and then make a mistake with mutual funds, don't complain. Like my uncle Yorgi would say, "You spoiled the broth . . . now you lie in it!" Man! I wish I'd said that.

Mutual fund resources

TIP

I can't tell you everything I want to write, but there are some great places to turn to for extensive information on mutual funds in general and in the great area of metals and mining. Here are some great websites for mutual fund investors:

>> Investment Company Institute (www.ici.org)

>> Investment Management Education Alliance (https://imealliance.com/)

>> Morningstar (www.morningstar.com)

>> MutualFunds.com (www.mutualfunds.com)

>> Value Line (www.valueline.com)

Selecting Exchange-Traded Funds

I love exchange-traded funds (ETFs). Really! I think that they're the best financial innovation in the past 15 years. The investing public must think so, too. More than $6.1 trillion had been invested in ETFs by mid-2020.

REMEMBER

First of all, what is an ETF? An ETF is like a mutual fund, but it trades like a stock:

>> It's like a mutual fund in that it has a basket of securities that it maintains, but the similarity ends there. The basket of securities in the ETF is typically a fixed basket of securities, while the mutual fund's securities are an actively managed portfolio. In other words, the mutual fund's basket of securities (such as stocks, bonds, and so on) isn't static; the securities are regularly bought and sold as well as held.

>> The ETF also trades like a stock, another difference it has with mutual funds. When investors buy or sell shares of a mutual fund, they deal directly with the fund. The ETF, on the other hand, is bought and sold like stock. Just like a stock, you can buy 1 share or 1,000 easily through any stock brokerage account.

In the following sections, I give you an overview of ETFs, specifically, precious metals ETFs.

The pros and cons of ETFs

ETFs have the following advantages:

>> **Diversification:** Depending on the industry, the ETF could have 20 to 50 different issues in its portfolio. Most ETFs tend to focus on a specific industry or sector.

>> **Personal control:** You decide how many shares you want to buy. You decide whether to hold or sell. You can even use brokerage orders such as stop-loss orders or virtually any brokerage order that applies to a stock.

>> **Tax advantages:** Because the ETF's basket of securities is a relatively fixed portfolio, it's tax-efficient in that the individual securities are seldom sold. (Flip to Chapter 17 for the basics on taxes.)

>> **Liquidity:** Just as with a stock, you can buy or sell it very easily.

>> **Flexibility:** You can dictate how many shares and be able to buy the right amount in your account whether you have a large or small account.

>> **Lower costs:** ETF fees are relatively low and a small percentage of the portfolio (especially when compared to mutual funds with high loads).

>> **Ownership benefits:** You own an ETF as though it's a stock; you can use it as collateral (ETFs are marginable), and you use it to write covered call options (options are covered in Chapter 13).

Those are great benefits. Just thinking about them makes the tears well up in my eyes. Okay, let's get back down to earth. Here are some of the drawbacks:

>> **The shortcoming of diversification:** Diversification reduces risk, but it can also reduce gain. A single stock may have great risk, but if you're right about it, it has great potential for gain. Yes, there are trade-offs.

>> **Industry or sector risk:** If you choose an ETF in an industry that is having a rough time, it will cause the ETF's price to fall.

There's a unique risk with ETFs that specialize in the metal itself. Investors need to invest only in ETFs that specialize in transparency. In other words, do they fully disclose that they're holding 100 percent physical metal? Major ETFs, for example, such as the SPDR Gold Shares ETF (symbol: GLD) and the iShares Silver Trust ETF (symbol: SLV) do lend out or lease the metal in their possession, so it's not clear about the actual holdings of physical gold and silver.

My personal preference is that GLD and SLV are great trading vehicles and that for long-term considerations, conservative investors are better off with ETFs that have greater transparency and make a major point of holding accountable, physical bullion. See some good examples later in this chapter.

The world of precious metals ETFs

Because ETFs are an excellent way for investors and speculators to participate in the precious metals arena, here are all the ETFs (so far!) that you should be aware of.

The gold ETFs

Investing in gold gets easier and easier. These are the primary gold ETFs in order of trading volume (with their trading symbols):

>> SPDR Gold Shares (GLD)

>> Invesco DB Gold Fund (DGL)

>> Aberdeen Standard Physical Gold Shares (SGOL)

The gold ETFs act like the metal but in paper form. In other words, the gold ETFs allow you to get involved in gold, but as a paper investment that you can transact much like a stock. You see, you can't normally (or at least conveniently) buy physical gold through a stock brokerage account (or through an IRA if it is in, say, a self-directed brokerage account or a mutual fund). But with the advent of gold

ETFs, you can now participate in the gold market conveniently and as easily as any stock or bond.

The silver ETFs

For those who are excited about the potential profits in silver (like me), these silver ETFs are worth considering:

>> iShares Silver Trust (SLV)

>> Sprott Physical Silver Trust (PSLV)

>> Aberdeen Standard Physical Silver Shares (SIVR)

Here again is the same point as with the gold ETFs in the preceding section. The silver ETF gives investors and financial institutions the ability to include silver as an investment choice inside the realm of a brokerage account or IRA.

Other precious metals ETFs

The following are metals-oriented ETFs that add a level of diversification. They have more than just one metal:

>> Sprott Physical Gold and Silver Trust (CEF). This is a great way to invest in both metals with just one ETF.

>> Aberdeen Standard Physical Precious Metals Basket Shares (GLTR). This fund primarily holds gold and silver also includes minor holdings of platinum and palladium.

Other ETFs for the metals-minded

For the sake of completeness, I want to include some ETFs that have metals as an important component but that have other nonmetal components as well. I do this because investors should be aware of other securities that aren't necessarily a pure-play involving 100 percent precious metals. The reason is that an ETF can have diversification for those investors who want to hedge their bets, so to speak, about precious metals.

>> VanEck Vectors Gold Miners ETF (GDX) mirrors the 30-plus global gold mining stocks tracked in the ARCA Gold Miners Index (GDM).

>> Invesco DB Precious Metals Fund (DBP) is an ETF that concentrates in gold and silver futures contracts. This makes it more speculative than other ETFs that focus on physical bullion or stocks.

All the preceding ETFs (here and in earlier sections) have generally performed well during the past few years of the metals' bull market. If you're looking to participate in precious metals with some measure of safety, this is the venue for you. Just ask Uncle Yorgi.

TIP

Oops! Before I forget, I want you to investigate options on ETFs. Some of the greatest profits in recent years for myself and my clients and students have not just been in ETFs; they have also been with options on ETFs. You can profit with options in a variety of ways, and there are options strategies suitable for virtually any investor. To find out more about options, see Chapter 13.

ETF resources

As ETFs proliferate, so will the information and opinions about them. Here are among the best resources to help you choose. I'm sure you'll see a lot more coming out of the woodwork in the future.

The exchanges

Most of the ETFs you'll come across will most likely emerge on either Nasdaq (www.nasdaq.com) or the New York Stock Exchange (www.nyse.com). You'll find a lot of details on ETFs, and you have the ability to download prospectuses (in Adobe PDF file format).

The issuers

Because the ETF universe keeps expanding, you should get to know the major firms that issue ETFs. These firms do the heavy lifting of creating the ETFs, listing them on the stock exchanges, and maintaining them. See Table 8-2 for an extensive listing of ETF issuers in alphabetical order.

Peruse the extensive list of ETF issuers and their roster of ETFs. More are added constantly, and due to the boom in natural resources in general and metals in particular, you have (and will have) a great selection of precious (and base) metals–related ETFs.

WARNING

Investors are best served if they stick to ETFs that are very liquid. (Yes, there is a water ETF, but that's not what I mean!) In other words, stick to ETFs that have a large market (many buyers and sellers) so that it's easier to buy and sell your ETF. Judging the liquidity can be as easy as looking at the trading volume. (Most active ETFs have a daily volume of more than 50,000 shares.) Low liquidity or low activity sometimes results in unfavorable prices due to matters such as a wide bid/ask spread or a difficulty to fill an order quickly.

TABLE 8-2   **ETF Issuers**

The ETF series	The Financial Firm That Creates and Maintains It	Website
Fidelity	Fidelity Investments	www.fidelity.com
First Trust	First Trust Portfolios, L.P.	www.ftportfolios.com
Invesco	Invesco Ltd.	www.invesco.com
iShares	BlackRock, Inc.	www.ishares.com
Market Vectors	Van Eck Securities Corporation	www.vaneck.com
SPDRs	Standard & Poor	www.sectorspdr.com
Sprott	Sprott Inc.	www.sprott.com
Vanguard	Vanguard Group	www.vanguard.com
Wisdom Tree	Wisdom Tree	www.wisdomtree.com

Newsletters

The ETF part of the financial landscape is here to stay, and it will continue to grow. Their limitation is set only by the imagination of the issuers. You can find an ETF for almost any purpose.

TIP

The large publishers such as Forbes, Weiss Research, and Value Line have newsletters and research reports that cover ETFs (and mutual funds) with in-depth data. Well-stocked business libraries carry their publications. And of course, you can use a major search engine to find them and other sources. Here are newsletter publishing sites to visit:

>> Agora Financial (www.agorafinancial.com)

>> Forbes (www.forbes.com)

>> Stansberry Research (https://stansberryresearch.com/)

>> Value Line (www.valueline.com)

>> Weiss Research (www.weissratings.com)

Websites

Fortunately, the same financial information websites that tell you about the economy in general and the financial markets, in particular, will likely have lots of information on ETFs (and mutual funds) and how each one is faring lately. Here are some to start you off:

» Bloomberg (www.bloomberg.com)

» ETF Trends (www.etftrends.com)

» ETFdb.com (www.etfdb.com)

» MarketWatch (www.marketwatch.com)

3

Looking at Other Gold and Silver Investing Vehicles

Find out how to invest safely in actual physical metals through bullion (great for beginners).

Understand the pros and cons of numismatic (coin-collecting) vehicles.

Kick it up a notch and speculate in gold and silver through leveraged (and inverse) exchange-traded funds (ETFs).

Enter the high-risk, high-profit potential world of futures and options.

IN THIS CHAPTER

» Sizing up gold and silver in troy ounces

» Digging in to the benefits of physical metals

» Checking out gold and silver bullion

» Discovering commemorative coins

» Finding dealers and resources

Chapter 9

Going Direct: Buying Bullion

Most folks know something about gold and silver and can figure out to some extent what bullion coins and bars are. Although a wide variety of choices are available, even in this apparently narrow area of the precious metals world, it actually won't be that difficult to choose. Buying and selling can be as easy as a phone call or a visit to a website. In this chapter, I explore the various ways you can buy metals directly.

Weighty Matters: Troy Ounces

The most common measure of weight that you'll come across is the ounce, but you need to understand what kind of ounce. There are troy ounces and avoirdupois. My goodness — who thought that up? Probably the same guy who called cave exploring *spelunking*. Anyway, precious metals are measured in troy ounces.

Regular weight that you and I and the guy at the deli counter are familiar with is the avoirdupois. *Avoirdupois* (why don't they change that to *regular weight*?) is 16 ounces to a pound, while that same 16 ounces is 14.58 in troy ounces. The troy ounce is roughly 10 percent heavier than the avoirdupois equivalent. The use of troy ounces started in the Middle Ages and is still in use today with precious metals. It's used as the standard unit of measurement over the avoirdupois ounce to ensure purity standards and other common measures necessary for precious metals.

REMEMBER

Bullion coins and bars are those in which you pay every cost above the actual metallic content. Gold may be $1,700 an ounce, but that same ounce as a bullion gold coin or bar may be a few bucks more (due to fabrication costs). Bullion coins and bars are about as close as you can conveniently get to tracking 100 percent of the price of that metal, be it gold or silver (or other precious metals such as platinum and palladium). Bullion coins and bars are generally bought purely because of the metal content and little else.

WARNING

Keep in mind that 10 percent weight difference between the troy and avoirdupois (or regular) ounce because it has been a source of confusion and fraud. If an unscrupulous bullion dealer sold you a silver bar, for example, that weighs 10 regular ounces and charged you as if it were troy ounces, you can easily overpay by 10 percent due to the difference since 10 regular ounces are equivalent to 9 troy ounces. Make sure you're paying for and getting troy ounces.

Making the Case for Physical Ownership

Physical ownership means having the actual asset in your possession. This contrasts with paper assets where most investors have greater familiarity. Examples of paper assets are stocks, bonds, and mutual funds (covered in Part 2). In the world of bullion, there's paper in the form of silver (or other precious metal) certificates and pooled account programs.

In a paper asset, you have a claim on an asset via that piece of paper. The paper derives its value from the value of the underlying asset. For example, if you owned 100 shares of Gobbledegook Corporation, you own a small sliver of that company, and the value of your shares rises and falls with the fortunes (or lack of fortune) of the company involved. If the public goes gaga over Gobbledegook (it happens more often than you think), then your shares will go up. If the company has problems or goes bankrupt, your shares will end up no better than bits of paper. Paper assets have potential problems quite different from owning the physical asset. For many investors, having the physical in your possession is more desirable.

Let's make the paper versus physical comparison more relevant because having, say, silver coins and having shares in a stock (even more specifically, a silver mining stock) can be an example of comparing apples to oranges. Whenever investors are debating the merits of physical ownership, they're most likely talking about physical metal and *paper representing the physical metal*.

Since the 1970s, ownership in precious metals has taken various forms. The most obvious is the subject of this chapter, which is physical ownership. In addition, competing forms of ownership exist through paper. Some examples are

>> Silver certificates and warehouse receipts (can be allocated or unallocated)

>> Perth Mint Bullion Certificates (unallocated)

>> Perth Mint Bullion Certificates (allocated)

>> Pooled accounts (unallocated)

Note the terms *allocated* and *unallocated* in the preceding list:

>> Allocated to metal means that it's segregated from other assets held by that company. It usually has its own serial number, and you're charged more for this type of arrangement. The safer of the two is allocated.

>> Unallocated means that you have an ownership share along with others in a large pooled amount of metal that's not segregated and is not separately numbered. It's like when you go to a baseball game, and you see the difference between prestigious box seats and the bleacher seats out in right field. Well, I hope you got that. Anyway, the unallocated usually has lower transaction and storage charges.

TIP

For those who want to consider these venues, at least make sure that the companies you deal with have a long and unblemished record. A good example is The Perth Mint (based in Australia; www.perthmint.com.au). Some other places to consider are Sunshine Minting (www.sunshinemint.com), Monex (www.monex.com), and Kitco, Inc. (www.kitco.com).

What could go wrong with paper assets?

When I talk about what could go wrong with paper assets, I emphasize the point that a clear distinction exists between physical metal and paper representing the physical metal. You'll run into both. Because metals-related paper investment vehicles come in many forms, I think it's helpful to summarize what could go wrong with paper assets versus the physical metal.

The most obvious potential pitfall with paper assets is the risk of default. The second potential pitfall is fraud. When you buy physical silver, for example, and you have it delivered, you have the physical silver. Period! With paper silver, you need to keep in mind that the paper is a promise to deliver the underlying asset or to otherwise have a claim to that asset or to beneficial ownership, be it silver, gold, or other precious metal. For potential pitfalls of the various categories of paper assets, see Table 9-1.

TABLE 9-1   **Paper Assets and Potential Risks**

Type of Paper Asset	Potential Risks	Get More Details in . . .
Certificate for pooled account	Default, fraud	This chapter
Silver (or gold) certificate	Default, fraud	This chapter
Unallocated account	Default, fraud	This chapter
Warehouse receipts	Default, fraud	This chapter
Stocks	Company bankruptcy, financial difficulties may cause falling stock price, and so on	Chapter 7
Exchange-traded funds (ETFs)	Market risk based on what happens to mining stocks in portfolio	For stocks, Chapter 7; for ETFs, Chapter 8
Mutual funds	Same as stocks except choices made by the investment firm; fees may erode returns	Chapter 8
Futures contract	Volatility, default	Chapter 12
Options	Could expire worthless; if you're wrong, could drop in value drastically	Chapter 13

Bullion versus numismatics

Let's get physical. How does bullion stack up versus numismatic coins? The prime benefit of buying bullion is that you get 100 percent correlation with the asset itself. If you have silver bullion and silver goes up 20 percent or down 10 percent, then your silver bullion will perform accordingly. It's a pure play on the asset.

Numismatics involve far more than just the metal content. The metal content, even if it was a precious metal, may still be a secondary or even minor factor in the value. A good example is some uncirculated gold double eagle coins. You could easily see a coin valued at $50,000, but the intrinsic metal value portion of the coin could be far lower. That coin may have only an ounce of gold, and if the market price of gold is $1,750, then the intrinsic metal value would be only $1,750. What would account for the remaining $48,250 of value in that double eagle? The other factors, of course, such as scarcity, condition, and popularity. Chapter 10 goes into greater detail about numismatic coins.

The downside to numismatic coins can be the cost and the potential for problems in areas such as grading and dealer markups. Numismatic coins have a wholesale and a retail price that could have a wide margin that could be 30 percent or more (the premium over dealer cost). Bullion coins have a lower premium that could range from 2 to 10 percent. Bullion bars could have an even lower premium. Of the two, the coins have a higher premium because they aren't just lumps of metal; they are minted coins, so the cost of fabrication is a factor.

REMEMBER

When you're buying bullion coins, you pay a small premium over the metal content cost, and it could vary depending on the dealer. Also, keep in mind that when the time comes to sell your coins, you will get the price of the metal and some premium as well. Of course, you'll receive a lower premium than you paid, but at least you get something extra. This is why bullion coins (and especially numismatic coins) should be held for the long term so that enough appreciation builds up to hopefully more than offset the transaction costs you incur at the time of purchase.

The risks of owning physical metals

WARNING

The biggest concern of owning the physical outright is safeguarding it. Keeping the physical entails two risks:

>> **Someone could steal it.** This is the most likely risk.

>> **The government could confiscate it.** This may seem unlikely or very improbable, but it's not impossible. History has shown that government encroachment has happened before and it could happen again. Heck! If I told you in 2004 that local governments would have the power to take the home of a law-abiding, tax-paying citizen and that person could have no recourse (the eminent domain issue, authorized and expanded by the Supreme Court in 2005), you'd have thought I was crazy.

In safeguarding your precious metals, how you secure it is also important. If you have gold and silver stored in a bank safe deposit box, the government can confiscate under certain conditions. Many folks prefer putting it in a secure place at home or their business. Use your discretion.

TIP

If keeping precious metals at home is a little unsettling for you, then consider an alternative that many precious metals investors have used in recent years: James Turk's Goldmoney program at www.goldmoney.com. The metals are allocated and insured.

Going for Gold Physical Bullion

The first area of bullion to consider is with the ancient metal of kings: gold. With its beauty, reputation, and long history as a store of value and safe haven investment, holding some in your hands is a great experience. Fortunately, there are plenty of ways to do it, starting right here in the United States.

One of the first things you learn about is karats (also known as carats but definitely not known as carrots). The *karat* is a measure of fineness. A karat in gold is equal to ¹/₂₄ part of pure gold (in an alloy). Here's a rundown of how many karats you need to be aware of:

>> **24-karat gold:** Equals pure gold (100 percent gold).

>> **22-karat gold:** Equals ¹¹/₁₂ gold and ¹/₁₂ other (such as copper). A bullion coin or bar that is 22-karat gold is roughly 92 percent pure gold.

>> **18-karat gold:** Equals ¹⁸/₂₄ gold (the other ⁶/₂₄ is copper or other metal). Basically 75 percent of the item is pure gold.

>> **14-karat gold:** Means that ¹⁴/₂₄ of the item is gold. In other words, 58.3 percent of it is pure gold.

One hundred percent pure gold is too malleable (soft) for regular use, and it needs to be hardened by alloying it (mixing or combining it) with another metal such as copper or silver (or other metal). Twenty-four-karat jewelry, for example, needs to be handled with much greater care than 22-karat (or lower) jewelry. This is why I try to get my wife to buy 0-karat jewelry because, you know, it's a heck of a lot more durable — really. But I haven't succeeded in presenting my case. Oh well.

American Eagle Gold Bullion Coins

For gold investors, this coin is the first bullion vehicle to look into. In 1986, the U.S. Mint first starting minting the Eagle coin series (22 karats). The gold eagle caught on very fast, and it's the top-selling gold eagle in the country today. They are beautiful coins. The coin's design echoes the original design of the $20 gold eagle done by Augustus Saint-Gaudens as commissioned by then-President Teddy Roosevelt. Check it out in Figure 9-1.

FIGURE 9-1:
Gold Eagle Coin.

The authenticity, content, weight, and metallic purity of gold eagles are guaranteed by the U.S. government, which makes them an acceptable investment not only to American investors but also in international markets.

REMEMBER

The advantages of gold eagles are numerous. Many financial advisors see them as a good way to diversify the typical portfolio. Gold is well known as an inflation hedge, and gold eagles are a convenient way to add this benefit to long-term investment strategies. Gold eagles are very popular and the market for them is very large, so buying and selling them isn't a problem. Buying or selling them is usually private and nonreportable when done in small quantities.

Gold eagles are typically sold as 1-ounce bullion coins. However, you can also get them in ½-ounce, ¼-ounce, and ⅟₁₀-ounce denominations. This makes gold affordable for just about any portfolio.

TIP

Sites such as the US Mint's page at `www.usmint.gov/coins/coin-medal-programs/american-eagle/gold-bullion` provide more details.

The American Buffalo Gold Bullion Coin

As gold rose in value in recent years, the interest in gold bullion picked up. Because the gold eagle was hitting record sales levels, why not other gold coins? It was at that point that the newest gold bullion kid on the block showed up: the 24-karat American Buffalo Gold Bullion Coin.

The face value of the coin is $50, and for the first time ever, investors can get 1 troy ounce of pure gold in bullion coin form. These coins were manufactured by the U.S. Mint at West Point, and they come in special protective holders. (Remember that pure gold is soft.)

TIP

For more details on this coin, head over to www.usmint.gov/coins/coin-medal-programs/american-buffalo-coin-program/bullion.

The Krugerrand

Issued in 1970 by South Africa, the Krugerrand (see Figure 9-2) was the world's first gold bullion coin. Since their issuance, nearly 55 million coins have been bought and sold across the globe. The 22-karat coins are available in 1-ounce, ½-ounce, ¼-ounce, and $\frac{1}{10}$-ounce denominations. Because they have a huge market and are highly liquid, buying and selling them is easy. For more details on the Krugerrand, go to www.realkrugerrand.com/.

FIGURE 9-2:
Krugerrand.

Content: © doublematt/123RF.COM

The Canadian Maple Leaf

Issued by the Royal Canadian Mint, the Maple Leaf (see Figure 9-3) is one of the world's most popular gold bullion coins. Guaranteed by the Government of Canada for its authenticity and metallic content, the Maple Leaf has a purity extremely close to 24 karats: It's 99.99 percent gold, making it the world's purest gold coin. In addition to its reputation and quality, the Maple Leaf is also very liquid and accepted internationally.

FIGURE 9-3:
Canadian Maple
Leaf Coin.

Content: © Steven Heap/123RF.COM

TIP

You can get more details for this coin at `https://mint.ca/store/mint/about-the-mint/bullion-1300002`.

Other gold bullion

Gold bars (see Figure 9-4) are popular and safe choices for investors and have relatively lower premiums than minted coins. It's a good idea to buy them from sources that get these bars manufactured by Pamp Suisse and Credit Suisse (I list sources later in this chapter). The gold bullion bar available sizes are

» 400-ounce bullion bars

» 100-ounce bullion bars

» Kilo bullion bar (32.15 ounces)

» 10-ounce bullion bars

Seeking Out Silver Physical Bullion

I like silver, and I'm very bullish on silver, especially during 2020–2022. I think that long term, it's a good part of virtually any portfolio. Silver bullion is the best and easiest way to start participating. I give you several ways to get involved in silver in the following sections.

American Eagle Silver Bullion Coins

The U.S. Mint started minting these beautiful coins in 1986. With nearly 135 million coins sold since then, the American Eagle Silver Bullion Coins (see Figure 9-5) have become the world's bestselling silver coins. The design of these 1-ounce coins (0.999 silver content) was inspired by Adolph A. Weinman, the designer of the 1916 Walking Liberty half-dollar.

A primary advantage of the silver eagle is that it's very liquid, so buying and selling are easy and convenient. A primary disadvantage is that the premium can run as high as $2 over the metal content value (depending on the dealer).

TIP

The Silver Eagle is profiled at `www.usmint.gov/coins/coin-medal-programs/american-eagle/silver-bullion`.

One-ounce rounds

These bullion coins weigh 1 ounce and are 0.999 pure silver. They're like the silver eagle in the previous section, but they have lower premiums. Private mints create them, and the premium is typically 40¢ to 50¢ above the metal content value. Silver rounds aren't as well known as silver eagles, but they make good choices for investors who want to get more silver bang for the buck. You can acquire these rounds at many of the dealers listed in Appendix A.

Junk silver bags

This may sound like an odd way to invest in silver, but it's actually a great consideration. A junk silver bag has $1,000 of face-value silver coins issued in 1964 or earlier. It has a that less-than-appealing name because the coins in the bag are in poor condition, and you won't find any coin that's rare or has numismatic value. The coins are generally worn down from usage and wouldn't be considered at any numismatic grade above good. For more information about grading and numismatic coins, see Chapter 10.

The $1,000 bag weighs about 55 pounds and contains about 715 ounces of pure silver. What kinds of coins are in the bag? If half-dollars were used, there would be 2,000 coins. If the coins were quarters, then there would be 4,000 coins. Dimes? 10,000 coins. Because the bag of coins is bought as a bullion investment, the price of the bag would move in correlation with the price of silver. Many firms (like the sources I list later in this chapter) can sell you half bags that have $500 of face-value silver coins to make it easier for storage and handling.

Even though these old coins are generally priced as bullion, they are coins that are no longer minted. That tells you that the supply is finite, so prices for these bags could rise further if demand increases.

The difference between the buy and sell is fairly constant, and there are investors who buy bags when premiums are cheap or negative and trade them when premiums increase substantially. Keep in mind that you're required by law to report your sale of $1,000 face value 90 percent bags on IRS Form 1099B. Smaller quantities of 90 percent aren't reportable. (Ninety percent silver means that all the coins are 90 percent silver content and are typically U.S. dimes, quarters, and/or halves issued 1946–1964.)

The $1,000 bag of silver dollars

This interesting play in silver isn't exactly a bullion investment, but it's not a rare coin investment either. Circulated silver dollars struck between 1878 and 1935 carry higher premiums, yet they're a prime source of legal tender silver coins because they're so recognizable. These early dollars are divided into two price categories: the more expensive Morgan dollars struck between 1878 and 1904 and the Peace dollars struck between 1921 and 1935.

The Peace dollar being the less expensive is quoted by the bag. Such coins are always in average condition and grade VG (Very Good). A Morgan dollar bag and better-quality coins are available at slightly higher prices, so it pays to ask questions before placing an order. This option is popular because silver dollar bags have represented real, portable wealth for more than 100 years.

The 40 percent silver bag

The last silver coin the United States made for general circulation was the 40 percent silver clad 50¢ struck from 1965 through 1969. This is another popular way to own silver bullion in legal tender form. Like circulated 90 percent coins, these $1,000 face value bags are traded primarily for content. Because they're 40 percent pure, a bag contains substantially less silver (296 troy ounces), which is reflected in a lower selling price.

The 40 percent silver bag has a number of advantages:

>> These are real U.S. coins and therefore are legal tender. In an emergency, this could be significant.

>> The bag has a high face value ($1,000), which limits the money anyone could lose should silver move lower. This is easily seen in a down market because premiums almost always move higher.

>> Unlike 90 percent silver bags, you're not required to fill out IRS Form 1099B on 40 percent bags when you sell.

Silver bars and ingots

In terms of getting the most silver metal content against the purchase price (in other words, paying the least amount of premium over metal content), bullion bars are the way to go. Ingots are really just small bars that are imprinted with designs to make the bar attractive and/or collectible. Ingots are more appropriate for collectors rather than for investors. In the following list, I concentrate on bars (uh, bullion bars, not adult drinking places):

>> **1,000-ounce silver bars:** These bars tip the scales at about 68 pounds. They're typically used to settle the delivery obligations of futures contracts at NYMEX (the New York Mercantile Exchange, which is part of the CME Group found at www.cmegroup.com; more about futures contracts in Chapter 12). A typical futures contract is tied to 5,000 ounces of silver, so five of these bars will cover the physical requirements for delivery. The bottom line is that this size isn't practical for average-sized or small transactions typically done by investors. Besides, why get sued by the delivery guy for his backache?

>> **100-ounce silver bars:** Another popular way to own bullion silver is the 100 troy ounce bar, which is 0.999 fine. At a tenth of the size, it's also a tenth of the weight: 6.8 pounds. This is the most typical weight for large retail transactions among investors.

>> **10-ounce silver bars:** These are popular and the most common for small investors. They come with a slightly higher relative cost, but as an absolute transaction, they fit the small investor's budget.

There are other bar sizes (such as odd-weight retail bars), but these are the best sizes due to their acceptability in the marketplace and the high degree of liquidity (being able to convert to cash).

The common popular brands that most investors will come across are Engelhard (www.allengelhard.com) and Johnson Matthey (www.matthey.com). There are more obscure sources, but these two have a long-time reputation for their standards such as metallic quality and authenticity.

So what kind of silver is best?

Some of this is tied to your preference. Those who are purists like the bars and 1-ounce rounds. Those who want a more popular, more liquid, and easier bullion transaction would opt for the U.S. Eagle coins. Your budget will also dictate the transaction. Some buy a large lump sum now. Still, others will allocate a portion of their monthly budget and do some dollar-cost averaging.

REMEMBER

Serious investors may consider a portion into bullion as a part of their precious metals foundation and then allocate a portion of their investable funds among some of the paper assets (such as mining stocks and ETFs). Over the long haul, accumulating your investing among the different classes of physical and paper assets will prove rewarding as the precious metals bull market unfolds.

Gold and Silver Commemorative Coins

I could have easily put the topic of commemorative coins in Chapter 10 on numismatics, but I thought it fit better here. Why? Commemorative coins weren't issued for circulation, and the modern commemoratives had greater value due to their metal content. But these coins can indeed be collectible. These coins could easily become a beer commercial debate. (Tastes great! Less filling!)

The real answer is that commemorative coins have something to offer both the collector and the bullion investor. There are two types of commemorative coins: early commemoratives issued 1892–1954 and modern commemoratives issued from 1982 to the present. The early commemorative coins are highly collectible (they have both numismatic and investment value), while the vast majority of modern issues aren't. The vast majority of modern commemorative coins don't fetch any substantial value beyond their metal content. For serious investors, the early issues are where the numismatic and investment action is.

WARNING

The public is offered newly issued commemoratives that are very overpriced. The price is frequently ten times (or more) the value of the actual bullion content if it's marketed with a recently deceased celebrity or famous event. It may be touted as a collectible, but, either way, it's overpriced or simply a rip-off. The bottom line is that if you see it being marketed in expensive venues such as television, then the items sold will be too expensive.

Among the more popular commemoratives are the 1892 Colombian Exposition half-dollar (the first commemorative coin authorized by Congress) and the half-dollar commemorating George Washington Carver (issued during 1951–1954). During 1892–1954, the U.S. Mint produced commemorative coins for 53 different events and honored individuals on a total of 157 different gold and silver coins.

TIP

The same sources (listed throughout this chapter) that sell bullion coins usually sell commemorative coins. For more information on quality commemoratives, you can turn to the sources listed in Chapter 10 (on numismatic coins) as well as the U.S. Mint (www.usmint.gov) and the dealers listed in Appendix A.

Bullion Costs, Fees, Dealers, and Resources

REMEMBER

When you're buying bullion coins or bars, you'll come across "bid" and "ask" prices. The difference between the bid and ask amounts is the spread. Generally, coins and bars that are actively bought and sold have a relatively small spread. Coins and bars that are in a slow or thinly traded market tend to have wider spreads. This you need to know: When you're buying, you pay the ask price. When you're selling, you receive the bid price. The bid and ask prices vary greatly from dealer to dealer.

In addition, find out about fees that cover costs such as shipping, storage, and any transaction fees. The size/quantity of the order will matter. The premium per ounce on a 1,000-ounce bar order will be relatively lower than the premium on a 100-ounce bar order, which in turn will be relatively lower than for the 10-ounce bar order.

Even in the realm of precious metals, the advice from every consumer guide in the history of humanity says, "shop around for the best price." Hey, the best advice isn't always the most original!

Fortunately, finding dealers and shopping around is easier than ever before. Now you can search for a coin shop near you online. The following are some dealers with websites to help you do your shopping:

>> American Gold Exchange (www.amergold.com; 800-613-9323)

>> APMEX (www.apmex.com; 800-375-9006)

>> Investment Rarities (www.investmentrarities.com; 800-328-1860)

>> To find a local coin shop, you can search by name, by state, or by zip code at www.coininfo.com.

TIP

To get consumer reports on how to avoid scams in precious metals or buying tips on silver (and other) bullion, go to www.PreciousMetalsInvesting.com. The site regularly features consumer tips on buying coins, avoiding scams, and so on. More resources are in Appendix A.

Lastly, for those who want to consider buying physical gold and silver for your individual retirement account (IRA), head over to Chapter 17.

Chapter **10**

Numismatic Coins and Collectibles

N umismatics. Who thought up that name? Why not call coin collecting, uh, coin collecting? And then there's stamp collecting: philately (probably from the same renaming genius). Why stop there? Why not call wine tasting *grapeology* or skydiving *splat-o-lympics*? Anyway, coin collecting — er, numismatics — is a great and interesting way to get into precious metals. Don't confuse it with bullion coins and bars (as covered in Chapter 9) because the metal content is only part of the reason that you get into numismatic coins.

In 2002, a 1933 gold double eagle coin sold at a Sotheby's auction for $7.59 million. Whew! Now that's not chump change. But it does attest to the clout of investment-grade numismatic coins. Rare, high-quality coins can command prices of five, six, or even seven figures, so it certainly pays to consider the power of coins in your portfolio, especially in an era of growing demand and inflation.

Numismatic coins offer some of the same advantages as other investment vehicles such as scarcity, marketability, and appreciation. But another dimension comes into play: It can be an interesting and absorbing hobby. For years, I was an active numismatist who was initially drawn by the opportunity for long-term appreciation but came to see the other appealing features of the world of coin collecting.

In this chapter, I compare numismatic coins and collectible coins, point you to helpful coin groups and services, and give you tips on selling coins.

Understanding the Basics of Numismatic Coins

REMEMBER

Numismatic coins are coins that have achieved value due to their rarity. As you may recall if you read Chapter 9, bullion coins are primarily acquired for their metal content. For numismatic coins, you need to consider (or be aware of) the following:

>> **Metal content:** This is first in this list only because this is a major consideration in this book. The major types of precious metals are silver and gold. Other metals exist (base metals such as copper and nickel), but they're not a factor in the value as is the case with precious metals.

>> **Rarity:** The fewer there are of a particular coin, the greater the potential value. Many old coins are valuable because of their rarity.

>> **Grade (or condition):** The better the condition, the higher the value. The grade is a crucial factor in the coin's value (more on this appears later in this chapter).

>> **Age:** This is a relatively minor issue, but it's worth listing. All things being equal, a 100-year-old coin has greater value than a 1-year-old coin.

>> **Popularity:** Some coin series are more popular than others. The coin's popularity may be attributed to its beauty or historical significance.

>> **Mint mark:** Coins were minted at a variety of minting facilities throughout U.S. history. A coin in the same year but from a different mint could be more scarce, hence more valuable.

As you find out in the following sections, numismatics can be a little bit more complicated than just the age and/or metal content. Of course, if you have an old coin made of a precious metal such as gold or silver that's in excellent condition and is rare and popular, then you have a winner!

Aiming for profitable coin investing

REMEMBER

If you're going to be successful in coin investing (certainly financially successful), some golden rules will enhance your efforts:

>> **Stick to precious metals.** Because of other factors covered in this book (such as inflation), it will enhance your long-term profitability to stick to gold and silver coins due to the metals' appeal for a variety of reasons. As contemporary coinage becomes more debased (the government is using cheaper metals to keep coin mintage costs low), that means that more valuable coins will keep rising in price.

>> **Specialize.** It's hard to keep track of all the coin series. It's advisable to stick to a single popular series (certainly in the beginning anyway) such as Mercury dimes or Morgan dollars. Get to know the key dates and grades. (Find out more about grades as well as gold and silver coin series later in this chapter.)

>> **Focus on quality.** Buy the higher grades because they'll fetch a higher price. Investors will generally look at the uncirculated and proof grades first (grading explanations are in the next section). Depending on the year and mint, an uncirculated Morgan silver dollar, for example, could easily be worth thousands of dollars more than the same coin in good or fine condition.

Making the grade

Grading is a reference to a coin's physical condition. The grading system referred to as the Sheldon Scale (named after William Sheldon, who standardized coin grading in 1948), is an industry standard that helps dealers, collectors, and investors find an easier way to determine the coin's condition. The Sheldon Scale (see Table 10-1) works on a numeric system ranging from 1 to 70, with 70 being the highest and most flawless level.

TABLE 10-1   **Sheldon Scale Rundown of Grades**

Level	Grade	Comments
AG-3	About Good	Lowest grade. You can barely make out the features on the coin. This is fine if you're seeking coins for their metal content but the worst (and cheapest) choice for numismatic investors.
G-4	Good	This isn't good in the true sense. It's a notch above the worst. This is a poor condition.
VG-8	Very Good	In this condition, you see all the basic features of the coin, but they're very worn.
F-12	Fine	The fine grades are still low grade. Much better condition than the good grades but not investment grade.
VF-20	Very Fine	This and the next two grades have strong definition of major features, but the intricate details are worn out.
VF-30	Choice Very Fine	
EF-40	Extra Fine	
EF-45	Choice Extra Fine	Choice Extra Fine is okay if you're talking steak, but in the world of coins, it isn't investment grade; it's fine if you're just a collector.

(continued)

TABLE 10-1 *(continued)*

Level	Grade	Comments
AU-50	About Uncirculated	Now you're talking. Uncirculated means that the coins are in excellent condition. All the features are strong with very little wear and some nicks.
AU-55	Choice About Uncirculated	This is a level better than AU-50. Some minor wear and nicks keep it below investment grade.
AU-58	Very Choice About Uncirculated	This level is almost indistinguishable with higher grades, but there are noticeable nicks and very slight wear.
MS-60 to 70	Uncirculated or Mint State (MS)	This should be the lowest level for investors seeking coins with high desirability. The better the grade, the higher the price at sale time.
MS-70	Proof	This is the top grade. The coin has a mirrorlike look and is in superb condition with no blemishes, nicks, or other signs of wear or contact.

The grades of MS-1 to MS-59 could really be called the collectible grades. For collectors who are simply seeking to add to or complete their coin collections, these grades are okay. Because the grades are low, the prices are also generally low, so coins at these levels are affordable.

TIP

Those seeking coins with the best potential for investment gain need to concern themselves with the higher grades of MS-60 to MS-70. To get a truly good idea about these investment grades, it's best to get it from the source, of course. You can find full descriptions straight from the Fifth Edition of *Official ANA Grading Standards for United States Coins*, published by the American Numismatic Association (www.money.org).

Checking out information sources

TIP

As with most things in life, the more information you have, the better off you're going to be. The top sources of information on numismatic coins are

>> Krause publications. Krause publishes *World Coin News, Numismatic News* (www.numismaticnews.net), and *Coins Magazine*.

>> Coin World (www.coinworld.com)

>> CoinWeek (www.coinweek.com)

>> Daily Numismatic & Gold Investment News (www.cointoday.com)

>> Numisma-Link (www.numismalink.com)

Considering Collectible Coins

Once you get a good understanding of the coin market and important features such as the grade (quality) and mintage (quantity), you can choose what coin series you want to get involved with. In this section, I won't cover every series that's out there because there are a lot of coins to deal with. It's important to stick to those series that have a large, popular market because it will make it much easier to buy and sell when the time comes.

REMEMBER

Collectible coins have a grade between 1 and 59, as explained in the earlier section, "Making the grade." Anything graded 60 to 70 is considered a numismatic coin. These levels are also referred to as "investment grades" because investors are more apt to get these higher-quality conditions.

Gold coins

Although the U.S. Mint (www.usmint.gov) has minted gold bullion coins in recent years, the last numismatic gold coins were issued in the early 1930s. One of the most popular gold coins is the $20 Saint-Gaudens coin issued 1907–1933. It's still a very popular coin for collectors and investors, and it serves as the quintessential gold coin. Here are the most popular numismatic gold coins:

>> The $20 Saint-Gaudens double eagle (see Figure 10-1)

>> Liberty head $1 gold

>> Liberty capped bust $2.5 gold

>> Indian $2.5 gold

>> Indian $5 gold

>> Indian $10 gold

TECHNICAL STUFF

By the way, some of the coins are referred to by the designer's name. The $20 gold double eagle coin was designed by Augustus Saint-Gaudens. Later in this chapter, you see a reference to coins such as the Barber halves. Before you look for the razor and shaving cream in the design, keep in mind that it's another reference to a coin designer, Charles E. Barber. Barber designed many of the coins in the late 1800s.

Credit: United States Mint Image

FIGURE 10-1:
The ultra
high relief
$20 Saint-
Gaudens double
eagle gold coin
issued in 2009.

Silver coins

Silver coins were more prevalent than gold coins and were in common circulation until 1964. From the early days of the United States' history to 1964, there were silver dimes, quarters, halves, and dollar coins. These coins were 90 percent silver. An exception was Kennedy halves that still contained 40 percent silver during 1965–1970. After that, all common coins in circulation were made from base metals.

The most common silver coin series are

>> Early silver dollars (1794–1804)

>> Early halves (1794–1807)

>> Liberty bust dimes (1796–1837)

>> Draped bust quarters (1796–1838)

>> Liberty bust halves (1807–1838)

>> Liberty seated dollars (1836–1873)

>> Liberty seated dimes (1837–1891)

>> Liberty seated quarters (1838–1892)

>> Liberty seated halves (1839–1891)

>> Trade dollars (1873–1885)

>> Morgan Silver Dollars (1878–1921)

>> Barber halves (1892–1915)

>> Barber dimes (1892–1916)

- » Barber quarters (1892–1916)
- » Standing liberty quarters (1916–1930)
- » Mercury dimes (1916–1945)
- » Walking liberty halves (1916–1947)
- » Peace Silver Dollars (1921–1935)
- » Washington silver quarters (1932–1964)
- » Roosevelt silver dimes (1946–1964)
- » Franklin Halves (1948–1963)

To get much more detail on these and other coin series, consult the various coin resources and publications in this chapter.

Other coins

Beyond gold and silver (there are no platinum numismatic coins, only platinum bullion coins), there's little else in the way of precious metals for collectible coinage. However, you'll find plenty of base metals used. Copper, zinc, and nickel are common in coinage, and there are plenty of choices here for collecting and investing. Here are the most common collectible series with base metals:

- » Large cents (1793–1857)
- » Flying eagle cents (1856–1858)
- » Indian cents (1859–1909)
- » Shield nickels (1866–1883)
- » Liberty nickels (1883–1913)
- » The Lincoln wheat cents (1909–1958)
- » Buffalo nickels (1913–1938)
- » Jefferson nickels (1938–present)

Keep in mind that even coins with base metals have risen in value very nicely in recent years. The same things that have a positive impact on precious metals (such as money supply growth and price inflation) have a similar impact on base metals. A good example is the Lincoln wheat cent.

The original Lincoln cent was 100 percent copper. During World War II, copper was so necessary for the war effort that Lincoln cents were made primarily with steel instead of copper temporarily in 1943. In recent years, the price of copper rose dramatically, and copper is only a miniscule part of pennies today. The increase in the price of copper was just another reason the older Lincoln cents rose in value.

A special category: Commemoratives

One area of the coin world that I don't want to leave out is commemoratives. These aren't coins in the normal sense — that is, they're not issued for general circulation. Every coin that I've written about in this chapter can actually be used as regular money in that you can use these coins to buy stuff at the store but — *please* — don't do that! Anyway, commemoratives are just that; they commemorate a person, organization, or event. Gold and silver commemoratives are a large market for collectors and investors. Some of the same rules apply (such as scarcity, metal content, and grade).

TIP

It's important to stay with commemoratives that have a substantial market so that buying and selling are easier. Stick with quality and with reputable dealers. For more information, check out the same websites and resources indicated in this chapter. Some sources for information on commemoratives are the U.S. Mint (www.usmint.gov) and the sites and organizations listed throughout this chapter.

Exploring Coin Organizations and Services

When you have your bearings on numismatics and are ready to dive in, it pays to survey the best sources of both numismatic information and to find out about grading services — especially if you're going to spend some big bucks on (hopefully) high-grade, investment-worthy coins. This section helps you navigate your major coin acquisitions.

Information sharing

TIP

If you're serious about numismatics as a long-term investment vehicle, then it pays to join one or more of the organizations in this specialized area. As you find out, numismatic coins are more complicated than bullion coins (see Chapter 9), and you need to keep informed. The first place to start is the associations:

>> American Numismatic Association (ANA; www.money.org)

>> The American Numismatic Society (ANS; http://numismatics.org)

>> Professional Numismatists Guild (PNG; https://pngdealers.org)

The associations provide a lot of information and guidance to collectors and investors. Member benefits usually include newsletters, books, and conferences. Meeting other members is easy, and you can quickly get information from others on the particular coins that you're focusing on. Speak to experienced members and ask a lot of questions about grading, mintage, rarity, selling tips, and so on.

Besides the associations, the internet has another venue for you to meet folks and exchange opinions and information on numismatics. Use your favorite search engine to find newsgroups. One of the more active ones is Coin Talk Forum (www.cointalk.org).

Grading services

TIP

Because grading can be such a touchy and delicate matter — a single level difference in grade could mean thousands of dollars — it's recommended that you consult a grading certification service. A reliable grading certification service is crucial whether you're buying or selling your coin. The service can certify not only the grade of the coin but also authenticate it. The following are the major coin grading services in the industry:

>> Numismatic Guaranty Corporation (NGC; www.ngccoin.com)

>> Professional Coin Grading Service (PCGS; www.pcgs.com)

>> American Numismatic Association Coin Service (www.anacs.com)

>> Independent Coin Grading Company (www.icgcoin.com)

Generally, they'll request that you fill out their form and send it in with the coin(s) and their fee. Depending on how busy they are, expect to receive your coin back with their certification in several weeks or longer. Here are some questions that you should consider asking right after you ask "How much does it cost?" and "When will my coin collection be worth a million bucks?"

>> How many years have you been grading and authenticating coins?

>> Does your firm offer a guarantee in your grading and authenticity service?

>> What type of holders (containers) do you use to safeguard the coins?

>> What grading standard do you use?

>> What established dealer or collector groups use your services?

>> Where do your firm's certified items trade (auctions and so on)?

>> What's the capital of Bolivia? (Just kidding!)

Selling Your Coins

Understanding what you're buying is important, but what better way to end this chapter than understanding selling your coins? After all, the whole point of buying collectible coins (at least from an investment perspective in this book) is to gain by selling it at a higher price later on. The following sections help you understand potential buyers and pricing information.

REMEMBER

For maximum investment gain, it's best to hold your coins long term to give them adequate time to appreciate in value. Coins aren't really appropriate as tradable vehicles.

Potential buyers

Keep in mind that to achieve maximum gains with your coins, the issue isn't just when to sell (again, later is better than sooner); it's also important to understand whom you sell to. The following sections give you guidance.

Dealers

The most convenient way to cash in your coin investments is to sell to a coin dealer. The reputable ones are members of the long-standing organizations such as the Professional Numismatists Guild (see the earlier section "Information sharing"), and you shouldn't have a problem making a fast and efficient sale. However, keep in mind that what you're seeking to get paid isn't the same as what dealers are willing to pay.

WARNING

I'm sure that after you pored over all the price listings in coin publications, you have a preconceived idea of what your coins are worth. Keep in mind that you're probably looking for the retail price while the dealers are looking to pay only a wholesale price. Oh sure, you read the dealer's ad stating, "We pay the highest prices in the industry," and it may even be 100 percent true, but in reality, the point is highest wholesale prices. Dealers are in business, and they need to make a profit to stay in business. If you think that the value of your coin should be, say, $100 (that's what you saw in those coin publications), then the amount you'll likely be offered will be in the $50 to $65 range. This is why you should consider your coins to be a long-term investment to give them enough time to appreciate. The difference will mean another 30 to 40 percent in the price to cover the difference between wholesale and retail.

Of course, if the coins you're seeking to sell were found in your attic or inherited, then the wholesale/retail price difference may not mean much to you because your purchase price was effectively zero.

TIP

Dealers will generally pay a wholesale rate for your coins. Therefore, if you're settling for dealers to make a fast and convenient sale, call several dealers to size up the offers.

Other investors

If you want to gain a higher price, then it may behoove you to skip past the middleman and go straight to the buyer: another investor. You may say, "Great! The heck with the dealer; I'll go directly to the buyer and get more money!" Here's where you discover the trade-off. If you want to realize more money from the sale of your coins, then you'll need to put in the time, effort, and diligence. Realizing a higher price entails more marketing and sales efforts on your part.

You can find coin investors in a variety of places, and the internet makes it easier to locate would-be buyers. There are numismatic clubs and chat rooms. There are markets for buyers and sellers of coins at websites such as www.coinmasters.net. You can also go to coin shows and conferences (check out www.coinshows.com).

TIP

Selling directly to individuals will be easier if you get your coins certified. Investors are more apt to make a deal with you if a credible organization (see the grading services covered earlier in this chapter) has certified the coin and its condition and authenticity.

eBay and other auctions

Online auctions are one of the most active areas of the internet. Unless you've been spelunking (a weird word that means exploring caves) for the past dozen years, you've heard of eBay (www.ebay.com). It is, of course, the premier online auction site, and lots of coins are bought and sold there regularly. A lot of great information sources are available on how to buy and sell on eBay, and it's the first place to look when you're considering selling your stuff online.

TIP

eBay is a horizontal auction site, which means everyone sells all sorts of stuff to everyone else. If you can't sell your coins on eBay, then consider finding a vertical auction site. This type of auction site means the buying and selling are in a narrow niche or specialty. There are auction sites that specialize in coins. Also, keep in mind that some dealers and auctions do consignment sales. Consignment means that you sell your item through a sales agent, but you still retain ownership of the item until the sale is made.

Here are some of the major coin auction websites:

>> Stack's Bowers (www.stacksbowers.com)

>> Heritage Auction Galleries (https://coins.ha.com)

>> Spink (www.spink.com)

>> Auction Zip (www.auctionzip.com)

Pricing information

Whether you're buying or selling, the price is everything. You shop around if you're going to buy. If you're going to sell, you need to verify with reliable sources regarding the market value of your coin(s). The following sources have pricing information that can help:

>> NumisMedia Fair Market Value Price Guide (www.numismedia.com)

>> PCGS Coin Price Guide (www.pcgs.com/prices/us)

>> Coin News (www.coinnews.net)

TIP

A book that achieved renown as the bible for coin prices and values is the *Red Book*. The full title is *The Official Red Book: A Guide Book of United States Coins*. It's inexpensive and compact. Although it gets updated annually, that's enough. Coin values aren't that volatile, so an annual book is sufficient for most folks. Find it at your favorite bookstore.

CHECK YOUR CHANGE

Check your pocket change every day. You'd be surprised by what you can find that has greater value than you think. Many years ago when I was a kid, I went into a bank and gave them 20 bucks and asked for some rolls of halves. Being a coin collector and a hunter, I always checked my change and even went to the bank to check their change, too! In those rolls of half-dollar coins, I was delighted to find over half of the coins were Kennedy 40 percent silver halves.

Even today, you can still spot the occasional silver dime or wheat cent. Maybe you'll be like the 16-year-old who found a Lincoln copper 1943 cent that was sold at auction for $1.7 million. It was one of only 20 cents made from copper in 1943 (they were made from steel that year because copper was a necessary war material). It's like finding real money.

Chapter **11**

Leveraged and Inverse ETFs

For those who want some of the firepower of speculating with futures and options (see Chapters 12 and 13) but are also wary of the potential of significant losses, let me introduce leveraged exchange-traded funds (ETFs).

You may have already read about the general benefits of regular ETFs in Chapter 8 (at least I hope so). If not, make sure you read it as a prerequisite before you "up" your gain to the more speculative and volatile variations covered in this chapter — not only leveraged ETFs but also inverse ETFs and inverse leveraged ETFs.

Feeling Bullish: Leveraged ETFs

You know that if you were positive on gold, you'd simply buy gold as a good diversification in your portfolio. If you were bullish and you wanted to add some "oomph" into your stock portfolio, you'd buy stocks and gold-related ETFs. But if you were really, *really* bullish on gold but too skittish to get into futures or call options, then the most appropriate candidate for your purposes would be a gold-related vehicle such as a leveraged ETF in either the metal itself or in gold mining stocks.

The following sections define leveraged ETFs, describe their advantages versus futures and options, and provide a real-life example of how they work.

Discovering what makes an ETF leveraged

As you find out in Chapters 12 and 13, futures and options are ultra-speculative vehicles that have the potential for outsize gains (which rewards you for the associated risk). Futures and options are derivatives, which means that they don't have their own value; they derive their value from an underlying asset (such as gold and/or silver, as in the case of this book). Given that, a leveraged ETF will contain derivatives to turbocharge the potential gain but have the mirror effect of having a greater-than-average potential for loss.

Here's a general example of how a leveraged ETF works: Besides having the asset (a stock or physical metal) within its portfolio, the ETF also has derivative vehicles such as futures contracts and call/put options that can serve to magnify moves; these vehicles are volatile and have the power to make aggressive moves (up or down) to a greater extent than simply the primary asset or stock themselves. If a mining stock, for example, were to go up 10 percent in a week, then call options on that stock would have the potential to go up 15 percent, 20 percent, or more in the same time frame.

The following sections describe two other types of leveraged ETFs beyond a basic one: double bullish and triple bullish.

Double-bullish leveraged ETFs

A double-bullish (or 2x) leveraged ETF is structured to attempt to double the potential move in the underlying asset. For example, if the underlying asset is gold and it goes up 5 percent, then your 2x bullish leveraged ETF would go up, say, 10 percent. Of course, the opposite can be true, too. If gold goes down, say, 8 percent, then your ETF could go down as much as 16 percent. Yes, a 2x bullish leveraged ETF can be a double-edged sword — great in a bull market but painful in a bear market. This means that you need to be sure in your research that the underlying asset is indeed heading upward ultimately.

Here are some examples of 2x bullish leveraged ETFs to analyze whether you're bullish on gold and silver:

>> ProShares Ultra Gold (UGL)

>> DB Gold Double Long ETN (DGP)

>> ProShares Ultra Silver (AGQ)

TIP

Don't assume that the preceding leveraged ETFs are the only ones (they're just the only ones I found in August 2020). It's not unusual for more leveraged ETFs to get issued during a bull market for a particular underlying asset. When the investing public's interest in the underlying asset grows (as it can when a popular asset experiences a bull market), more ETFs can be created and available for investors. Make it a habit to do a search for new leveraged ETFs using the resources at the end of this chapter as well as the resources in Appendix A.

Triple-bullish leveraged ETFs

Okay, now it's time to put on your helmet and shoulder pads and have some nausea meds by your side (preferably near your snug seat belt). The triple-bullish (3x) leveraged ETF is seeking to triple the move of the underlying asset. For example, if the underlying asset goes up 5 percent, then the ETF is structured to attempt to gain 15 percent. Of course, the downside potential is also there. If that asset goes down, say 7 percent, then your 3x leveraged ETF could potentially go down 21 percent (3×7 percent). As with the 2x leveraged ETF in the preceding section, do your homework on the underlying asset, and time your purchase accordingly.

Here are some examples of 3x leveraged ETFs for gold and silver:

>> VelocityShares 3x Long Gold ETN (UGLD)

>> VelocityShares 3x Long Silver ETN (USLVF)

WARNING

Although the leveraged ETFs will say they are "double leveraged" or "triple leveraged," don't assume a precise mathematical result — you won't get it. A 3x leveraged ETF won't exactly result in three times the move; the portfolios inside the 3x (or 2x) leveraged ETF strive for that potential move but will fall short because market moves are really precise moves. You may find that when you do the math, your 3x bullish leveraged ETF didn't triple the move; more likely it ended up being 2.6x or 2.7x or a closer approximation, so be aware of that. It will depend on how well the derivative portfolio is structured, which isn't always an exact science. Perhaps the derivatives mix inside that leveraged ETF may accomplish a gain that did better than 3x (unlikely). Regardless, don't sweat the difference; just monitor that you're generally getting the results you're expecting with the overall market move.

Some advantages of leveraged ETFs versus futures and options

REMEMBER

As risky and as volatile as leveraged ETFs can be (which your financial advisors and financial planners will continue to warn you about), they can have some of the following advantages that you optimize in your trading approach:

>> **No expiration:** As futures and options have near-term expiration dates, leveraged ETFs don't have a nominal expiration date. The managers of the ETF keep rotating and repositioning the securities within the portfolio continuously.

>> **Stop-loss orders:** Just as with other stock and ETF securities, you can enter orders to help you limit potential losses, such as entering stop-loss orders or trailing stops. More on these orders that are done through your stock brokerage account is in Chapter 16.

>> **Generate option income:** Because many leveraged ETFs are optionable, that could be put in your favor as an income strategy. The two most common income strategies are covered call writing and selling puts. I cover resources on doing this later in this chapter.

TIP

These advantages also apply to inverse ETFs, which I discuss later in this chapter.

Checking out a real-life example of a gold and silver leveraged ETF

For my clients, readers, and students (and for myself, of course), I look for opportunities, especially if I think a bull or bear market is unfolding. Because the opportunity I uncovered is with the gold and silver bull market that was unfolding in early 2020, I was excited with a leveraged ETF that was well situated for a bull run. The Direxion Daily Junior Gold Miners Index Bull (JNUG) is a leveraged ETF whose portfolio reflects the portfolio that represents the junior mining stocks index.

REMEMBER

As you find out in the following sections, I stress two things (some of my "golden rules") to my students and clients about researching speculative opportunities:

1. **Be a contrarian.**

   When the public is selling, you may have a buying opportunity. When the public is buying, you may have a selling opportunity.

2. **You don't need a crystal ball to view the future.**

   Just notice the reality in front of you at that moment.

REMEMBER

Keep in mind that although I describe this as a real-life example, take it as a learning example and not as advice because it's a speculative vehicle (discuss it with a qualified financial professional).

Being a contrarian

Figure 11-1 shows what the chart looked like for JNUG at the time I first came across it. Whew! It's a pretty ugly chart! If your doctor saw this as a medical chart for your health, you'd probably get the advice, "Don't buy green bananas" or "Sure, go ahead and max out your credit cards." Meanwhile, seasoned speculators would see "green" all right, a color they often associate with the colors "gold and silver."

JNUG Overview

Direxion Daily Junior Gold Miners Index Bull 3X Shares ◇ 6.44 +0.84 (+15.00%)

FIGURE 11-1: JNUG chart December 2019 to February 2020.

During January/ February 2020, my extensive research told me that gold and silver's unfolding bull market would pick up steam during spring/summer 2020. I wanted to get my portfolio (and my clients' portfolios) positioned for that strong bull market. In Figure 11-1, you can see where the price of JNUG was during that brief time frame. JNUG's share price was at a very low $5 (give or take), which means that if you bought 100 shares, it would cost you a total of $500 (not including commissions). So the choice to speculators was clear — the absolute worse that could happen was that you could lose $500, but what if you were right? Even mildly, right? You could make a great profit.

At that moment, you were a contrarian. The market-at-large either ignored or exited this security. All the selling sent JNUG down almost through the floor. An experienced speculator takes the contrarian view and says, "How bad can it go? Really?" An experienced speculator would see the reality of that moment and say, "Why not?"

Seeing the reality in front of you

The next point is realizing that a bull market is unfolding, right in front of you. The planets and stars aligned so well that an astrologer would be green with envy. Those two "golden rules" of speculating lined up nicely, so what happened? As you view Figure 11-2, my clients and I started buying JNUG at that time in early 2020 (late January into February and March). I had bought 50 shares at $7 per share, then 50 shares at $6, then more shares at $5. So what happened next?

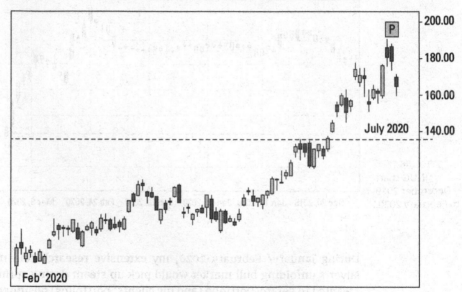

Direxion Daily Junior Gold Miners Bull 2X Shares

FIGURE 11-2:
JNUG chart
February 2020 to
July 2020.

© John Wiley & Sons, Inc.

WARNING

Around March 2020, the issuer of JNUG announced a 10-for-1 reverse split. A reverse split for stocks is generally a negative event for stocks, a sign that the company is in difficulty and is trying to boost its share price. A reverse split means that, for example, if the stock is $1 and you have 100 shares, and the reverse split is 10-for-1, that means that afterward, your 100 shares at $1 will now be 10 shares at $10. In both cases, the nominal value is still $100, but what changed? Companies do this type of split because selling forced the stock down to levels that some exchanges (such as the New York Stock Exchange) would delist it if the stock price fell to $1 per share — not a good development for a company.

However, a reverse split is indeed a different animal in the world of ETFs. The issuer and manager of the ETF may do a reverse split so that the ETF would still qualify to be in mutual fund portfolios that have a share price criteria (such as "We invest only in ETFs with share prices north of $10 per share"). Those who had 100 shares of JNUG (bought at $6 per share) now have 10 shares of JNUG at $60. The issuer (Direxion) actually did this reverse split at the time for a dozen of its ETFs, so ultimately, this was a nonissue.

Note: Keep in mind that the only reason I mention a reverse split here is because it actually happened. It's usually not in your mix of factors that you're seeking or preparing for. In actuality, it wasn't a factor in the educational point being made here for the budding speculator.

The bottom line is that by July, JNUG was $175 per share. Had you held your 10 shares of it at $60 per share (the post–reverse split price), you'd have made a great profit. Your $600 investment (10 shares × $60 per share) becomes worth a total of $1,750 (10 shares × $175 per share) for a total gain of $1,150 (a percentage gain of 192 percent) in less than five months (cool!). Just imagine how many green bananas you could buy with that!

Feeling Bearish: Inverse ETFs and Inverse Leveraged ETFs

Say that you're bearish on a particular asset (or industry or the general market). Then you may do what many speculators would tend to do: Explore the possibilities of making some gains through bearish strategies (bets that the underlying asset will go down in the near term). If it's a stock or ETF, some will either "go short" on that particular asset (very risky and *not* recommended for novice investors or speculators) or perhaps buy put options (making a speculative bet that the underlying asset will go down), which is a slightly safer bearish bet.

In the scope of this chapter, consider another way: using an inverse ETF. An inverse ETF is structured to gain a corresponding amount in the event that the underlying asset goes down. Let's say that you're bearish on silver, and you seek to gain in the event that silver goes down. A silver inverse ETF would then essentially mirror the opposite move. If silver goes down 5 percent, for example, then the silver inverse ETF would go up by 5 percent. An example of a gold inverse ETF is DB Gold Short ETN (DGZ).

TIP

An inverse ETF would typically use vehicles such as put options and related derivative strategies. The best time for speculators to be in an inverse ETF is either when the underlying asset is about to enter a bear market (an extended downward move in the price of the asset of 20 percent or more) or when the asset is still in an intact long-term bull market but may experience some temporary corrections (a short-term and modest downward move of the asset typically 5 to 15 percent) along the way. Sometimes in a bull market, the asset may have moments of being "overbought," which some speculators see as a short-term opportunity to gain a bearish profit before the asset resumes its upward trajectory.

Now for those of you who are really, *really* bearish, this could be your cup of tea. A leveraged inverse ETF (which could be 2x or 3x) is a vehicle that can bring you a greater profit when the underlying asset either corrects or enters a bear market. Here, the gain is magnified in a similar way as with the bullish 2x or 3x ETFs but with the inverse (or opposite) impact.

Say that you became bearish in gold and wanted to have a magnified gain (again, 2x or 3x) in the event its price declines. If gold indeed goes down 10 percent, then an inverse 2x leveraged ETF would be structured to go up 20 percent. You get the picture.

Here are some examples of gold and/or silver inverse leveraged ETFs:

>> ProShares UltraShort Gold (GLL)

>> DB Gold Double Short ETN (DZZ)

>> ProShares UltraShort Silver (ZSL)

Using Leveraged and Inverse ETFs during the Market's Ups and Downs

Figure 11-3 has a fairly typical bull market trajectory for a given asset. Assume that the asset tracked is gold for the purpose of this section. Keep in mind the speculative golden rules mentioned earlier in this chapter. Take a look at the inflection points on the chart labeled A, B, and C. They are typical peaks and troughs as the asset zigzags upward.

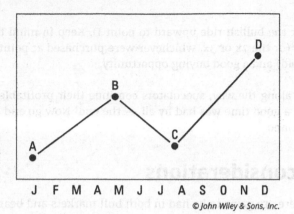

FIGURE 11-3:
Typical highs and lows include A start, B upleg, C downleg, and D higher upleg.

© *John Wiley & Sons, Inc.*

The choices that investors and speculators have today are amazing! Here are a few strategies to get you thinking about leveraged and inverse ETFs during the ups and downs of the market.

Bullish moves

At the beginning (point A in Figure 11-3), you're bullish (remember, you looked at the fundamentals), and your research and best judgment indicate that a bull market is about to unfold. At this point, you get some shares into a regular ETF (discussed in Chapter 8) or you see a screaming bull market, so you get some bullish leveraged ETFs as covered earlier in this chapter.

For long-term investors, they'll simply hold on and not be concerned with the occasional pullback. They may even buy some more shares when they see corrections along the way (as with point C) as the bull market zigzags upward.

Bearish moves

Speculators may be bullish at point A in Figure 11-3 and may indeed be there for the long term, but they'll keep an eye open for every point that presents an opportunity. At point B, their research may indicate that gold is "overbought" according to their technical analysis (covered in Chapter 15), so they decide to buy some shares of either an inverse gold ETF or (if they're truly bearish) a leveraged inverse gold ETF. Presume that they still have their original bullish ETF and will hold onto it for the full bull market ride. They then decide to cash out their profitable inverse ETFs at point C. Now they have the cash to add to their original bullish ETFs and are ready for the bullish ride upward to point D. Keep in mind that the original bullish ETFs (or the 2x or 3x, whichever were purchased at point A) are down in price (oversold) and a good buying opportunity.

With profits along the way, speculators continue their profitable ride upward to point D, and a good time was had by all — the end! Now go and buy that snazzy retirement condo.

Other considerations

Note that there are gains to be had in both bull markets and bear markets, and a variety of tactics to deploy along the way. When some speculators, for example, see that gold was overbought at point B in Figure 11-3, they may deploy a trailing stop or stop-loss order to minimize the downside. Had gold declined and hit the stop-loss order, they may then put in buy orders at the lower price. (See Chapter 16 for more about these orders.)

Still, other speculators may employ call and put options to profit from those points. This chapter really "peels back the onion under the hood" (that sounds right to me) for these speculative vehicles, but here's where I put the "cherry on top": Many of these ETFs are also optionable. That's right. It's like finding a nuclear hand grenade that's also filled with nitroglycerin — mind-blowing! Imagine buying a call (or put) option on a leveraged ETF. This is like a leveraged vehicle that is, uh, leveraged. If you're correct, you could have an amazing profit! But — you can see this coming — it would get riskier, too. Do your homework here and tread lightly. More on options is in Chapter 13.

Looking at Resources for Leveraged and Inverse ETFs

Hopefully this eye-popping chapter gives you plenty of vehicles, ideas, and strategies to mull over and act on for your own profitable pursuits. Of course, the chapter isn't complete and I could write an entire course on it . . . hmmm. I'll mull over that one, and I hope to see you at my website down the road. Meanwhile, here are some further considerations.

TIP

To find out more about ETFs in general and also for an extensive, searchable database of ETFs, here are some places to start your research:

» ETF Database (www.etfdb.com): The database is regularly updated, and you can find out about new ETFs in general or about the latest leveraged and/or inverse ETFs. You'll also find out about ETFs that are no longer available and plenty of posts about ETFs and how to invest in them.

» ETF Trends (www.etftrends.com): This great site is loaded with ETF news and views along with education and webcasts on ETF events.

» ETF Guide (www.etfguide.com): This site has podcasts and a blog covering the happenings in the ETF industry.

Shameless plug: My book *High-Level Investing For Dummies* (Wiley) has in-depth chapters on leveraged and inverse ETFs and a full section on call and put options. For more resources, check out Appendix A.

Chapter **12**

Focusing on Futures

Fasten your seat belts and put your trays in the upright position. Check your helmets. Grab some bromo-seltzer and put away any sharp objects. You're now ready for the world of futures! And if you've seen the roller-coaster moves of world markets in 2020, then you have a good idea. Fortunes can be made quickly. They can be lost even faster. Let's dip our collective toes in the water of this exciting corner of the financial world.

Back to the Futures

Commodities and futures are mentioned as though they're synonymous, but at the risk of nit-picking, they are truly different:

» Commodities make up the raw stuff that is indeed the building blocks of society. Commodities encompass food, building materials, precious metals, energy, and more. Commodities range from the typical (wheat, soybeans, sugar, and so on) to the odd-sounding (pork bellies?). Commodities end up in their ultimate forms as produce and processed foods found at the local supermarket or in other venues such as the gasoline you get at the local gas station or the components found in the circuits of a computer or cellphone. They are in every corner of modern life.

>> Futures are nothing more than commodities that come in a standardized quantity and are delivered in the future at a specified price and a specified date in the future (hence, the term *futures*). The word *futures* is technically shorthand for *futures contract* because futures contracts are really legal claims to an underlying asset (the commodities).

A BRIEF HISTORY OF FUTURES

In the mid-1800s, merchants began organizing centralized markets to make the act of buying, selling, and trading commodities much easier. These places gave them the ability to set standards for quality and quantity. The first commodities to be commonly traded were grains and other agricultural products. By the mid-1900s, more than 1,500 markets or exchanges had been set up at every major port and rail station. As the United States became industrialized, these exchanges went beyond agricultural commodities into almost anything that had an active market.

The major commodity hubs sprung up during the 19th and 20th centuries at two large urban cities: Chicago and New York. In New York City, circa 1872, a group of dairy merchants came together to create a formal exchange, which came to be called the Butter and Cheese Exchange of New York.

As they added commodities, the exchange grew and so did the name. It became the Butter, Cheese, and Egg Exchange. I would hate to think what the local supermarket would have been called then, but fortunately, they made it a convenient name in 1882 when it became the New York Mercantile Exchange (NYMEX). A second exchange, Commodity Exchange, Inc., was established during the Great Depression in the early 1930s. This came to be called COMEX, and it specialized in hard goods and metals such as copper, silver, and tin.

Because the federal government banned private ownership of gold during the Great Depression, it wasn't available for futures trading on the COMEX until December 1974. New York's two largest commodities exchanges, COMEX and NYMEX, merged in August 1994. The two exchanges became two divisions of one entity:

- The NYMEX Division traded energy (such as crude oil, heating oil, gasoline, and natural gas) and the precious metals platinum and palladium.

- The COMEX Division covered gold, silver, copper, aluminum, and several stock indexes.

In the early days (the 1800s and early 1900s), transactions were primarily in cash on the spot for immediate delivery (the spot market) and in forward contracts (described later in this chapter) before the advent of futures contracts.

The reality then is that commodities are real stuff while futures are paper. So futures contracts are derivatives; they derive their value from the underlying asset. This is a crucial distinction (you'll see why later in this chapter).

I think that a good way to remember the difference between commodities and futures is somewhat like the difference between a car and a car title. The car is the underlying asset, and the car title is a formal piece of paper that has a legal claim to a car. In the same way that a futures contract precisely describes what it's a claim to (a certain quantity and quality of a commodity), a car title precisely describes what it's a claim to (a 1987 Ford Torino, its serial number, and so on).

Although the futures market may sometimes look like a crazy and haphazard market, it's actually an orderly market that performs important functions in the overall economy, as you find out in the following sections. Although futures are a speculative and risky market for beginner investors' purposes, it's actually a market that removes risk and uncertainty for those in industry who need the underlying commodities to keep making the stuff that you and I need on a daily basis.

How the futures market works

The futures market operates in a centralized, auction-style marketplace called the futures exchange. The exchange makes sure that the market works smoothly. Those floor brokers are there to match buyers and sellers with the best prices. Each of the stations represents a batch of commodities, and the chaotic crowd that hovers around the stations is making buy and sell bids based on the open cry system. In that crowd are brokers who are buying futures for their clients or for their own accounts. Those shouting for the buyers are looking for the lowest prices. Those shouting for the sellers are looking for the highest prices. This method has real and beneficial impact not only for those in futures but also the economy at large. Of course, the physical "shouting" has been replaced with "digital shouting" as market technology keeps improving and buy and sell orders are sent with keystrokes instead.

Two very important events occur on the floor of the exchange with all these brokers:

>> **Price discovery:** Because of how competitive it is, the futures market becomes an important way to determine prices based on current and future estimated supply and demand. The futures market receives a nonstop flow of information from around the world, all of which gets absorbed and ends up being reflected in the price through the bidding process. This is how the price is discovered. This helps the rest of the economy figure out prices and values of an entire range of goods from A to Z. Capitalism at its finest!

>> **Risk reduction:** The futures markets provide a place for commerce and industry to reduce risk when making purchases. Risk is reduced because the price in the futures contract is set, which helps those who want delivery of the underlying asset know exactly what they're buying (or selling), how much they're paying (or receiving), and when delivery can (or should) be made. Some examples appear later in this chapter (see the section on hedging).

That's right. Futures can reduce risk. Your response might be, "Reduce risk?! Are you crazy?! I lost a fortune going long on umbrella futures just before the drought! How can futures possibly reduce risk?" Glad you asked. Technically, risk isn't reduced; it's transferred. Merchants and manufacturers seek to reduce the risk in buying their raw materials, and the folks who take on this risk for them are the speculators. Speculators take on risk because of the incentive to possibly make a lot of money.

The futures market is a crystal clear example of the age-old equation of risk versus return. Desiring a greater return on your money means tolerating greater risk. If you don't want more risk, then you have to tolerate a lower return on your money (yep, it can be a vicious cycle).

What can be traded as a futures contract

The average person would be surprised at the range of things that can be traded as futures (the average person is also annoyed at being called average). Although this book concentrates on precious metals (notably gold and silver), it's important for you to see the range because many traders do two or more commodities (or other tradable entities such as currencies and financial instruments). A trader may, for example, take positions in gold and the U.S. dollar to take advantage of opposing price moves. It's important for you to know what's available for trading opportunities or to just plain diversify your futures account:

>> **Precious metals:** The basic ones are gold, silver, platinum, and palladium.

>> **Base metals:** Copper, aluminum, zinc, lead, tin, and nickel (the nonferrous metals).

>> **Steel:** A ferrous metal (not to be confused with a Ferris wheel).

>> **Currencies** (also known as Forex, which is short for foreign exchange): The most actively traded are the U.S. dollar, euro, Japanese yen, Canadian dollar, British pound, Australian dollar, and others.

>> **Indexes:** The S&P 500, E-Mini S&P, Nasdaq, Dow Jones, FTSE, DAX, and others.

>> **Grains:** The most active are corn, wheat, soybeans, soy meal, bean oil, oats, rice, rapeseed, barley, and others.

- » **Financial instruments:** Treasury notes, treasury bonds, muni-bond, eurodollar, BUND, Schatz, Euroyen, and others.

- » **Food and fiber:** Coffee, cocoa, sugar, cotton, orange juice, lumber, and others.

- » **Energy:** Crude oil, Brent Crude, West Texas Intermediate Crude, natural gas, unleaded gasoline, propane, and others.

- » **Meats:** Live cattle, pork, lean hogs, and others.

- » **Plastics:** That includes . . . uh . . . plastics.

- » **Stocks:** There are futures on single stocks.

- » **The unusual:** Hurricane (you read that right), home prices, and who knows what else they'll think up.

The futures market is such a growing area, I wish there were futures on futures (maybe in the future).

The Players in the World of Futures

The main players in the world of futures are the exchanges, speculators, hedgers, and regulators. Check out the sections that follow for more information on each.

REMEMBER

To make all this great futures activity happen, you'll need a broker and an account approved, funded, and ready to go. I could write a whole chapter on brokers, so I did (see Chapter 16).

The U.S. exchanges

The CME Group (www.cmegroup.com) is the primary organization in the United States that runs a marketplace for futures, and it does so by operating four futures exchanges. The exchanges are centralized markets that make the buying and selling efficient and liquid. Here are the major futures exchanges in the United States:

- »» New York Mercantile Exchange (NYMEX): This is the most active exchange for precious metals (www.cmegroup.com/company/nymex.html).

- »» Chicago Mercantile Exchange (CME; www.cmegroup.com/company/cme.html).

- »» Chicago Board of Trade (CBOT; www.cmegroup.com/company/cbot.html).

- »» COMEX (www.cmegroup.com/company/comex.html).

Don't forget that the CME Group's exchanges also offer options on futures contracts. Speak to your broker about futures options because they're great tools for speculators. Personally, I prefer futures options because they have less risk than outright futures contract trading. Options on futures have the same general features as options on other vehicles; you can find out more about options in Chapter 13.

The international futures exchanges

The primary international marketplace where you can trade gold and silver futures contracts (and options on them) is done at the London Metals Exchange (www.lme.com), and futures in other markets are done at London's Intercontinental Exchange (www.theice.com).

As the world becomes a more global market, more and more exchanges will either spring up or existing exchanges will make available their own offerings in precious metals. Exchanges ranging from Dubai (pronounced do-BUY; hopefully, they "do sell") to Shanghai are already trading in precious metals such as gold and silver.

Keep in mind that all this international futures trading will benefit you even if you don't buy or sell a single ounce of any precious metal. As more investors across the globe get involved, that will increase demand. Couple this with limited supply, and you have yet another bullish factor for precious metals.

Speculators

This is the category that you and I belong to. We don't want to take delivery of 25,000 pounds of copper — we just want to profit from its market action. As market participants, speculators are out to profit from the futures market's risk and volatility. Speculators aren't involved in some business that needs the goods tied to the futures contract; they're looking for cash transactions. Depending on the market, only 1 to 5 percent of futures contracts result in a physical delivery. Speculators aren't seeking safety but the financial benefits that could accompany the risky side of the market.

Hedgers

Hedgers aren't landscapers. That is just a term for those who practice hedging, which is a practice of making an order to reduce the risk of an unfavorable price move in an asset or commodity by taking an offsetting position in a related security (such as a futures contract). The odds are that the hedger is an organization in commerce or industry (such as a manufacturer or an agricultural business) that regularly buys raw materials for its production facilities.

Here's an example: Baubles Galore, Inc. (BG), is a gold jewelry manufacturer that must secure some gold before the holiday season to produce earrings and necklaces for retail consumers that are already being marketed in catalogs and websites with prices already publicized. Say that season is six months away. What happens if the price of gold goes up during that time? The prices that the consumers would be paying are already set. If gold goes down in that period, not a problem. BG would end up making more money. But the real problem is if prices go up. That is a real risk for BG because it can't pass along the higher cost to its customers. What can the company do?

Fortunately, the company can hedge or diminish the risk of the potential gold price increase by entering the futures market and purchasing a gold contract that would settle in a suitable time frame (such as August) and lock in a price. Let's say that time has passed and it's now August, and the price of gold is up $50 per ounce. Fortunately, BG isn't affected by the increase in the price of gold because the futures contract locked in the lower price.

REMEMBER

Now you see the value of hedging and how the firms that do take delivery benefit from a futures contract. Locking in a price protects you from unforeseen price increases. Hedging with futures contracts can protect buyers and sellers. When you understand who has the incentive to lock in a lower price (or a higher price), you can understand the economic value of futures contracts to hedgers. Cattle ranchers would hedge against lower meat prices, while a large restaurant chain would hedge against higher meat prices. In each case, the risk was transferred to the other side of those futures contracts, the speculators.

Regulators

America's futures market is regulated by the Commodity Futures Trading Commission (CFTC; www.cftc.gov), a federal government agency. The market is also subject to regulation by the National Futures Association (NFA; www.nfa.futures.org), a private, self-regulatory body authorized by the U.S. Congress and subject to CFTC supervision. The NFA primarily oversees the brokers and enforces a code of business ethics.

A futures broker (the firm and those individuals employed as brokers) must be registered with the CFTC to issue or buy or sell futures contracts. Futures brokers must also be registered with the NFA and the CFTC to conduct business. The CFTC has the power to seek criminal prosecution (through the Department of Justice) when it thinks that the law may have been violated. The NFA can permanently bar a company or an individual from dealing on the futures exchange because of violations of business ethics and the NFA code of conduct.

TIP

Investors and speculators should become more informed about how futures should work and aware of anything improper. To find out more, head to the websites for the CFTC and the NFA. You'll find great consumer information on choosing a broker and educational materials for how the market works. If you feel that you've been victimized by fraud or improper behavior, you should contact the CFTC and the NFA for assistance.

The Fundamentals of Futures Contracts

At the core of futures trading is the futures contract. The futures contract derives its value from the underlying asset (corn, gold, silver, and so on). In this respect, a futures contract is really a derivative. A derivative sounds complicated, but the essence of a derivative is that it (a paper contract, for example) derives its value from something tangible.

In a futures contract, the agreement is between two parties. Party #1 agrees to deliver a commodity (referred to as the short position). Party #2 agrees to receive a commodity (referred to as the long position).

REMEMBER

So what is being traded? The futures contract is a paper vehicle with the underlying promise to deliver the goods, which are the commodities involved. A buyer of a futures contract may or may not want delivery, though. It depends on why they're buying into the futures contract. Buying the futures contract is also referred to as going long. There are two basic reasons that a buyer will buy a futures contract:

>> The buyer is an organization that may want to see a delivery of the physical commodity made. Maybe the organization is a jewelry manufacturing firm that needs raw materials (such as gold or silver) to make jewelry.

>> The buyer is a speculator seeking profit. He or she doesn't want the underlying commodities (who wants a ton of pork bellies or copper dumped on their lawns anyway?); they're just looking for making some money betting on the price move of the underlying commodity.

Like any contract, a futures contract is an agreement. It's a salable contract, and it's made on the trading floor of a formal futures exchange. The contract is for the buying or selling of a particular commodity (in our case, metals, including gold and silver) at a predetermined price at a specified delivery date in the future. The following sections describe the features of a futures contract.

A specified size

Futures contracts get standardized for the same reason when you go to the store to get a loaf of Wheat-O brand bread — it's the exact same as any other loaf of the same type.

The futures contract is tied to an asset with a set size. Each futures contract has a set size. The size of the futures contract is determined by the regulated exchange on which the contract trades (I list different exchanges earlier in this chapter). For example, a futures contract for a single stock may be based on a hundred shares of that stock. If prices are reported per share, the value of the contract would be the price times 100.

Specified quality

Not just any old batch of stuff can be an underlying asset to a futures contract. The exchange is usually pretty vigorous about quality. Take the Chicago Board of Trade (CBOT) and its silver futures contract. The description of the underlying metal states clearly that it must be "5,000 troy ounces (±6%) of refined silver, assaying not less than 0.999 fineness, in cast bars weighing 1,000 or 1,100 troy ounces each." (Troy ounces are the standard measurement for precious metals versus avoirdupois or "regular" ounces. A troy ounce is 10 percent heavier than an avoirdupois ounce. For more details, see Chapter 9.) You can't just slap on some silver paint to a copper brick and expect it to be acceptable. Buyers and sellers expect a standardized quality.

Specified prices

The prices of futures contracts are usually quoted the same way prices are quoted in the underlying asset. For example, a contract for an individual security would be quoted in dollars and cents per share. Contracts for indexes would be quoted on an index number, usually stated to two decimal points.

Each futures contract has a minimum price fluctuation (called a tick), which may differ from product to product or exchange to exchange. For example, if a particular futures contract has a tick size of one dollar, you can buy the contract at $100 or at $101 but not at $100.50.

A specified delivery date

Futures contracts on precious metals will continue to be traded right through the delivery month until trading is terminated on a day specified by the exchange near the end of the month. Up until expiration, you may liquidate an open position by offsetting your contract with an equal and opposite contract that expires in the same month. If you don't liquidate an open position before it expires, you'll be required to make or take delivery of the underlying security or to settle the contract in cash after expiration.

Although futures contracts on a particular security may be listed in and traded on more than one regulated exchange, contract specifications may not be the same. Also, prices for contracts on the same security or index may vary on different regulated exchanges because of different contract specifications.

Because each futures exchange has slightly differing terms for its contracts, review the contract specifications at the exchange's website. Discuss it with your broker so you're not surprised.

Metals Futures Contracts

You can find futures contracts for both precious as well as base metals, and you can also get in the futures games with a smaller amount of dough by using mini-futures contracts. In the following sections, I discuss these futures contracts as well as special considerations, such as margin and leverage, that you should keep in mind if you decide to get involved in futures.

Precious metals contracts

There are futures contracts on gold, silver, platinum, and palladium. There are more obscure precious metals (like rhodium), but their markets are very thinly traded and not really practical for the average investor. Table 12-1 gives you a run-down on the main precious metals futures contracts (at NYMEX).

TABLE 12-1 **Precious Metals Futures Contracts**

Metal	Contract Size	Delivery Months	Symbol	Tick	Point Value
Gold	100 oz	G, J, M, Q, V, Z	GC, RGC	10 points = $10	1 point = $100
Silver	5,000 oz	F, H, K, N, U, Z	SI, RSI	50 points = $25	1 point = $50

For delivery months, the column reads with letters that the exchange uses to symbolize the delivery month. Table 12-2 gives all the months and their accompanying letter (symbol).

TABLE 12-2 **Delivery Month Symbols**

Delivery Month	Symbol Letter
January	F
February	G
March	H
April	J
May	K
June	M
July	N
August	Q
September	U
October	V
November	X
December	Z

As an example of how a particular contract is symbolized, a gold contract for the delivery month December 2021 would be "GCZ21," where GC is for gold, Z is for December, and 21 is for 2021. NYMEX's website (www.cmegroup.com/company/nymex.html) gives you full details on the futures contracts and their delivery dates and margin requirements.

Trades on a futures contract continue through its delivery month until a final date specified by the exchange. Gold futures contracts for December 2020 are terminated for trading as of the last trading day in December 2020.

Mini-futures contracts

For those of you who think you need a zillion bucks to get into futures, think again. The exchanges have something for those who would like to speculate with less money, which also means less risk. By the way, if you do have a zillion bucks, they would welcome you with the same hospitality as your neighborhood casino!

Recently, some of these mini contracts had margin requirements of less than $500, which makes it more affordable to speculators with limited funds. Of course, check with your broker because initial margin can change. The next section has the scoop on margin.

See Table 12-3 for a list of mini-futures contracts.

TABLE 12-3 **Mini-Futures Contracts**

Metal	Exchange	Contract Size	Symbol
Gold	CME	33.2 troy oz	YG
Gold	NYMEX	50 troy oz	QO
Silver	CME	1,000 troy oz	YI
Silver	NYMEX	2,500 oz	QI

Pass the margin

A futures contract is an obligation and not an asset; it has no value as collateral for a loan. Because of the potential for a loss as a result of the daily mark-to-market process, however, a margin deposit is required of each party to a futures contract. This required margin deposit also is referred to as a performance bond. This performance bond or margin is security for the broker.

The basic margin requirement is 20 percent of the current value of the futures contract. Some types of futures strategies may have lower margin requirements. Requests for additional margin are known as margin calls. Both the buyer and seller must individually deposit required margin to their respective accounts.

WARNING

It's important to understand that individual brokerage firms can, and in many cases do, require margin that is higher than the exchange requirements. Additionally, margin requirements may vary from brokerage firm to brokerage firm. Furthermore, a brokerage firm can increase its house margin requirements at any time without providing advance notice, and such increases could result in a margin call.

For example, some firms may require margin to be positive the business day following the date of the deficiency, or some firms may even require deposit on the same day. Some firms may require margin to be on deposit in the account before they'll accept an order for a futures contract. You should get very familiar with the customer agreement with your brokerage firm before entering into any transactions in futures contracts. (Find out more about brokers in Chapter 16.)

WARNING

Brokerage firms generally reserve the right to liquidate a customer's futures contract positions or sell customer assets to meet a margin call at any time without contacting the customer. Brokerage firms may also enter into equivalent but opposite positions on your account to manage the risk created by a margin call. Some customers mistakenly believe that a firm is required to contact them for a margin call and that the firm isn't allowed to liquidate securities or other assets in their accounts to meet a margin call unless the firm has contacted them first. This is not the case.

While most firms notify their customers of margin calls and allow some time to deposit additional margin, you're not required to do so. Even if a firm notifies the customer of a margin call and sets a specified due date for a margin deposit, the firm can still take action as necessary to protect its financial interests, including the immediate liquidation of positions without advance notification to the customer.

TIP

For speculators who want to avoid the problems inherent in margin of your account, consider options on futures. Generally, options on futures for retail investors and speculators can be bought with cash and done so without margin. Options on futures have the same basic volatility and can offer great profit potential but can be done without the risks of margin. You can lose money in options, but at least the worst-case scenario is that losses are limited to the price of the option and no more. See Chapter 13 for more about options. Almost every precious metal and base metal covered in this book has options available. Explore this investing option (pun intended!) with your broker.

Leverage: The double-edged sword

The futures market can offer leverage that can magnify your gains (or your losses). Leverage is the ability to retain control over a valuable asset with a relatively small amount of money. Most people are familiar with leverage in real estate: You gain control of a property valued at $250,000 by making a small down payment of, say, 10 percent ($25,000) and borrow the remaining 90 percent ($225,000). Then if the property goes up to $300,000 in value (a gain of $50,000), your initial invested amount of $25,000 at that point made you 200 percent.

In futures, you get similar leverage. On the plus side, you don't have to use as much money as in real estate, and you don't have to wait a long time to see results. On the negative side, the leverage can work against you, and you can lose money big time. I tell you, there's always a catch!

In futures, the down payment is your initial deposit (not really a down payment, just comparing it with the prior example). As in the previous example, the initial deposit or margin is a small sum that, in turn, controls a valuable asset as represented by the valuable futures contract.

Take a futures contract on gold. The contract's underlying asset is 100 ounces of gold. If gold is $1,700 an ounce, then the contract would be worth $170,000 (100 ounces times $1,700 an ounce). Say the initial margin is $20,000, and you're going long on the gold futures contract (meaning that you're bullish on gold futures and believe the price will go up). If gold rises to $1,850, then that contract would be worth $185,000 (100 ounces times $1,850 an ounce). Because the price increase would be $15,000, your profit percentage would be 75 percent (the $15,000 gain is 75 percent of your initial margin deposit of $20,000).

Again, if gold fell in that example, you'd lose money as your broker makes that margin call so that you can kick in more funds to maintain margin.

Basic Futures Trading Strategies

The whole point of speculating in futures contracts is an attempt to figure out what the price will be in the near future and profit from that move. Your strategies all flow from what your expectation is. Although you can choose from many sophisticated strategies with futures (especially when you combine them with options on futures), that's something you can look forward to learning after this book. For now, the basics will be covered. Very basic. But some of the best strategies are indeed simple.

Basic strategy #1: Going long

In going long, the speculator is making a bullish bet (thinking that the asset will go up in price) on that futures contract. The speculator gets into the contract by agreeing to buy and receive delivery of the underlying asset at a set price. The bet is that the market price will rise above the set price and the profit is the difference.

Say that Howard the speculator is bullish on gold. Howard would, therefore, go long on a gold futures contract. Presume that he starts with an initial margin of $15,000 in August. He buys one December contract with gold at $1,600 per ounce. Because the contract is for 100 ounces of gold for a total contract value of $160,000, and because Howard is going long in August, he's expecting (hoping?) that the price of gold will go up by the time the contract expires in December.

Say that gold rises by $250 to $1,850 in October. He decides to sell the contract to lock in a profit. The contract would be worth $185,000, and the profit would be $25,000. That $25,000 would be a profit of 167 percent on his initial $15,000 in about two months.

Of course, gold could go down. If it had gone down $250 per ounce instead, then the contract would be worth $135,000 (100 ounces times $1,350 per ounce) and Howard would realize a significant loss, and a margin call would be made because he would have to kick in more margin. Howard would be very unhappy.

Basic strategy #2: Going short

In going short, the speculator is making a bearish bet (thinking that the asset will go down in price) on a futures contract. The speculator gets into the contract by agreeing to sell and deliver the underlying asset at a set price. The bet is that the market price will fall below the set price and make a profit on the difference.

Let's say that after doing some research, Sally expects the price of silver to go down in the next few months. It's September, and she decides to sell (go short on) a January futures contract. Starting with an initial margin deposit of $3,000, Sally would then sell a contract today, in September, at the higher price of $25,000 and buy it back after the price declined and before January. Keep in mind that going short is a strategy to profit in a declining (or bear) market.

By November, the price of silver had gone down, and the contract's market value had subsequently declined to $20,000. After buying back her short position, she nets a gain of $5,000 ($25,000 less $20,000). Of course, if silver rallied (gone up), she would have lost money. Say that silver's rally caused the futures contract's market value to rise and hit $31,000 in November. Sally would have lost $6,000 (yes, the margin call would have been painful). She would be best advised to get out of that contract in the event that silver keeps going up and watching the loss get painfully bigger.

Basic strategy #3: Spreads

Going long and going short are out-and-out directional strategies. In other words, you're 100 percent committed to a particular direction, either up or down. Once you get past those two, you get into strategies that offer some hedging opportunities for you, the speculator. This means the next strategy: spreads.

Speculators can use spreads to take advantage of the price difference between two different contracts of the same underlying asset. Spread strategies are less risky than directional strategies, which may make them good considerations for speculators with limited funds. Check out the three common spreads in the following sections.

The calendar spread

In futures, the calendar spread is also called an intracommodity spread because it's done within the same commodity or asset. Say that Eddie is doing a calendar spread on silver futures. He'll buy (go long on) the further-out month while selling (going short on) the closer month. Table 12-4 gives you an idea of how the trade looks.

TABLE 12-4   **Calendar Spread Trade***

Direction	Asset	Price per ounce*	Delivery Month	Contract Symbol	Contract Value
Going Long	Silver	29.234	Dec 21	SI Z21	146,170
Going Short	Silver	29.008	July 21	SI N21	145,040

* Prices in this example are from the CME Group website as of 9/1/2020.

As you can see, the contract for Dec '21 is valued at $146,170, and the July '21 contract is $145,040. The difference is $1,130. There's a difference because the market places greater value on the December contract.

In this spread, Eddie anticipates that the price difference between July and December silver futures will widen. Ideally, he'd like to see the short position (on July silver) go down and his long position (on December silver) go up. More likely, the two contracts' prices will move in the same direction, but Eddie is betting that the latter month contract will rise more so than the earlier month. He starts with initial margin of $600.

The spread between July silver (at $29.008 an ounce) and December silver (at $29.234) is 22.6 cents. Because a silver futures contract is on 5,000 ounces of silver, the total spread is then easy math (5,000 × 22.6 cents = $1,130).

As time passes and we get closer to July, Eddie is ready to cash out his calendar spread. Both prices rise, but as Eddie anticipated, the December contract increased more than the July contract. Presume that July silver rose by 20 cents and that December silver rose by 35 cents. After you do all the math, July silver is $29.208 and December silver is $29.584. The contracts are now worth $146,040 (July) and $147,920 (December). The spread has widened to $1,880. Eddie closes out the spread. The loss on the short position was offset by the greater gain on the long position. His profit is $750.

REMEMBER

In the case that silver went down, the value of his position would go down, but he could still realize either a smaller loss or a partial profit because his short position would become profitable. In the calendar spread, you have two positions that are like bets against each other. In a spread, you're hoping that your winning position is more successful than your losing position.

The inter-market spread

In the calendar spread, I provide an example to flesh out the concept to show you how a basic spread works. That gives you the gist so I won't have to beat you up with more detailed examples. Beyond that, other spreads are the same basic structure, but they may have some twist.

An inter-market spread is a spread with two contracts of the same month but two different markets. You go long in one market while you go short in another market. For example, you can go long on one oil futures contract and short on one natural gas futures contract.

The inter-exchange spread

This is another type of spread in which you go long on a contract in one futures exchange while you go short on another contract in a different futures exchange. For example, the speculator may go long on a contract on the Chicago Mercantile Exchange (CME) and go short on a contract on the London Mercantile Exchange (LME).

And if you go long and short on two dairy contracts, then I believe it's called a cheese spread (but don't quote me).

Using Fundamental and Technical Analysis with Futures

Fundamental analysis is usually used for stock investing, but it's also done with futures. With stocks, fundamental analysis involves reviewing and analyzing the company's finances, operations, and market to determine how well its stock will perform. As a side point, it's recommended for long-term investing (measured in years).

The same methodology is used for futures, but instead you're looking at the factors affecting its market price, such as supply-and-demand data, along with economic and political variables that could influence its value. As a side point, futures tend to be more short term (usually measured in days, weeks, or months). In general, futures typically have a shorter time horizon than stocks.

Technical analysis is based on the idea that market data, such as charts of price, volume, and open interest, can help predict the future (usually short-term) direction of market prices. The folks who use technical analysis believe that they can accurately predict the future price of a stock by looking at its historical prices as recorded in charts and accompanying data. In part, technical analysis makes the assumption (with the data) that market psychology influences trading in a way that enables predicting when futures prices will rise or fall. See Chapter 15 for more on technical analysis.

Comparing fundamental versus technical analysis reminds me of that beer commercial where the two sides heatedly exchange those immortal words, "tastes great!" and "less filling!" That humorous debate made it sound as if it were one versus the other. But who says that you couldn't have both? I think that investing and speculating can taste great and be less filling. Well, you know what I mean.

In the financial world, fundamental versus technical analysis is a long-time debate, but it's not a heated one. No fights break out in the bleachers, and one group doesn't throw water balloons at the other one (at least not to my knowledge).

Considering my background and what has worked for me, I can be rightly called a fundamental analyst because I use an approach labeled value investing. Because stocks are predominantly a long-term pursuit, fundamental analysis works extremely well for me and others. For people with a long-term perspective, fundamental analysis generally wins out over technical analysis. As proof, in the historical pantheon of investors, you'll find far more familiar names that are proponents of fundamental analysis and value investing (or some variation of these) versus those that use technical analysis and charting methods.

In the short term, it's a far different picture. Technical analysis has shown to be valuable, and using it to determine short-term buy-and-sell trading decisions has shown some fruitful results. A great way to show these two approaches in action is to view an illustrative example. Here are the gold charts for the year 2019 (Figure 12-1) and for the longer time frame 2000 to 2020 (Figure 12-2). Combined, these two charts give a compelling perspective.

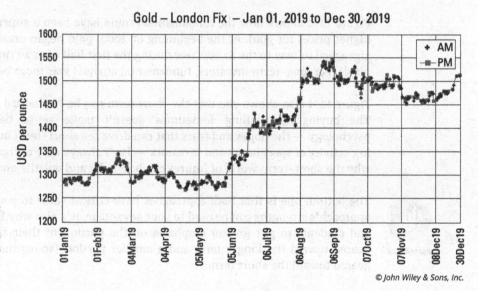

FIGURE 12-1: Chart of gold price as it ebbs and flows across 2019.

FIGURE 12-2: Chart of gold from 2000 to 2020. It's bullish and slopes upward.

As you can see, gold was a trader's dream in 2019 (Figure 12-1): some solid rallies (up moves in the price) and some steep corrections (down moves in the price). Technical analysis was useful in determining conditions such as oversold and overbought, which worked much like red flags to be careful and green lights that indicated a good entry point. During 2019, the fundamentals were very strong for gold, but that didn't stop the short-term price corrections that are really present in most bull markets (and certainly present in precious metals).

Figure 12-2 shows how the fundamentals could have been a superior catalyst to higher prices for gold. At the beginning of 2000, gold began under $300, and it zigzagged its way to the $1,700 area during the first half of 2020 (up 500 percent-plus!). For long-term investors, fundamental analysis was more beneficial.

Figure 12-1 also shows you that the short term can be haphazard and irrational. The buying and selling sometimes doesn't make sense because market psychology — the hopes and fears that can drive the short-term buying and selling activity of speculators and investors — isn't always easy to figure out. This is why the short-term world of futures can be a risky and volatile one.

REMEMBER

The bottom line is that both approaches have critical value to you because each approach's strengths can be used to your advantage. It's also why I tell my clients and students to put greater emphasis on the portion of their financial assets geared toward the longer term and a smaller portion (sometimes no portion!) geared toward the short term.

WARNING

One of the biggest factors in the short-term volatility in futures is the very fact that futures contracts are paper assets. Because they're paper, you can create a lot of it, and a lot of it can be bought and/or sold. Because relatively few contracts result in physical delivery, there's little standing in the way of creating more contracts than there are physical assets. Imagine that you have a market with 1 million cars (the underlying asset); what if 2 million car titles were being bought and sold? If too many car titles are being sold (going short), then that would temporarily and unusually drive the price down. If too many car titles are sold, then it would have the same effect upward. (The CFTC is there to prevent excessive events such as these.) Too much paper can warp the market price, causing it to go unnaturally higher or lower as the case may be. The bottom line is that futures can cause more radical swings in the price in the short term that you should be aware of.

Futures versus Options on Futures

If you've read the earlier sections of this chapter, you're aware of the good, the bad, and the ugly of futures. It's a great market but it can be a scary one as well. You've seen the statistics about how 80 percent of all speculators lose money in futures and that some of them end up in insane asylums singing Ethel Merman tunes while drinking Bosco without milk (it's tragic). Darn it — I don't want you to end up like that. So let's add some sanity to this topic.

Futures trading is great, but it's obviously not for everyone. I think that if beginners and those with limited funds want to experience the action of the futures market, let me give you a strong recommendation to make your entry into this market a little less stressful. Consider long-dated options on futures.

As I've written earlier in this chapter, futures options can have some of the same characteristics as futures. Generally, options (covered in more detail in Chapter 13) are considered a short-term market, much like the futures market. But notice that I write *long-dated* options. This is a reference to a category of options referred to as LEAPs.

LEAP stands for Long-term Equity AnticiPation securities. They're almost exactly like regular options but with one small yet major difference: LEAPs have a much longer time frame or shelf life. Typical options can be up to nine months before expiring; LEAPs can go out up to three years (and sometimes longer).

Take the example on silver in the earlier section, "The calendar spread." There I use silver futures contracts with delivery dates in 2021, but there are options on other silver futures contracts that go out to December 2022 and even into 2023. You'd have to speak with your broker about availability because sometimes the exchange may issue futures contracts and options for faraway dates, but there may not be an active market yet for those securities. Granted, futures may have more profit potential, but to me the difference in profit potential isn't that attractive because options on futures has very significant profit potential (with significantly less downside potential).

REMEMBER

The bottom line is that long-dated options on futures (LEAPs) are a good way to play the futures market and still have the benefit of more time so that you can work the market as if it were an investment (albeit an aggressive one).

Futures Resources

TIP

I hope you take note of all the specific futures-related websites I list in this chapter. Most of them have great educational materials, resources, and links that will be invaluable to you (or is that valuable?). Check out these additional futures-related websites that I think have merit for your research:

» Futures Buzz (www.FuturesBuzz.com)

» Futures.io (www.Futures.io)

» Goldprice.com (www.goldprice.com)

» INO.com (www.ino.com)

» Investing.com (www.investing.com)

Listed here are some general sites that have great information on the basics of futures, including explanations for beginners on futures terminology:

» CME Group (www.cmegroup.com)

» Futures Magazine (www.futuresmag.com)

» Inside Futures (www.insidefutures.com)

» Investopedia (www.investopedia.com)

IN THIS CHAPTER

» **Understanding how options work**

» **Placing option orders**

» **Using options for gains and income while minimizing risks**

» **Looking at profitable options combinations**

» **Exploring options on metals and finding helpful resources**

Chapter **13**

Considering Options

O ptions are a very versatile speculative vehicle. They are, in fact, excellent adjuncts to your gold and silver investing strategies. When I do my national seminars on options, it does my heart good to see bright-eyed and bushy-tailed budding investors in the room have their faces light up when I discuss the possibilities in their portfolios with options.

In general, options are extraordinarily versatile. They could be used for short-term or long-term purposes. Options can be used for gains or for generating income. You can use options for speculative purposes or for defensive or conservative purposes. Options can be used for that home-run shot where you can make a lot of money very quickly or more to protect the position in your portfolio. You can use options to make money in up markets or in down markets. Heck, you can even use options to make money on flat or boring markets. In my eyes, options are perfect for virtually any portfolio depending on the type of strategy and the suitability.

Options are perfect vehicles for the portfolio of any precious metals investor no matter how aggressive or conservative. Options can help juice up the returns on your precious metals stocks or futures contracts or to get help removing some of the risk and volatility that are part and parcel of the world of precious metals. I give you the full scoop in this chapter.

Discovering How Options Work

An option is a contract. That means that it doesn't have its own value; it derives its value from the underlying asset. Two parties are in this contract — the buyer of the contract and the seller or writer of the contract — and you can get an option on virtually any marketable securities that are assets available in the marketplace today.

As you find out in this section, the two types of options contracts are calls and puts:

>> A call gives the holder or buyer of the options contract the right but not the obligation to buy the underlying asset at a specific price during the life of the options contract.

>> A put gives the holder or buyer of the options contract the right but not the obligation to sell the underlying asset at a specific price during the life of the options contract.

WARNING

The most important risk to be aware of when you buy an option, whether it's a call or put, is that it has a finite life, and it can if you're not careful, expire worthless.

The call option

A call option is a contract that allows the buyer to buy a particular security or asset at a specific price on or before a certain date. Just like the name implies, it's an option; the person doesn't have to buy the underlying asset but can if she wants to. Buying a call option is basically a bet that the underlying asset will be going up. The call buyer is also betting that the up move will occur before the option expires. It may sound a little complicated or legalistic, but when you think about it, you've probably bought options in the past. The following sections explain how call options work in more detail.

REMEMBER

An option is a contract that's called a *derivative.* A derivative is nothing more than an investment vehicle that derives its value from something else; in the case of options, it's the underlying asset.

Real-world examples of options

A good example of a call option is, believe it or not, a lottery ticket. A lottery ticket doesn't have its own value; after all, it's a small piece of paper with printing on it that doesn't have any intrinsic value. So why would you buy a lottery ticket? A lottery ticket is like a call option on a set of numbers. A lottery ticket derives its value from that particular set of numbers. It's also like options because it has a finite shelf life; that lottery ticket will expire on the specific date whether or not those numbers come out.

If those lottery numbers don't come out, then a lottery ticket is worth nothing. The lottery ticket is worth nothing because it derives its value from numbers that are worthless. Now, how much would that lottery ticket be worth if the numbers did come out? Obviously, that lottery ticket would, at that point, be worth a lot of money, maybe even millions. That lottery ticket would then derive its value from some very valuable numbers. Of course, if the winning numbers come out after the date of a lottery ticket, then that ticket will expire worthless.

Another example of a derivative is a car title. A car title has very little of its own intrinsic value; it's just a piece of paper with some printing on it. The car title derives its value from the underlying asset, which is an automobile. Now, if that automobile is a brand-new luxury car with all the bells and whistles, then that car title is a very valuable piece of paper. Because the underlying asset (a snazzy car) is very valuable, that piece of paper is valuable. Now if that car title is attached to a 1987 Ford Torino that was in several major car crashes and had a dozen paint jobs, then that car title would derive, uh, much less value.

Possible outcomes for the call buyer and the call writer

In a call option, there's a call buyer and the call writer (the seller). The call buyer pays money (called the premium) to the call writer for the right but not the obligation to buy the underlying asset at a specific price before the call option expires.

WARNING

When you buy an option, whether it's a call or a put, it has a finite life. The remaining life may be a few weeks or a few months, or even a few years, but an option will expire sooner or later. The great danger with buying an option is that you could easily lose 100 percent of your money in the option if you're not careful. For this reason, I don't call an option an investment. Buying options isn't investing; it's really speculating. Speculating is a form of financial gambling and is much different from investing. Investing means you're putting your money into an asset (such as stock or real estate) that has changeable value, is appropriate for your situation, and can be held for the long term. This asset may fluctuate but, if chosen wisely, will keep trending upward. An option, on the other hand, is a wasting asset; as the clock keeps ticking, the option's time value will keep shrinking until it expires.

Table 13-1 summarizes the rights and obligations of call buyers and writers.

TABLE 13-1 **Call Options: Rights and Obligations**

Buyer	Seller (the Writer)
Pays premium	Receives premium
Has the right to buy a security (such as stock or a futures contract) or an asset (such as gold or oil) at a predetermined price on or before a defined date	Grants right to the buyer so has the obligation to sell the security or asset at a predetermined price at the buyer's sole option
Expectation: Rising prices	Expectation: Neutral or falling prices

The following are all the possible outcomes for a call option buyer:

» **The option can expire worthless.** This is the worst case. Because options can be relatively inexpensive (versus buying the underlying investment outright), it's not a huge loss.

» **You can exercise the option.** Exercising means that you formally request the buying (or selling) of the underlying security at the strike price (see the next section).

» **The option goes up a lot.** You can cash out the option and make a large profit.

» **The option goes up a little.** The asset is moving in your direction, and you cash out the option and still make a profit.

» **The option goes down.** You can still cash out the option and take a loss and at least recoup some of your investment.

The following are all the possible outcomes for a call option writer (seller):

» **The option can expire worthless.** You'd like this outcome because it means that you get to keep 100 percent of the option premium.

» **You may have to fulfill your obligation.** The buyer may exercise the option, forcing you to make good on your obligation to buy or sell the underlying security.

» **The option gains value.** You can let the option trigger your obligation, or you can buy back the option at a loss.

» **The option loses value.** You can let the obligation keep losing money, or you can buy it back at a profit and remove your obligation.

» **You want to get out of your obligation regardless.** You don't want the risk of the option being exercised by the buyer so you buy back the option at a loss (or gain) depending on the price of the option.

The strike price and being out of, at, or in the money

The strike price is the agreed-upon price in the call options contract. Say that you have an option on a stock called Juggernaut, Inc. Presume that the stock is at $50 per share and that the strike price in the option is $55. Say that the option will expire in nine months (for this example, assume that the expiration date is December 31, 2021), and the option buyer paid $200 for this option. The option buyer is making a bet that Juggernaut will rise toward $55 (and hopefully exceed it) before the expiration date of December 31, 2021. In this case, the stock's market price ($50 per share) is $5 away from the strike price. I like to remember it as the market price striking the target price, in this case $55.

If the stock stays at $50 or rises a little to $51 or $52 or falls lower, then the odds are that the option will expire worthless. After all, what good is an option that gives you the ability to buy the underlying asset at $55 if the market price is much lower? As you can see, the relationship of the asset's market price to the option's strike price is critical.

In the world of options, the relationship of the asset's market price to the option's strike price is referred to as being one of the following:

>> **Out of the money:** With Juggernaut at $50 and the strike price at $55, it is out of the money (or OTM). OTM options don't have much value.

>> **At the money:** If Juggernaut rose to $55, it would be called at the money (or ATM) because the market price of the asset and the strike are basically equal. ATM options are usually more valuable than OTM options.

>> **In the money:** If Juggernaut rose to, say, $60 per share, then the option would be referred to as being in the money (or ITM). The ability to buy a $60 stock for only $55 (the option's strike price) makes that a valuable option. An ITM option would have both time and equity value. Not sure what that means? Read on.

Time and equity value

So what does the buyer get with the premium that he or she pays? The call buyer gets some combination of time and equity value, such as the following, given the three different types of options:

>> **Out of the money (OTM):** The premium you pay for an OTM option is 100 percent time value. There's no equity value. You've paid for the duration of the option's life span. An OTM is the riskiest option because, basically you're hoping that the underlying asset will hit the strike price before it expires. OTM options are the cheapest options but also the riskiest. Fortunately, the full

amount at risk is only the premium you paid for the option, which is probably not that much. Because with an OTM option, you're buying time; the longer the option period, the more time you're paying for. A one-year option, for example, is more valuable than a six-month option. In a nutshell, an OTM option is 100 percent time value and 0 percent equity value.

» **At the money (ATM):** Because the market price of the asset and the option's strike price are equal or at parity, the value of the ATM option is definitely higher than the OTM (all things being equal). An ATM option has a greater chance of becoming an ITM option, of course, than the OTM option. The value of the ATM is still more time value than equity value, but at least it has some equity value. How much equity value it has depends on the marketplace.

» **In the money (ITM):** Because the market price of the asset is higher than the option's strike price, the value of the ITM option is higher than either the ATM or the OTM. The ITM option will have plenty of equity value and will still have some time value, of course, depending on how much time is left.

REMEMBER

Keep in mind that the time premium is the amount buyers are willing to pay for the options contract above its intrinsic value on the chance that, at some time prior to its expiration, it will move into the money. OTM options all carry a time premium because their intrinsic value is zero, as is that of ATM options. The time premium for the ITM options contract is the amount that exceeds the option's intrinsic value and reflects the possibility that the options contract may move deeper into the money. The time value of an options contract shrinks as the expiration date approaches, with less and less time for a major change in market opinion and a decreasing likelihood that the options contract will increase in value.

The put option

The put option is making a bet that the underlying asset is going down in price (see Table 13-2). Officially, a put option is a contract that gives the buyer (or holder) the right to sell a certain quantity (such as 100 shares of stock) of an underlying asset (such as stock or a commodity) to the writer (or seller) of the options contract at a specified price (the strike price) on any business day during the life of the option.

Put options are great tools for both investors and speculators. Puts can be used to generate gains (when the underlying asset falls), create income (by selling or writing them), or protect your positions (such as buying a put on your own asset or stock just in case it goes down).

TABLE 13-2

Put Options: Rights and Obligations

Buyer	Seller (the Writer)
Pays premium	Receives premium
Has the right to sell a security (such as a stock or an exchange-traded fund) or an asset (such as silver or corn) at a predetermined price on or before a defined expiration date	Grants right to the buyer so has the obligation to buy the security or asset at a predetermined price at the buyer's sole option during the life of the option
Expectation: Falling prices	Expectation: Neutral or rising prices

If you think that silver, for example, had a great rally and is poised for a correction or a temporary downward move in the near term (and you want to profit from this down move), then you can buy a put option on it. Speculators may buy put options on a silver futures contract, for example, or someone with a stock brokerage account can buy a put option on a silver exchange-traded fund (ETF; see Chapter 8) or buy a put on a mining stock. For beginners, I always emphasize buying options that are long-dated, meaning that the option has a long shelf life of a year or longer such as a LEAP (covered later in this chapter).

Writing a put option is a consideration for those who want to generate income. Unlike the put buyer, who buys a put option because he's expecting (or hoping for) a downward move in the underlying asset, the put writer basically takes the "opposite position" and is writing an option in hopes that the asset has already gone down and expects (or hopes) that the asset goes up. If the option loses value or expires worthless, the money that the put writer received from writing the put option isn't exercised, and he can keep it.

Conversely, a put option writer takes on the obligation of buying the underlying stock in the event that the stock does indeed go down and hits (or passes) the strike price in the option. In that event, the put writer still keeps the premium income from writing the put but, in addition, must buy the underlying asset (such as buying 100 shares of a stock). Given that, you should only write a put option on a stock that you would love to own (or are bullish on).

Lastly, a put option can be a great way for an investor to add some "insurance" or "protection" to a stock or asset that she owns (also referred to as a "protective put"). Say that you own 100 shares of an optionable mining stock and you're concerned that it may be correcting or going down temporarily in the near term. Given that, a good consideration is to buy a relatively inexpensive short-term put option on your own stock. Why? Because if the stock does indeed go down, the put option will go up and can be sold at a profit. Your profitable put in that scenario could offset either partially or fully the temporary down move in your stock. Keep in mind that you don't want to see your stock go down; in this scenario the put merely acted as a form of insurance to add some protection to your position.

Placing Orders for Options

If you want to go forward with options, you'll need to open an account first. The account will need to be funded and approved for options.

REMEMBER

For options on stocks, stock indexes, and exchange-traded funds (ETFs), a standard stock brokerage account will suffice. For options on commodities and futures, you'll need a futures brokerage account. Both accounts are covered in Chapter 16.

When you're ready to make your options order, the brokerage firm has information, customer service, and so on to help you. Just keep in mind the following order types to make sure you're transacting what you truly want:

>> **Buy to open:** When you initially buy an option (either put or call), you're essentially paying for a contract that you're opening. This is called buying to open.

>> **Sell to open:** When you're writing an option (either put or call), you'll receive income (as in selling) for opening a contract. This is called selling to open.

>> **Buy to close:** When you want to end or close out an option that you had initially sold, then you need to buy back your option to close it out. This is called buying to close. This completes the process of selling to open.

>> **Sell to close:** When you want to cash in an option that you had initially bought, then you need to close out the options contract. This is called selling to close. This completes the process of buying to open.

Options: Offering Something for Everyone

The great thing about options is not only their tremendous versatility and profit potential but also their ability to generate income and even act as insurance. This section covers important points for investors and speculators, and even worrywarts.

Keep in mind that gains occur when you buy or sell an asset or security, which is what occurs when you buy and then sell a call or put option. In the world of options, it's considered income when you write an option (call or put) and you receive the premium that the option buyer paid as income.

If, for example, you buy a call option at $100 and later sell it for $180, that is considered a gain of $80 (note that U.S. tax laws make a distinction between short-term and long-term gains, so find out about taxes in Chapter 17).

However, if you write an option (call or put), then the premium you received is considered income because that premium income isn't reliant on a realized sale. If you write a call option, say, for $100, it would be considered $100 of option income in the event that the option expired worthless. However, if you bought back that option before it expired and it was worth only $20, then you would realize income of $80 ($100 less the buyback price of $20).

For those seeking gains

If you're going to speculate, there's probably no better way than with options. With unlimited upside and limited downside, you have some powerful speculative advantages. In February 2020, I bought a call option on a silver futures contract for only $250, and five weeks later it was worth $1,250 — a gain of 400 percent. This is the power of leverage. To maximize your use of options, check out the resources at the end of this chapter and discover further trading techniques in Chapter 15 on technical analysis.

TIP

As I mention earlier, options are technically not an investment. They have a limited life, and you must do something with them before they expire. It's hard to invest with something that typically has a life span of only nine months. That's why I like to invest using Long-Term Equity AnticiPation Securities (LEAPs). They're the same in almost every way as regular, conventional options with one basic difference: the time span. LEAPs can be up to three years. You can find LEAPs on a given asset or security through the "option chain" feature in your brokerage account or at places such as the Chicago Board Options Exchange options quotes tables at www.cboe.com.

Income strategy #1: Writing covered calls

When you write a covered call option, you're doing so on a stock that you own. For every 100 shares of an optionable stock that you own, you can write (sell) a covered call, and you'll receive income (the premium) in exchange for an obligation to sell your stock at the strike price. Covered call writing is a safe strategy because you own the underlying stock, and you simply relinquish the stock if it hits the strike price during the life of the option. In other words, the call obligation is covered.

Say that you own 200 shares of Hokey Smoke Corp. (HSC). On July 17, 2020, the stock price was at $40.71. On that day, you could have written a September 2020 call with a strike price of $42.50 and received income of $60 (leaving out the brokerage commission to keep it simple). Because a call contract is tied to a round lot of 100 shares, you could write two calls (because you own 200 shares of HSC) and receive income of $120. In return, you take on the obligation to sell your HSC stock for $42.50 on any business day starting July 17 up to the third Friday in September 2020 (September 18).

It's a risk-free transaction for you in that there's no risk of financial loss. If HSC rises significantly between now and September 2020, the worst that happens is that you sell your stock for $42.50, which is a higher stock price than the $40.71 price back on July 17. In addition, you made the $120 income from the premium.

If HSC stays flat or goes down during that time frame, you get to keep the stock and the $120 from writing the two calls. Owning the HSC stock has the usual risk of stock ownership; it can go up, down, or stay at the same level. Writing the covered call itself was a risk-free way to generate income from your stock holding.

WARNING

It's possible to write an uncovered (or naked) call. This transaction is the same as the covered call except in one crucial way — you don't own the stock. You could still generate the $120 (in this example), but if HSC rises and hits $42.50, you have the obligation to provide the 200 shares. Because you didn't own the stock, you'd have to buy it at the market price (whatever price it is) and then sell the stock for the $42.50. If HSC rose to $50 a share, you'd end up losing $7.50 per share (on a 200-share transaction, you'd lose $1,500). In a naked call, you gamble to make the option income, but you risk having a loss that's potentially far higher. Most retail investors aren't allowed to do naked call writing because of the potential loss involved.

Income strategy #2: Writing puts

If you write a put, you'll receive the premium income, but in exchange you take on the obligation of buying stock if it hits the strike price. To be allowed to write a put in a stock brokerage account, you'd need to have enough cash (or marginable securities) in your account to handle the potential purchase. This is referred to as a cash-secured put. If you're using marginable securities, that's referred to as a portfolio-secured put. So-called naked puts — writing puts without sufficient cash or marginable securities in the account — aren't allowed for most retail investors.

When you write a put option, you're doing so typically on a stock that you don't own but wouldn't mind owning in the event that the option is exercised, meaning you'll be compelled to buy that stock (or other asset) at the strike price. When you write the put option, you'll receive income (the premium) in exchange for an obligation to buy the underlying stock at the strike price. Because writing the put option obligates you to buy that stock or asset, you must have funds in your account to cover the potential purchase.

Say that you wrote a put option on Hokey Smoke Corp. (HSC). On July 17, 2020, the stock price was at $40.71. On that day, you could have written a put option that expires in September 2020 with a strike price of $37.50 and received income of $50 (again, leaving out the brokerage commission to keep it simple). If HSC stays above $37.50 for the life of the option and you held the option until it expired in September 2020, then you would keep the $50.

However, if HSC falls to $37.50 (or below), then you would need to buy 100 shares of HSC at $37.50 per share or a total of $3,750 regardless of what price it dropped to. Therefore, make sure you have that sum of money in the account (the cash "covers the obligation" of the put option) and make sure you would like that stock at that price!

Suppose that HSC stays above $37.50 and even rises during the life of that option. The option would lose value. Say that it did so and in August 2020 (before the expiration), you saw that the put option lost value and was now worth only $10. Here's an opportunity to close out the option and remove the obligation to buy HSC if you decided. Buying back that put option at that moment means that you would end up with $40 income (the original premium income of $50 less the cost of buying it back at $10). Not bad! Doing so would lock in your $40 profit and remove the risk of HSC's stock price going against you (falling toward $37.50) during the remaining life of the put option.

TIP

You should write puts only on stocks that you'd personally enjoy owning. Writing a put option on a mining stock when it's at $35 and the put option's strike price is at $30 means that (in the worst case) you end up buying that stock at the bargain $30 price. The great thing is that the premium helped make the purchase more affordable. If you got $100 for writing the put and you need to buy the stock, you really had to shell out only $2,900 for those 100 shares ($3,000 total purchase price less $100 premium).

Minimizing Risks with Options

In other chapters (such as Chapter 16), I briefly discuss the defensive merits of stop-loss orders and the active strategy of trailing stops. (I discuss these orders in greater detail in the latest edition of my book *Stock Investing For Dummies*, published by Wiley.) But a great way to protect your stock position without having to sell the stock is to buy a put on your own stock. In this instance, the put that you bought would be referred to as a protective put. It becomes a form of insurance.

Say that you own 100 shares of Goldmines-R-Us Corp. (GMRUS). On July 17, 2020, GMRUS stock was at $25.85 per share. Let's say that you're nervous about market conditions for GMRUS during the summer, but you don't want to sell the stock because you bought it a few years earlier for only $8 a share, and you don't want to generate a capital gain and worry about the tax on the potentially large gain (the market price less the $8 original cost). Instead of selling, you could buy a put for that time period to give you some protection.

You could buy an OTM put with a strike price of $22.50 that expires in October 2020 for only $60 or an ATM $25 put (expiring that same month) for $140, depending on your expectation or budget. The bottom line is that you could buy insurance in the form of a protective put for very little money.

In the event that your concerns are realized, and the stock does go down in the near term, the put option would go up in value. The put option then becomes profitable. This gain then offsets either partially or fully the temporary downward move of the stock. The more the stock goes down, the more valuable the put option becomes. You then have the ability to cash out ("sell to close") the put option and realize your gain.

Trying Some Profitable Combinations

Options are very versatile, and after you figure out the ins and outs of a call option and a put option, then consider moving to the next level, combinations. There are literally dozens of options combinations. You can structure combinations to give you some exceptional profit potential. The following sections give you some ideas.

The zero-cost collar

The zero-cost collar is one of my favorite combinations, and it's an ideal strategy for those who are worried about some positions in their portfolios. It's done on a stock that you own and hold in your stock brokerage account. Simply stated, it's the act of buying a put option and selling (writing) a call option on your stock.

Let's say that you own 100 shares of Kabluki Corp. (KC) stock, and it's $30 a share. Say that the market is getting you concerned about your KC stock. Table 13-3 shows you the zero-cost collar for it.

Take a look at some of the advantages in Table 13-3. First of all, the zero-cost collar is protection that can be structured to cost nothing (I like that part). If KC stays flat or trades sideways, the options could expire. But you don't mind because the collar was zero cost.

TABLE 13-3 **The Zero-Cost Collar in Action**

Buy/Sell Action and Option Details	Type	Profit Direction	Cost
Buy 1 KC Put Strike price $27.50 Expires 10/19/20	Out of the money (OTM)	This is a protective put (you worry about your stock going down)	$100 (you are paying premium)
Sell 1 KC Call Strike price $32.50 Expires 10/19/20	Out of the money (OTM)	Bearish (you expect KC stock to go up)	$100 (you are receiving premium)
			Total cost = $0

What happens if your concern about your stock is realized? Although your KC stock would fall, the zero-cost collar helps offset the loss with a double profit. When KC falls, the put would increase in value, and the call would lose value. The put would be profitable. Now about that call, keep in mind that you didn't buy it; you sold it. Therefore, you don't mind it losing value. Now you can buy it back at a profit.

WARNING

The drawback of the zero-cost collar is if the stock goes up significantly during the options period. Because part of the combination was a covered call, that limited your upside because you would have to end up selling the stock at the strike price of $32.50.

The straddle

The straddle is a simple combination. It's buying both an at-the-money call and an at-the-money put (both have the same expiration date) on the same security or asset. Table 13-4 uses the example of XYZ Mining Corp. stock (price: $50/share) to illustrate the straddle.

REMEMBER

The basic point behind the straddle is very simple. You don't care where the stock goes (up or down); you just want the stock's price to go somewhere and to get there very fast. Certainly, you want it to happen long before the call and put options expire. Options strategies can be bullish, bearish, or, in this case, neutral. The buyer of the straddle combination is neutral and is actually seeking high volatility, a big move in either direction.

TABLE 13-4

The Straddle in Action

Buy/Sell Action and Option Details	Type	Profit Direction	Cost
Buy 1 XYZ Call Strike price $50 Expires 12/21/21	At the money (ATM)	Bullish (you expect XYZ stock to go up)	$300
Buy 1 XYZ Put Strike price $50 Expires 12/21/21	At the money (ATM)	Bearish (you expect XYZ stock to go up)	$300
			Total cost = $600

The bottom line is that you're hoping (in this example) that XYZ goes far enough (up or down) that one of the options in the straddle will be worth more than the two options combined. If, for example, XYZ skyrockets to $70, then the call will be very valuable while the put would be almost worthless. In the case of a $70 stock price, the call option would be worth at least $2,000 while the put option's value would be close to zero. In valuing the straddle, you can say that it went from a total value of $600 to an ending value of $2,000 (the $2,000 call plus the $0 put).

TECHNICAL STUFF

Keep in mind that technically the option combination that I just described is the long straddle. It's labeled long because you bought both options. Yes, there's a short straddle, but that goes beyond the scope of this chapter. Any and all the options terms, combinations, and so on are described more fully through the resources referenced later in this chapter.

Checking Out Options in the World of Precious Metals

The first half of this chapter goes into the generic world of options. That is necessary so that this section has more meaning for you. There are many ways to play precious metals, and few vehicles give you as much oomph as options, and when you combine precious metals with options, you get . . . ultra-oomph!

Options on mining stocks

When it comes to options in the world of gold and silver, the most obvious place to start is with mining stocks, of course. Many mining stocks have options available on them. Some of the stocks have a limited number of options issued and available for investors (many may have only 30 to 40 options going out nine months at most). Some of the larger and more active companies have 75 to 150 (or more) options available and stretching out two years or more (LEAPs).

Here are some examples of mining stocks and gold/silver ETFs with plenty of long-term options on them:

>> As of July 2020, the gold-mining company Newmont Goldcorp. (NEM) had options available all the way out to January 2022 (a full one and a half years of time value). By the time you read these words, options on that stock will be going out to mid-2022 or beyond.

>> As of July 2020, Wheaton Precious Metals (WPM) also has options stretching out to January 2022.

>> As of July 2020, VanEck Vectors Gold Miners ETF (GDX), an ETF that tracks a basket of mining stocks, had options available with expiration dates of January 2022.

>> As of July 2020, the Direxion Daily Junior Gold Miners Index (JNUG), an index that has a basket of junior mining stocks, has expiration dates available to January 2022.

TIP

These are mentioned as illustrative examples of what you can find. To find more, use the resources in Chapter 7 (on mining stocks) to locate and analyze the mining stocks. The same resources can tell you whether they have publicly traded options available. If the answer is yes, then you can go to the Chicago Board Options Exchange (www.cboe.com) and do your search. At the website, you can simply enter the stock symbol of your choice, and up will come the options available for you to buy (or write).

An option with no expiration?

As I explain earlier in this chapter, options are a derivative. But some stocks, especially those in the natural resource sector, can be considered derivatives of the resources they're involved with.

Here's an example. In 2019, I bought a stock that had substantial nickel reserves at about the time that industry reports mentioned supply problems with — you guessed it — nickel. That stock quickly shot up from less than $2 a share to more than $5 in a few weeks for a solid gain of more than 150 percent. That was a small company, and it had no publicly traded options. However, the stock acted like an option on the underlying asset. In that case, $200 would have gotten you 100 shares, and the best part is that, unlike options, there's no expiration date. For more information on small mining stocks, head over to Chapter 7.

Options on ETFs and indexes

Exchange-traded funds (ETFs) are explained in detail in Chapter 8, but I bring them up here because they're great underlying assets for options investors and speculators. Why make a bet on an individual security when you can bet on an entire industry or sector? You have the same options capabilities on ETFs as with stocks. You can buy or sell options (calls or puts).

The following are ETFs with options available (go to www.cboe.com for details):

» PowerShares DB Precious Metals Fund (DBP)

» PowerShares DB Silver Fund (DBS)

» PowerShares DB Gold Fund (DGL)

To find more ETFs for gold, silver, and other precious metals, do a search at the ETF Database (www.etfdb.com).

Some indexes also have options available on them. A good example of one is found at the Chicago Board Options Exchange: the CBOE Gold Index (GOX). It's an equal-dollar weighted index composed of ten companies involved primarily in gold mining and production. You can find out more about additional indexes that are optionable at the CBOE's site at www.cboe.com/index/.

Options on futures

For those who want the speculative, high-flying, ultra-aggressive, no-guts-no-glory, home-run, or strikeout type of vehicle, then you may want to consider options on futures. Check out Table 13-5 for a list of options on regular futures.

TABLE 13-5   **Options on Regular Futures**

Type of Asset	Size of Standard Futures Contract	Trading Symbol	Comments
Gold	100 troy ounces of gold	GC	Precious metal
Silver	5,000 troy ounces of silver	SI	Precious metal

Table 13-6 gives you a list of options on mini-futures.

REMEMBER

To do options on futures contracts, you'll need to open a futures account with a commodities brokerage firm, so head over to Chapter 16. You find details on futures and mini-futures in Chapter 12.

TABLE 13-6   Options on Mini-Futures

Type of Asset	Size of Standard Contract	Symbol	Comments
Gold	50 troy ounces of gold (NYMEX miNY Futures)	QO	Traded on NYMEX
Gold	50 troy ounces of gold (Chicago Board of Trade mini-sized futures)	YG	Traded on CBOT
Silver	2,500 troy ounces of silver (NYMEX miNY Futures)	QI	Traded on NYMEX
Silver	1,000 troy ounces of silver (Chicago Board of Trade mini-sized futures)	YI	Traded on CBOT

Following Golden Rules for Options Success

After watching this stuff for a few decades, teaching thousands of students, and actively doing this day in and day out, you get to see what works with options and what doesn't. You can take certain points to heart and apply to your own approach. After reading everything in this chapter (along with the referenced resources), here are my golden rules for options success:

WARNING

>> **Understand the risk in your strategy.** One speculator (I'll call her Betty) got a hot tip about Google and immediately bought 350 call options. Google didn't go the way she expected, and she lost more than $20,000. Yikes! The options she bought had only two months of time! That wasn't speculating — that was outright gambling. She may as well have taken the money to the local casino. Betty didn't realize the risk of too little time. Also, why risk so much and so quickly?

Sometimes the risk is not only in the vehicle (very short-term options) but also in the person. Impatience and acting without full information can be the kiss of death for your wealth-building aspirations.

REMEMBER

>> **Decide the most amount you'll put at risk.** In the previous example, Betty sadly told me afterward that the total amount she lost was a huge portion of her financial assets. It caused her hardship. As I've said before, buying options is a speculative pursuit, and you should know from the start how much you're willing to risk and no more. You should ask yourself "Will my lifestyle change drastically if I lose this money?" If that question makes you pause, then you may be risking too great a portion of your financial assets. For most people, 5 to 10 percent of your financial assets is a comfortable limit. As you grow in experience, confidence, and skill, you can certainly do more.

>> **Options buyers should get the longest time available and a strike price that's as close as possible.** What do you think has less risk — a two-month option or a two-year option? The more time, the better for you. What has a greater chance to be profitable — an ATM option or an OTM? The closer the strike price is to the market price, the better your chance of success. However, there's a better strategy — both! Your chance for success grows tremendously in your favor when the option you have has lots of time value and a strike price that's as close as possible to the market price.

>> **Options sellers should write options that are OTM and expire soon.** For those who are seeking income and want to minimize the risk of covered call writing (the chance that your asset could rise to hit the strike price and subsequently trigger the sale of your asset), then you need to do the mirror opposite of the call buyers' golden rule (see the previous paragraph). In covered call writing, you need to write options that are comfortably OTM and will expire in a relatively short period of time.

REMEMBER

>> **Don't wait too long to cut your losses.** Depending on the type of asset and the length of the option period, the options buyer shouldn't wait until the final 30 to 60 days of the option's remaining time value. Again, options are wasting assets, and they have the tendency to lose value dramatically in the final weeks. If you cash out the option while it still has some time value, then you can recoup some money and put the funds to work elsewhere.

>> **Take profits sooner if you've written options.** Say that you wrote a covered call, and you got a nice premium. If that stock had made a sudden yet temporary drop in price, consider taking some profits by buying back your covered call. Why wait? Make a profit, and now your stock is free and clear and available for the next covered call option.

TIP

>> **Focus on one area and become an expert in that area.** Ironically, the best advice I could give for options success actually isn't even an outright options-related recommendation. Note that options are derivatives. Options derive their value from the underlying asset, so it behooves you to become as knowledgeable and as proficient as possible in that underlying asset. Nine times out of ten, when you see someone who consistently succeeds with options, it's usually due to the fact that the investor or speculator focuses on that singular area and gets really good at understanding that particular market.

>> **Be patient.** Maybe it's a sign of the times and how people's behavior and attitudes have changed. Investors today are way too impatient and they're not allowing their strategies and investment choices enough time to bear fruit. Frankly, it has me scratching my head. It makes me compare today's investors with investors from the good ol' days. When I first started my financial

planning business (1981 — I hope I don't look that old), investors had a more realistic attitude toward time and money. Back then, long term was more than five years, intermediate term was one to five years, and short term was one year or less. Today, I think that investors measure long term in months, intermediate term in weeks, and short term in days. I asked one client what his idea of short term was, and he responded, "What time is it?"

Long-term investors and speculators have an easier time making money. When I say "long term," that doesn't necessarily mean you have to wait 57 years for something good to happen. It doesn't even have to mean a rigid time frame. It means giving the market *enough time to discover what you have.* One client I had bought a uranium stock in 2005. It went up nicely that year, but then during 2006, it stayed in a narrow trading range of $35 to $39 for many months. His impatience resulted in the sale of that stock, but guess what? Within a few months, that stock shot up to $56 a share for a gain of 43 percent in fewer than five months. The call options on that stock did even better. Over the years, I've seen many situations where impatience led some to prematurely sell (or buy) something, needlessly resulting in losses or missed opportunities.

Consulting Options Resources

TIP

The best places for information on options for beginners are the options exchanges and their trade association. I have visited their websites, and they have a tremendous amount of free educational materials, tutorials, publications, and so on. And for good reason: The exchanges make money each time an option is transacted. The more people doing more options transactions makes for a happy exchange. Given this, you may as well take advantage of the great stuff they offer:

>> **Chicago Board Options Exchange** (www.cboe.com/education): The place to turn to for extensive information regarding options on stocks, stock indexes, and exchange-traded funds (ETFs).

>> **Chicago Mercantile Exchange** (www.cmegroup.com): Offers extensive information on futures and options on futures.

>> **Options Industry Council's education site** (www.optionseducation.org): Lots of publications as well as free audio and online video programs well suited for beginners.

Other educational resources include the following:

» Many of the general financial websites such as www.investopedia.com and www.marketwatch.com have great how-to articles and tutorials.

» "Ultra-Investing with Options" (www.ravingcapitalist.com/options) is the online options course for beginners taught by yours truly.

» TraderPlanet (www.traderplanet.com) is an active site with blogs and news for traders.

» Modern Trader (www.futuresmag.com) is Futures Magazine's site with news and views for traders.

» Options and options combinations are covered in my book *High-Level Investing For Dummies*, published by Wiley.

» Commodities Futures Trading Commission (www.cftc.gov) is the government agency overseeing the futures marketplace. It has good resources and education for investors.

» The Ally Invest Options Playbook (www.optionsplaybook.com/) has great educational resources on options especially for beginners.

4

Digging into Gold and Silver Investing Strategies

Distinguish long-term and short-term investing, trading, and speculative approaches for the beginner. You'll also find out about the gold-to-silver ratio.

Use technical analysis and discover its value to short-term metals traders and speculators.

Get the lowdown on using brokers for your investment transactions.

Understand taxes and your portfolio as well as gold and silver retirement accounts for long-term investors.

Chapter **14**

Trying Out Trading Approaches

N o one can say that trading is boring. It's exciting — you just want any discussion on trading to remove the words *losing, terrifying,* and *depressing.* Of course, trading can be profitable. Some have successfully turned trading into a full-time pursuit, which takes a lot of preparation and the right frame of mind because it can be stressful at times. For a trader, *risk* and *volatility* aren't just words; they're a way of life.

Before you delve fully into the trading lifestyle, prepare yourself by first going through this chapter. I explain the various ways to prepare before you even begin trading and provide you with trading techniques to choose from. Preparing yourself and choosing the technique that best fits you should make the exciting life of trading more profitable and, well, exciting.

REMEMBER

Investing is long term (such as years) and primarily relies on the "fundamentals," which I cover in Chapters 3 and 7. Trading and speculating are generally short term and have greater emphasis on "technicals," which are covered more fully in Chapter 15.

Like a Scout: Being Prepared

You get the greatest benefit from trading before you risk a single copper cent (well, it used to be copper, but now it's an even baser metal) by simply preparing. Preparing for your trading pursuits puts you one step closer to successful trading. The sections that follow give you an idea of how to begin thorough preparations.

REMEMBER

Know the difference between trading and investing. *Trading* is a short-term play on the price moves of an asset. Whatever you're putting your money in, you'll be exiting this position relatively quickly. You just want someone to buy your stuff at a greater price and sooner rather than later. *Investing* means you're putting your money into an asset that has value today and that will essentially have long-term appreciation. This difference dictates your approach, and it dictates which philosophy will dominate your actions: fundamental analysis or technical analysis (covered in Chapter 15). For traders, price action is the name of the game.

Be a voracious reader

Paraphrasing the Bible, there is nothing new under the sun, and this is true in the world of trading. The technology may have changed radically, but the principles have remained the same. The successes and failures and strategies are there to learn from. The same way that investors should read the works of Benjamin Graham and Warren Buffett, traders should be reading about the exploits, strategies, and principles of great traders such as Jesse Livermore.

TIP

Two books worth checking out are *Reminiscences of a Stock Operator* by Edwin Lefèvre (Wiley) and *How to Trade in Stocks,* which is in Jesse Livermore's own words but republished by McGraw-Hill with updates and commentary by Richard Smitten. Livermore was a very colorful character, and he became the ultimate rags-to-riches trader as he made and lost four fortunes during the 1920s and '30s before he died by suicide in 1940. The amazing thing is that he started trading as a teenager with just five dollars (of course, five dollars was worth something back then), and he went on to make millions.

In today's market, some of the well-known traders include long-time veterans such as Larry Williams, Dick Diamond, and Roger Wiegand. There are more trading resources at the end of this chapter.

Have your plan

Making a trade with guesswork or your best hunch isn't enough, certainly not if you want to build wealth over time. You need to decide on a framework for your trading activity. Your plan needs to have clear and detailed answers to questions such as

>> How much risk capital will you be playing the trading game with?

>> What is your outlook on the asset in question (bullish, bearish, or neutral)?

>> Will you be focused in a single specialty or diversified in different assets (such as stocks, options, futures) or in different industries or commodities?

>> At what point will you enter a trade? What signals will you use (such as technical indicators explained in Chapter 15) as your entry points?

>> How long will you stay in your position? Will it be a fixed time period or until a particular event occurs (such as when it hits a certain price)?

>> Will you be doing any hedging (a way to reduce risk by having positions in your account that go up if your main positions go down)? If so, what kind of hedge?

>> What will you do if the position goes down in price during your time period? Buy more or get out?

>> If you buy more at the lower price, what will you do if the asset's price goes down even further? What price level or loss percentage will you tolerate before you decide to cut losses?

>> At what point do you cash out profitable trades? Is there a specific amount, or is it based on market events (such as technical indicators or news from the industry)? Will your advisory service or software tell you?

>> At what point will you say, "I can't take it anymore! I'm getting a job!"

REMEMBER

There are questions that no amount of research or professional guidance can answer for you. Much of what you do will be your own preferences and trading objectives. The point is to address these issues because the market will make mincemeat of traders who are throwing darts.

Decide your market

Until you're proficient and experienced with markets in general, your best bet is to get thoroughly familiar with a particular asset. Trading gold and silver futures is fine, but beginners shouldn't trade gold and silver along with grains, pork bellies, and natural gas. Commodities can be specialized, and the more you stretch yourself over more different markets, the less time you'll be able to become an expert in the markets that count.

Many of my clients and students get extremely knowledgeable about a particular market and then apply their trading strategies to take advantage of what they researched and studied. I know one trader who researched the oil market and turned $90,000 into $1.4 million in about 18 months during 2004–2005. He used bullish trading strategies such as buying call options that skyrocketed as oil prices nearly doubled during that time period. He did focused research (specialized in one market) and focused activity (buying call options), which paid off handsomely.

REMEMBER

Specializing in one market will make it much easier to succeed. After the learning curve to find out what's going on, you can monitor the market and implement your trades in minutes. Fortunately, precious metals investments have a lot to offer. You can specialize in different metals (precious or base) and in different vehicles (stocks, futures, and/or options). What will you concentrate on?

Practice with simulated trading

TIP

The various tools available to help you become more proficient are fantastic. In terms of technology, resources, and brokerage services available, it's a better time to be a trader than ever before. You can practically automate the process. The first thing to do before you commit funds to your trading activity is some simulated trading to get a comfort level before you actually trade. Here are some websites that can help you:

>> CME Institute Trading Simulate (www.cmegroup.com/trading_tools/simulator.html)

>> Trading Setups Review (www.tradingsetupsreview.com)

>> How the Market Works (www.howthemarketworks.com)

Picking Out Your Vehicle

I'm not putting the cart before the horse or — er — the car before the profits. Yes, you'll get a chance to pick out a shiny new toy if you make wise choices in trading, but this section deals with the *trading* vehicles you put your money in. Whether you're bullish, bearish, or neutral on precious metals, there are great choices for trading vehicles:

>> **Gold and silver stocks:** Done in a stock brokerage account (see Chapter 16), stock trading can be affordable, and plenty of precious metals mining stocks are tradable. You can probably start with a few thousand dollars and should concentrate on only a few stocks so you can watch them like a hawk. Choose them based on fundamentals and use technical analysis (see Chapter 15) for your entry and exit points.

Fortunately, most good brokers have a fully featured website and relatively low commissions. Services such as automated trailing stops and stock alerts that you can program make it easier for your trading activity. This venue can be as aggressive or as conservative as you prefer. Chapter 7 has more details on stocks for you.

>> **Gold and silver ETFs:** There are excellent trading and speculating opportunities in gold and silver exchange-traded funds (ETFs). The investable types are covered in Chapter 8, and the tradable and/or speculative ETFs are covered in Chapter 11.

>> **Futures:** Trading in futures contracts is, of course, the riskiest choice among the tradable vehicles. For a taste of volatility and a chance to make a great profit in a relatively short time frame (in days or weeks), trading futures is the one for you. You can either be aggressive or . . . very aggressive!

TIP

For beginners, a good approach is to do option spreads to limit your risk as you gain more knowledge and experience. The lowest appropriate amount to do futures is risk capital in the range of $10,000 to $20,000. For more information on futures, go to Chapter 12.

>> **Options:** This is my favorite area for traders. (Considering all the options seminars and workshops I do, it better be!) It has both the potential for large returns and the opportunity to take advantage of volatility. Combine this with limited risk, relatively low cost, and versatility (you can do options on stocks, ETFs, or futures contracts). Flip to Chapter 13 for more information on options.

Selecting Your Trading Strategy

The following sections indicate some trading strategies as they're matched up with your outlook. This is probably a better way to choose your strategy than to load you up with a batch of paragraphs (you're welcome!). I limit my examples with two tables: one on stocks with options (Table 14-1) and the second on futures contracts with options (Table 14-2). These tables provide a good cross section for beginners.

Choosing your market outlook

Yogi Berra said, "When you come to a fork in the road, take it." Of course, in today's market, that fork (preferably a silver spoon) gives you two options: buy or sell. Everyone has an idea about "where the market is going and what to expect for that asset's next price move." There are as many trading ideas and strategies as there are traders. What is your outlook? Your strategies (for either short-term trading or long-term investing) flow from your outlook: bullish, bearish, or neutral.

You should also decide the degree to which you have your outlook. For example, say that you're bullish. That's your outlook, but how bullish are you? Are you very bullish or moderately bullish? This affects your trading approach. If you think a stock will do well, then certainly you can buy the stock. If you were very bullish on the stock, then you can buy multiple call options on the stock with the same money. If you were moderately bullish, then you can buy the stock and put on a trailing stop to limit the downside while keeping the upside unlimited (of course, if the stock goes down, that can trigger the trailing stop and get you out). You get the picture.

TIP

Here are some excellent resources for traders on market outlooks and much more:

>> TraderPlanet (www.traderplanet.com)

>> TFC Commodity Charts (www.futures.tradingcharts.com)

>> DecisionPoint (www.decisionpoint.com)

>> *Stock & Commodities,* The Traders' Magazine (www.traders.com)

Stock trading coupled with options

Say that you're looking to trade stocks (and options on stocks). Your strategies will focus on a particular stock, the Mining Trading Corp. (MTC), which is $20 per share, and you have a stock brokerage account funded with $2,000. Presume that the calls and puts that you'd buy (or write) are all long-term options that will expire in a year, and they cost $200 per option contract. To make the math simple, presume no commissions. What could you do? Table 14-1 gives you some possibilities.

TABLE 14-1   **Possible Choices for Stock Trading with Options**

Your Outlook	Action*	Comments
Most bullish strategy	Buy 10 call options on the stock (total cost is $2,000)	If you're right, those call options would be very valuable because ten contracts is a leveraged play on 1,000 shares of MTC. Worst case, if you're wrong, you'd lose $2,000.
Very bullish strategy #1	Buy 100 shares of MTC (total cost $2,000)	If you're right and they go up, sell and take a profit. If they go down, you lost money. Simple!
Very bullish strategy #2	Buy a call for $200 and sell a put for $200 (total outlay is $0); the $2,000 sits as collateral (the synthetic long strategy)	If you're right and MTC goes up, you'd make a profit on both the call and the put. If you're wrong, then the money in your account would be used to buy MTC because writing a put obligates you to buy MTC stock.
Neutral strategy with high volatility	Buy an at-the-money call and put on MTC (the straddle); total outlay is only $400	You're hoping that MTC goes either way and very far and very fast. One option would lose money, but the other would be very profitable.
Very bearish strategy	Buy ten put options on the stock (total cost is $2,000)	If you're right, those puts would be very valuable because ten contracts is a leveraged bet on 1,000 shares of MTC going down. Worst case: lose $2,000.
Most bearish	Buy ten put options (total cost $2,000)	If you're correct, jackpot! If you're not, goodbye $2,000.

*Remember to use trailing stops and your broker's stock alert service where appropriate.

TIP

Table 14-1 has just examples and isn't even an extensive listing. All the preceding choices have variations, limited only by your education and creativity. These possibilities should whet your appetite and encourage you to look into a fascinating and potentially profitable area. Do your homework by starting with more information in Chapters 7 (stocks) and 13 (options) and resources in Appendix A.

Futures trading coupled with options

What kind of strategies could you implement in the futures market? Table 14-2 gives you a rundown of some strategies used by traders that are fairly simple and can be easily done in a futures brokerage account.

TIP

Alas, Table 14-2 barely scrapes the surface. There are many strategies, and there are many combinations of futures, call, and put options. Here, I give you some basic strategies that are very common and very popular. Get familiar with them for starters, and use the information and resources in Chapters 12 (futures) and 13 (options) for further details.

TABLE 14-2 **Possible Choices for Futures Trading with Options**

Your Outlook	Action*	Comments
Most bullish strategy	Buy (go long) a futures contract	Absolutely bullish. Besides the risk of losing money, you can also get a margin call from the broker.
Very bullish strategy	Buy (go long) a call option on that contract	Very bullish but not as bullish as the previous outlook. Because the call was fully paid in cash, no margin call risk.
Moderately bullish strategy	Buy (go long) a futures contract and buy an out-of-the-money put on the same contract	You're bullish; the futures contract and the put is a hedge. If the futures contract goes down, the put would act like insurance and go up in value.
Neutral strategy	Buy a call option and a put option on the same futures contract (called the straddle)	The straddle is a neutral strategy. You're making a bullish bet (the call) and a bearish bet (the put). You're hoping that it goes in either direction very strongly to make a net profit on the winning option.
Moderately bearish strategy	Sell (go short) a futures contract and buy an out-of-the-money call on the same contract	You're bearish. The futures contract and the call are hedges. If the futures contract goes up, the call would act like insurance and go up in value.
Very bearish	Buy (go long) a put option on that contract	Very bearish but not as bearish as the "Most bearish" option. Because the put was fully paid in cash, no margin call risk.
Most bearish	Sell (go short) a futures contract	Absolutely bearish. Besides the risk of losing money, you can also get a margin call from the broker.

Remember to use trailing stops and your broker's stock alert service where appropriate.

Trading the Gold-to-Silver Ratio (GSR)

In the precious metals world, one of the most watched indicators is the gold-to-silver ratio (GSR). It calculates how many ounces of silver is equal in price to a single ounce of gold. If the price of gold per ounce was, say, $500 and the price of silver per ounce was $20, then the GSR would be 25 ($500 divided by $20). If gold was $1,000 and silver was at $25, then the GSR would be 40.

Those who watch the GSR are looking to see whether one is more or less undervalued with the intent of finding a profitable buying opportunity in the undervalued one or possibly a selling opportunity in the one that's potentially overvalued. The following sections explain how the GSR is a worthy indicator in your gold and silver investing/trading/speculating strategies.

REMEMBER

Using the trading approaches covered here is not "set in stone," and there are no rigid rules for proceeding. You can be creative and modify any approach based on your personal and unique outlook and investment style.

Getting a little background on the GSR

For nearly two centuries (give or take a decade) from the late 1700s to the mid-1900s, the GSR was typically below 30. It was at about 15 for most of that time. It didn't rise dramatically until after 2000. In the year 2020, it peaked at an all-time high of 120 on March 18, 2020. An ounce of gold was the financial equivalent of 120 ounces of silver.

Say that on March 18, 2020, you heard that the GSR hit an all-time high of 120; what could you have done, and what result would have unfolded? With such a high GSR coupled with a bullish outlook for both metals (given supply and demand fundamentals at that time), the move was to sell your ounce of gold and buy the equivalent amount of silver.

On March 18, 2020, the price of gold per ounce was $1,498.20 (it was down that week), but the price of silver plummeted to a five-year low of $12.42. Given that, if you sold your gold, you'd have enough money to buy 120 ounces of silver; $1,498.20 divided by $12.42 equals about 120 ounces of silver (120.628 for the nudniks in the audience).

Then what? Fast-forward to, say, July 12, 2020, as I am writing this. Gold is at $1,801.50 per ounce, and silver is at $19.07, so the GSR is 94. Had you bought (or held) that gold originally at $1,498.20 (the March 18, 2020, price) and simply held it until July 11, 2020, it would have risen to $1,801.50 — a price increase of $303.30 or 20 percent in less than three months! Not too shabby! On an annualized basis, that cool gain comes in at about 80 percent.

However, had you traded the GSR and converted that ounce of gold (again, at $1,498.20) to silver on that day (again, at $12.42 per ounce), you'd have seen your 120 ounces of silver go from a total value of $1,498.20 to a total value of $2,288.40 (120 ounces of silver at $19.07 per ounce). Going from $1,498.20 to $2,288.40 is a gain of $790.20, or a whopping gain of 52.7 percent (annualized it would be almost 211 percent — woo-hoo!).

As of July 11, 2020, the GSR has gone to about 94, which represents a sharp dip from the all-time high of 120 (a decline of almost 22 percent). What if you were to trade this GSR and sell off your silver ounces to rebuy gold? What would happen?

Selling your 120 ounces of silver would get you $2,288.40, and if gold were at $1,801.50, you could then acquire 1.27 ounces of gold. As the GSR keeps rising and falling, you'd be able to compound your gains going forward, although it could be tedious going back and forth with gold and silver if you played the GSR trade in a strict physical gold/physical silver ongoing swap.

For the sake of convenience given standard stock brokerage accounts, there are more practical ways of profiting from the GSR. Keep reading.

Investing with the GSR

When the GSR hit an all-time high of 120 in March 2020, gold and silver were obviously in a bull market. This means that if gold was doing well relative to silver, the high GSR was suggesting that silver was undervalued at that time and offered a buying opportunity for investors. How could they have played this GSR moment?

The most obvious play was to buy either stocks (covered in Chapter 7) or ETFs (see Chapter 8). The high GSR suggests a good entry point in silver-related investment vehicles. The data shows that silver stocks and silver ETFs performed well in that same time frame and outperformed most stocks and ETFs as well.

REMEMBER

When the GSR is high (say, north of 50 or near 100), silver is considered more undervalued compared to gold, and investors should consider buying more silver rather than gold for optimal value. For those who trade or "rotate" between the metals, then consider selling gold and buying the equivalent value amount in silver. If the GSR is much lower, then gold is considered to be a better value. Given that, investors would buy more gold versus silver. For those who trade or "rotate," then consider selling silver for an equivalent value amount in gold.

Trading with the GSR

When silver did hit a low around March 18, 2020, I used it as a trading opportunity (as a short-term speculator). With silver in the $12 range, I immediately called my futures broker Charlie and bought a silver futures call option (at the time, about $260). Silver then rallied, and I sold that call about seven weeks later for $1,035 (a gain of $775 or about 300 percent). On an annualized basis, the percentage gain was an outrageous 1,900 percent.

TIP

When the GSR is relatively high (and both metals are in a bull market), then silver is the more bullish bet. Given that, traders and speculators would consider the following:

>> Buying a leveraged bullish ETF (see Chapter 11)

>> Buying a long-term call option (see Chapter 13)

>> Buying a junior mining stock (see Chapter 7)

When times look bearish for gold and silver, consider the following:

>> Buying an inverse ETF (see Chapter 11)

>> Buying a long-term put option (see Chapter 13)

>> Selling some of your gold and silver stocks and/or ETFs, or using trailing stops on them to minimize downside risk (see Chapter 16)

Chapter **15**

Using Technical Analysis

F or short-term moves (up and down) in the market, 2020 has been an eye-popping year. Technical analysis — the topic of this chapter — takes into effect short-term movements in both price and volume behavior of the asset in question. Simply stated, fundamental analysis is about the *what* and technical analysis is about the *when*. Getting in at a good price and getting out at a better price is the nature of the game for aficionados of technical analysis. Given how wild 2020 has been, knowing the ins and outs with technical analysis is as important as ever!

If you're buying stocks, exchange-traded funds (ETFs), and physical gold and silver for long-term investing (measured in years), technical analysis won't be a big factor. (With gold and silver, the fundamentals, including supply and demand, market factors such as mining data, global demand, currency issues, and so on, are very important considerations.) But if you're doing anything with short-term buy and sell considerations (measured in days, weeks, and a few months), then timing with technical analysis will be very valuable (or is that invaluable?). It's critical with vehicles such as

» Short-term stock and ETF trading (see Chapters 7 and 8)

» Trading leveraged and inverse ETFS (see Chapter 11)

» Futures (see Chapter 12)

» Call and put options (on any of the preceding three; see Chapter 13)

As for me, I embrace both the fundamentals and the technicals to optimize my approach, and it has worked well over the years. I think that the major content of this book is about fundamentals, so it's great to focus on the technicals in this chapter. This chapter will be particularly important to you short-term traders and speculators, so grab your favorite beverage and dive in!

Defining Technical Analysis

REMEMBER

Technical analysis tries to understand where an investment's price is going based on market behavior as evidenced in its market statistics (presented in charts, price, and trading volume data). Technical analysis doesn't try to figure out the worth of an investment; it's used to figure out where the price of that asset or investment is trending.

Because technical analysis is indeed technical, don't try to understand it all immediately. What normal person gets into stochastic oscillators and divergent and convergent who-z-what-is on the first day? "Not I!" said the author ("Amen, brother!"). Understanding technical analysis is like eating an elephant: You eat one bite at a time (and you put the rest in the trunk for later).

TIP

Technical analysis is most useful for those who are trading and/or speculating during a relatively short time frame measured in days, weeks, or months. It's not that useful when you're trying to forecast where the price will be a year or more down the road.

Comparing Technical Analysis versus Fundamental Analysis

WARNING

Although technical analysis is "the star" of this chapter, it's useful to take in its shortcomings and juxtapose it with fundamental analysis. The first and major drawback of technical analysis is that it's a human approach tracking human behavior in that particular market. In other words, just because it's called technical analysis doesn't mean that it's technical a la the law of physics. It's called technical analysis because the data you look at is technical, but the movement of the price of the underlying asset or investment moves due to the cumulative decisions of many buyers and sellers who are human and therefore fallible.

Why mention this? Everyone is looking to make money, and many trading systems and approaches are based on technical analysis. Unfortunately, making profitable investments isn't just 2 + 2 = 4. If technical analysis made things so easy that mere computer models or trading systems could give you a — voilà! — money-making decision, then everyone could and would do it. Yet that isn't the case. Let me give you my take.

I favor fundamental analysis for long-term investing. I've shunned technical analysis for choosing individual stocks because I didn't see the long-term value in it. In stock market history, if you did a nose count of successful investors and what approach they used, you'd find that those long-term investors who used some variation of fundamental analysis (as those who use a value-investing approach) are overwhelmingly the larger category. The legendary investors such as Warren Buffett and Peter Lynch rarely looked at a chart.

REMEMBER

But before you throw out the technical analysis with the bath water, read on. Those who use technical analysis in short-term trading or speculating in larger scope investments tend to do better than those who don't use it. What does that mean? What I mean is that if you apply technical analysis in something larger than a company, such as an index or a commodity, then you'll tend to do better. If you're getting into trading futures on entities such as grains or energy or precious metals, then understanding the basics of technical analysis will make you, overall, a better (hence, more profitable) trader. Because short-term market behavior and psychology can be very mercurial and irrational (human), then technical analysis will have usefulness.

The guts of technical analysis

When you're using technical analysis, understand how it operates and what you look at. Technical analysis, for the purposes of this book, is based on several assumptions.

The price tells all

The asset's market price provides enough information to render a trading decision. Those who criticize technical analysis point out that it considers the price and its movement without adequate attention to the fundamental factors of the company. The argument made favoring technical analysis is that the price is a snapshot that reflects in and of itself the basic factors affecting the company, including the company's (or asset's) fundamentals.

Technical analysts (also called technicians) believe that the company's fundamentals, along with broader economic factors and its market psychology, are all priced into the stock, removing the need to actually consider these factors separately. The bottom line is that technicians look at the price and its movement and extract from this a forecast for where it's going.

It's all about the trend

The price tends to move in trends. In the world of technical analysis, the phrase "the trend is your friend" is as ubiquitous as the phrase "you spoiled the broth, now you lie in it!" is in the restaurant industry. Uh, maybe more so. Following the trend is a bedrock principle in technical analysis, and the data is either there to support the trend or not. When a trend in the asset's price is established, the tendency is that it will continue. The three types of trends, as you see later in this chapter, are up, down, and sideways (but you knew that).

History repeats

Another foundational idea in technical analysis is that history tends to repeat itself, mainly in terms of price movement. The repetitive nature of price movements is attributed to market psychology; in other words, market participants tend to provide a consistent reaction to similar market stimuli over time.

Technical analysis uses chart patterns (covered later in this chapter) to analyze market movements and understand trends. Although many of these charts have been used for more than 100 years, they're still believed to be relevant because they illustrate patterns in price movements that often repeat themselves.

How about both?

REMEMBER

I think that a useful way to combine both fundamental and technical analysis is to use the strength of each. Fundamental analysis should help you understand "what" to invest (or trade or speculate) in, while technical analysis guides you as to "when" to do it. Because markets ebb and flow and zig and zag, technical analysis can help you spot low-risk points to enter or exit a trade. Technical analysis, therefore, helps stack the deck a little more in your favor. Considering how markets are going lately, every little bit helps.

Blending the two approaches to some extent has been done with success. Obviously, if the fundamental and the technical factors support your decision, then the chance for a profitable trade has more going for it. How could this blend occur?

For example, look at the concepts of oversold and overbought (see the later section on the relative strength index for details). If you were looking at buying a stock (or other asset) because you thought it would be a strong investment but weren't sure about when to buy, you'd want to look at the technical data. If the data told you that it was oversold, then it would be a good time to buy. *Oversold* just means that the market was a little too extreme in selling that particular investment during a particular time.

TIP

By the way, I like to think that the technical terms *oversold* and *overbought* have a parallel to fundamental terms such as undervalued and overvalued. Because fundamental analysis is a major part of a school of thought referred to as value investing, the concepts make sense (yes, I'm into value investing). Just as it's usually a good idea to invest in an undervalued stock, it's a good trading idea to buy a stock that's oversold. Presuming that an oversold stock is undervalued (all things being equal) is logical. Of course, the other terms (overbought and overvalued) can also run in tandem. I may as well finish here before you're overwhelmed and under-interested.

On the other hand, the fundamentals can help a technical analyst make a better trading decision. Say that a technical analyst has a profitable position in a mining stock called Digging Dirt Co. (DDC). If the technical indicators are turning bearish and the new quarterly earnings report for DDC indicates that net profit is significantly lower, then selling DDC's stock is probably a good idea.

The tools of the trade

When you roll up your sleeves and get into technical analysis, what will you be dealing with? It will depend on what type of technical analyst you are. Technical analysis has two subcategories: those who predominantly use charts (these technicians are called chartists) and those who predominantly use data (such as price and volume data). Of course, many technicians use a combination of both:

>> **Charts:** The neat pictures that graph price movements (such as chart patterns)

>> **Data:** Such as price and volume information (along with technical and behavioral indicators derived from it)

Keep in mind that technical analysts don't look at the fundamentals because they believe that the marketplace (as depicted in the charts, price, and volume data) already takes into account the fundamentals.

Tracking the Trend

Identifying the trend is a crucial part of technical analysis. A trend is just the overall direction of that security or commodity. Which way is the price headed? It's easy to see which way the asset is headed in Figure 15-1.

FIGURE 15-1: Generic chart sloping in a definite downward direction.

© John Wiley & Sons, Inc.

Unless you're a skier, that's not a pretty picture. The bearish trend is obvious. But what do you do with a chart like Figure 15-2?

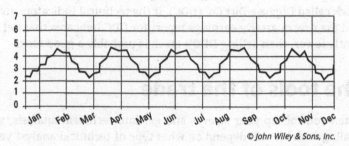

FIGURE 15-2: Generic chart showing a sideways pattern.

© John Wiley & Sons, Inc.

Yep. It looks like somebody's heart monitor while he or she is watching a horror movie. A sideways or horizontal trend just shows a consolidation pattern that means that the security or asset will break out into an up- or downtrend.

REMEMBER

Regardless of whether the trend is up, down, or sideways, you'll notice that it's rarely (closer to never) in a straight line. The line is usually jagged and bumpy because it's really a summary of all the buyers and sellers making their trades. Some days the buyers have more impact, and some days it's the sellers' turn.

REMEMBER

Keep in mind that there are formal definitions of the three basic trends:

>> **An uptrend or bullish trend** is when each successive high is higher than the previous high and each successive low is higher than the previous low.

>> **A downtrend or bearish trend** is when each successive high is lower than the previous high and each successive low is lower than the previous low.

>> **The sideways trend or horizontal trend** shows that the highs and the lows are both in a generally sideways pattern with no clear indication of trending up or down (at least not yet).

Figure 15-3 shows all three trends.

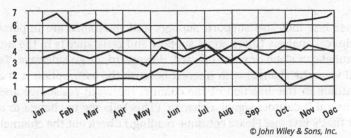

© John Wiley & Sons, Inc.

FIGURE 15-3: Chart that simultaneously shows an uptrend, downtrend, and sideways trend.

Technical analysts call the highs peaks and the lows troughs. In other words, if the peaks and troughs keep going up, that's bullish. If the peaks and troughs keep going down, it's bearish. And if the peaks and troughs are horizontal, then you're probably in California (just kidding).

Trend lengths

With trends, you're not just looking at the direction; you're also looking at the trend's duration or length of time that it's going along. Trend durations can be (you guessed it) short term, intermediate term, or long term. Generally, a short-term (or near-term) trend is less than a month. An intermediate term is up to a quarter (three months) long, while a long-term trend can be up to a year. And to muddy the water a bit, the long-term trend may have several trends inside it (don't worry; the quiz has been canceled).

A trend line is a straight line added to a chart to designate a clear path for a particular trend. The trend line simply follows the troughs in the trend to show a distinctive direction. Trend lines can also be used to identify a trend reversal or change in the opposite direction. Figure 15-4 shows a trend line.

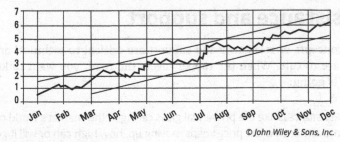

© John Wiley & Sons, Inc.

FIGURE 15-4: Chart that shows the jagged edge going upward along with the trend line.

Channels

Channel lines are lines that are added to show both the peaks and troughs of the primary trend. The top line indicates resistance (of the price movement), and the lower line indicates support. Support and resistance are important concepts in technical analysis (more about support and resistance is in the next section). The channel can slope or point upward, downward, or go sideways. Technical traders will view the channel with interest because the assumption is that the price will continue in the direction of the channel (between resistance and support) until technical indicators signal a change. (This tells me to change to a cable channel, but that's just me. Please continue reading.) Check out the channel in Figure 15-5.

10-Apr-2000 **Open** 80.91 **High** 82.80 **Low** 80.61 **Close** 81.50 **Volume** 1.3M **Chg** -0.36 (-0.43%)

Chevron Texaco 81.50 (Daily)

Main-trendline

Channel-line

© John Wiley & Sons, Inc.

FIGURE 15-5: Chart showing channel.

REMEMBER

As you're seeing the asset's price moving upward, you see where the price is on both the top and bottom. The channel shows you how the price is range-bound. The emphasis on trends is to help you make more profitable decisions because you're better off trading with the trend than not.

Resistance and support

REMEMBER

The concepts of resistance and support are critical to technical analysis the way tires are to cars. When the rubber meets the road, you want to know where the price is going:

>> *Resistance* is like the proverbial glass ceiling in the market's world of price movement. As the price keeps moving up, how high can or will it go? That's the $64,000 question, and technical analysts watch this closely. Breaking through resistance is considered a positive sign for the price, and the expectation is definitely bullish.

>> *Support* is the lowest point or level that the price is trading at. When the price goes down and hits this level, it's expected to bounce back, but what happens when it goes below the support level? It's then considered a bearish sign, and technical analysts watch closely for a potential reversal and expect the price to head down.

Both the resistance and support form the trading range for the asset's price. If the price continues in this range, then it's a sideways or horizontal pattern, and technical analysts watch for indicators that it will break out of the pattern and then either presume an upward or downward path.

Checking Out Charts

Charts are to technical analysis what pictures are to photography. You can't avoid them 'cause you're not supposed to. That's why you see more charts in this chapter than in others. But trust me, especially if you're serious about trading metals (or stocks or other commodities), charts and the related technical data will come in handy.

In terms of visualization and utility, the following are the four most common charts used in technical analysis.

Line charts

A line chart simply shows a series of prices plotted in a graph showing how the price moved over a period of time. The period of time could be a day, week, month, year, or longer. The prices that are usually chosen for a line chart are the closing prices for those market days.

I prefer to use a five-year chart because I like to encourage my clients, students, and readers to be focused on the longer term because positive results can be easier to achieve.

With a line chart, you can see how the stock has progressed during the 12-month period, and you can do some simple analysis. When were the peaks? How about the troughs? What were the strongest seasons for this stock's price movement?

Bar charts

Now we're getting a little fancier. Where the line chart gives you only the closing prices for each market day, the bar chart gives you the range of trading prices for each day during that chosen time period. Each trading day is a vertical line that represents the price movements, and you see the asset's high, low, and closing prices.

In a bar chart, the vertical line will have two notches. The notch on the left indicates the opening price, and the notch on the right indicates the closing price. If the opening price notch is higher than the closing price notch, then the line would be in red to indicate that the closing price of the asset declined versus the opening price. An up day would be in black and the closing price notch would be higher than the opening price notch.

Candlestick charts

Candlestick charts have been all the rage in recent years. They're basically bar charts but with a little more complexity to them. The full name for them is Japanese candlestick charts because they originated as a form of technical analysis in the 17th century during trading in rice markets. Candlestick charts are too involved to adequately describe in this space, so continue your research with the resources provided at the end of this chapter.

It stands to reason that because candlestick charts provide more information in a visual form than bar charts, they can provide more guidance in trading.

Point and figure charts

A more obscure chart that chartists use is the point and figure chart. When you look at it, you'll notice a series of Xs and Os. The Xs represent upward price trends, and the Os represent downward price trends.

Picking Apart Chart Patterns

Chart patterns like those in the following sections are very interesting and are the graphical language of technical analysis. For technical analysts, the pattern is important because it provides a potential harbinger for what's to come. It's not 100 percent accurate, but it's usually accurate better than 50 percent of the time as odds go. In the world of trading, being right more than 50 percent of the time can be enough. Usually a proficient technician is better than that.

Head and shoulders

The head and shoulders pattern is essentially bearish. It's usually a signal that an uptrend has ended and the pattern is set to reverse and head downward. Technical analysts consider this to be one of the most reliable patterns. The pattern shows three peaks and two troughs.

The first components of this pattern are the three peaks that break down into the tall center peak (the head) and the shorter peaks (the shoulders) that are on each side of the center peak. The two troughs form the neckline.

The head and shoulders pattern tells technical analysts that the trend that just preceded this pattern basically ran out of gas. The selling pressures build up and overpower the buyers. Hence, the price starts to come down. The shoulder on the right is like a last effort for the bullish trend to regain its traction but to no avail. Keep in mind that the neckline in this pattern is the support. As support is broken, then the tendency is that it's a bearish expectation.

Reverse head and shoulders

As you can infer, this pattern is opposite to the prior chart pattern, and it's essentially bullish. This pattern signals that a downtrend has ended and is set to reverse and head upward. In this pattern, you have three troughs and two peaks. The middle trough is usually the deepest one.

In this pattern, buying pressures build up and form a base to spring upward. Note that a bullish pattern is a series of higher highs and higher lows. In the reverse head and shoulders pattern, the neckline is resistance. When resistance is broken, then the expectation is for an upward move.

REMEMBER

Keep in mind that with this chart (as with all charts), there isn't 100 percent reliability or guaranteed accuracy. Technical analysts don't say that the next step after a particular pattern is a certainty; it's a probability. Probable outcomes, more times than not, tend to materialize. Increasing the probability of success for more profitable decision-making (entering or exiting a trade) is the bottom-line mission of technical analysis.

Cup and handle

This pattern is generally bullish. In the pattern, the price first peaks then craters into a bowl-shaped trough (the cup) and peaks at the end of it with a small downward move (the handle) before it moves up.

This pattern basically tells the technician that the security's price took a breather to build support and then continue the bullish pattern.

Double tops and bottoms

Both the double top and the double bottom chart patterns indicate a trend reversal:

>> The double top is essentially a bearish pattern as the price makes two attempts (the double top) to break through resistance but fails to do so. The bottom of the trough between the two peaks indicates support. However, the two failed attempts at the resistance level are more significant than the support at the trough, so this pattern signals a potential downturn for that asset's price.

>> The double bottom is the opposite reversal pattern. It's a bullish pattern because the support level indicators are stronger than the resistance. This signals a potential upturn in the asset's price.

TECHNICAL STUFF

As a further variation, there are also triple tops and triple bottoms. These are sideways or horizontal patterns that do portend a trend reversal. Don't even think about quadruple tops and bottoms.

Triangles

A triangle is formed when the resistance line and the support line converge to form the triangle point that shows a general direction in the asset's price movement. There are three types of triangles: symmetrical, ascending, and descending.

The symmetrical triangle points sideways, so this tells you it's a horizontal pattern that becomes a setup for a move upward or downward when more price movement provides a bullish or bearish indicator. The ascending triangle is a bullish pattern, while the descending triangle is bearish.

Of course, if you see a divergent trapezoidal and octagonal candlestick formation supported in a bowl-shaped isosceles triangle, then do nothing! Just take two aspirin and try again tomorrow.

Flags and pennants

Flags and pennants are familiar chart patterns that are short term in nature (usually not longer than a few weeks). They're continuation patterns that are formed immediately after a sharp price movement and then usually followed by a sideways price movement.

Both the flag and the pennant are similar except that the flag is triangular while the pennant is in a channel formation. Because these patterns are so short term, they're usually considered continuation patterns.

Wedges

The wedge pattern can be either a continuation or reversal pattern. It seems to be much like a symmetrical triangle, but it slants (up or down) while the symmetrical triangle generally shows a sideways movement. In addition, the wedge forms over a longer period of time (typically three to six months).

Gaps

A gap in a chart is an empty space between two trading periods. This happens when there's a substantial difference in the price between those two periods. Say that in the first period the trading range is $10 to $15, and then the next trading session opens at $20. That $5 discrepancy will be a large gap on the chart between those two periods. These gaps are typically found on bar and candlestick charts (described earlier in this chapter). This may happen when positive (or negative) news comes out about the security or commodity in the interim and initial buying pressure causes the price jump with the subsequent period as soon as trading commences.

There are three types of gaps: breakaway, runaway, and exhaustion. The breakaway gap forms at the start of a trend, and the runaway gap forms during the middle of the trend. So obviously, what happens when the trend gets tired at the end? Why, the exhaustion gap, of course! See, this stuff isn't that hard to grasp.

Assessing Moving Averages

In terms of price data, a favorite tool of the technical analyst is the *moving average*. A moving average is the average price of a security or commodity over a set period of time. This is done because frequently a chart shows price movements as too jumpy and haphazard, so the moving average smooths it out to show a clearer path for the price. This helps decipher its trend. There are three types of moving averages: simple, linear, and exponential.

Simple moving averages (SMA)

The first (and most common) type of average is referred to as a simple moving average (SMA). It's calculated by simply taking the sum of all the past closing prices over the chosen time period and dividing the result by the number of prices used in the calculation. For example, in a ten-day simple moving average, the last ten closing prices are added together and then divided by ten.

An example of the ten-day moving average

Say that the prices for the last ten trading days are (in order) $10, $11, $12, $10, $11, $13, $14, $12, $12, and $14. It's hard to derive a trend from that, but a moving average can help. First, you add up all the prices; in this case, the total is $119. Then you take the total of $119 and divide it by ten (the total number of trading days). You get an average price of $11.90. As you do this with more and more price data (in ten-day chronological sets), you can see a trend unfolding.

Say that on the 11th day, the closing price is $15. At this point, the next ten-day trading starts with $11 (this was the closing price from the second day in the first example) and ends with a new closing price for the tenth day, $15. Now when you add up this new ten-day range, you get a total of $124. Once you divide that number by ten, you get the average of $12.40 ($124 total divided by 10 days). In this brief and simple example, you see that the ten-day moving average tells you the price trend is up (from $11.90 and moving to $12.40).

Of course, you need to see a much longer string of ten-day sets to ascertain a useful ten-day moving average, but you get the point. These averages can also be plotted on a graph to depict the trend to help render a trading decision. The more time periods that you graph, the easier it is to see how strong (or weak) the trend is.

REMEMBER

Moving averages are very useful in plotting out the support and resistance levels in the trend. They're very helpful in figuring all the various peaks and troughs necessary in analyzing the trend's direction.

The most common simple moving averages

Technical analysts most frequently use 10-day, 20-day, or 50-day for short-term trading. To confirm longer-term trends, they also watch the 100-day and 200-day moving averages. Of course, there are other time frames as well, but these are common.

REMEMBER

The longer-period moving averages help put the short terms in perspective so that the trader can still view the big picture. In other words, you may have an asset correct and see its price fall significantly, but does it mean that a trend has reversed? If the asset is in a long-term bull market, it's common for it to violate or go below its short-term averages (such as 10-, 20-, or 50-day moving averages) temporarily. The more serious red flags start to appear when it violates the longer-term averages such as the 200-day moving average. And if it violates the ten-year moving average — watch out!

Other averages

TECHNICAL STUFF

Some critics believe that the SMA is too limited in its scope and, therefore, not as useful as it should be. This is why more involved variants are also used, such as the linear weighted average (LWA) and the exponential moving average (EMA). It would be too involved to cover these averages adequately in this chapter. You can get more details on them through the resources at the end of the chapter. For beginners, the SMA is sufficient.

Investigating Indicators

An *indicator* is a mathematical calculation that can be used with the asset's price and/or volume. The end result is a value that's used to anticipate future changes in prices.

There are two types of indicators: leading and lagging.

>> Leading indicators help you profit by attempting to forecast what prices will do next. Leading indicators provide greater rewards at the expense of increased risk. They perform best in sideways or trading markets. They work by measuring how overbought and oversold a security is.

>> Lagging (or trend-following) indicators are best suited to price movements that are in relatively long trends. They don't warn you of any potential changes in prices. Lagging indicators have you buy and sell in a mature trend when there's reduced risk.

Oscillators

Oscillators are indicators that are used when you're analyzing charts that have no clear trend. Moving averages (described earlier in this chapter) and other indicators are certainly important when the trend is clear, but oscillators are more beneficial when the asset is either in a horizontal or sideways trading pattern or has not been able to establish a definite trend because the market is volatile and the price action is very uneven.

The relative strength index (RSI)

As you read earlier, the technical conditions of overbought and oversold are important to be aware of. They're good warning flags to help you time a trade, whether that means getting in or getting out of a position. The relative strength index (RSI) is a convenient metric for measuring the overbought/oversold condition. Generally, the RSI quantifies the condition and gives you a number that acts like a barometer. On a reading of 0 to 100, you can see that the RSI becomes oversold at or about the 30 level and overbought at or about the 70 level.

Moving average convergence/divergence (MACD)

The moving average convergence/divergence (MACD) is a lagging indicator that shows the relationship between two moving averages of prices. The MACD is calculated by subtracting the 26-day EMA from the 12-day EMA. A nine-day EMA of the MACD, called the signal line, is then plotted on top of the MACD, which acts as a trigger for making buy and sell orders.

TIP

That's the technical definition of the MACD, but don't worry if you didn't understand it on the first round. The MACD indicator is usually provided by the technical analysis software or trading service that you may use. It's fortunately not something that you have to calculate on your own.

Crossovers and divergence

A crossover is the point when the asset's price and an indicator intersect (or cross over). This is used as a signal to make a buy or sell order. Say that a stock, for example, falls past $20 per share to $19, and the 20-day moving average is $19.50. That would be a bearish crossover, and it would indicate a good time to sell or risk further downside. The opposite is true as well; there are crossovers that indicate a good time to buy.

Divergence occurs when the price of an asset and an indicator (or index or other related asset) part company and head off in opposite directions. Divergence is considered either positive or negative, both of which are signals of changes in the price trend:

» Positive divergence occurs when the price of a security makes a new low while a bullish indicator starts to climb upward.

» Negative divergence happens when the price of the security makes a new high, but bearish indicators signal the opposite and instead close lower than the previous high.

Bollinger bands

A band plots two standard deviations away from a simple moving average. The Bollinger band works like a channel and moves along with the simple moving average.

Bollinger bands help the technical analyst watch out for overbought and oversold conditions. Basically, if the price moves closer to the upper band, it's an overbought condition. If the price moves closer to the lower band, it's an oversold condition.

Focusing on the Short Term versus the Long Term

I hope this chapter gives you a good taste of technical analysis without making you scratch your head. I'm personally an adherent of fundamental analysis and a value investing approach. Over the long term, history tells us that the fundamentals ultimately win. This has usually been true, even though in the short term, the zigs and the zags can fool you. When the fundamentals are in your favor, any short-term move against you is a buying opportunity (provided that you chose wisely from the start). But unfortunately, too many investors aren't patient and they get too busy with the short-term trees to be bothered by the long-term forest. Yet that long-term forest has a lot more green, if you know what I mean. (I hope I'm not meandering here.)

In other words, a long-term investor doesn't have to bother with things such as triangles, pennants, cups and handles, or other paraphernalia. Long-term investors just ask questions like, "Is the company making money?" or "Are financial and economic conditions still favorable for my investment?"

Now the short term is a different animal. It requires more attention and discipline. You need to monitor all the indicators to see whether your investment is on track or whether the signals are warning a change in course. The technicals can be very bearish one month, very bullish the next month, and then give you mixed signals the month after that. Being a proficient technician ultimately requires more monitoring, more trading, and more hedging, which in turn likely means more commissions. For more on brokerage orders and services that can aid your short-term trading, turn to Chapter 16.

REMEMBER

Keep in mind that all this activity also means more taxes and administrative work (tax reporting, and so on). After all, who do you think will pay more in taxes — someone who buys and holds for a year or longer, or someone who makes the same profit but by jumping in and jumping out based on which way the technical winds are blowing? Short-term gains don't have the same favorable rates as long-term gains. Sometimes the issue isn't what you make but what you keep (taxes are covered in Chapter 17).

Resources for Technical Analysis

TIP

Use the following resources to discover more information about technical analysis:

>> StockCharts (www.stockcharts.com)

>> Incredible Charts (www.incrediblecharts.com)

>> Robert McHugh, PhD (www.technicalindicatorindex.com)

>> Technical Analysis at Commodity.com (https://commodity.com/technical-analysis/)

>> *Technical Analysis of Stocks & Commodities* Magazine (www.traders.com)

>> International Federation of Technical Analysts (www.ifta.org)

>> Elliott Wave International (www.elliottwave.com)

>> *Technical Analysis For Dummies,* 4th Edition, written by Barbara Rockefeller and published by Wiley (www.dummies.com/personal-finance/investing/online-investing/technical-analysis-for-dummies-4th-edition/)

WARNING

Technical analysis isn't infallible, and don't assume it's like a crystal ball or tea leaves (which are also fallible!). Make sure you study it and do "paper trading" or simulated trading before you risk capital because short-term movements in an asset's price can be very unpredictable. Technical analysis will certainly be beneficial in providing clues into what may be the most likely movements, but 100 percent accuracy will never be achieved. Do plenty of research and education before you devote substantial capital, and be disciplined (keep your emotions out of it). Now go forth and prosper!

Chapter 16

Using Dealers and Brokers

S o now that you got to this chapter, I can read your mind: "Holy smoke, I gotta get me some gold . . . or silver . . . or mining stocks . . . or exchange-traded funds . . . or gold futures . . . . or options on silver . . . or gold . . . but gee whiz, where do I go?" So glad you asked! It's time to cover those folks you need to know so you get what you want: dealers and brokers.

In this chapter, I break down dealers and brokers into three main categories, to cover the main vehicles involved:

» **Precious metals dealers:** For buying physical bullion first, I provide some buying tips in transacting with precious metals dealers. Appendix A has an extensive listing of dealers that specialize in gold and silver.

» **Stockbrokers:** I clue you in on how to deal with stockbrokers so you can buy mining stocks, exchange-traded funds (ETFs), mutual funds, and call and put options on stocks and ETFs.

» **Futures brokers:** I cover the turbocharged world of futures brokers for the riskier vehicles of gold and silver futures (and options on them).

REMEMBER

Before your roll up your sleeves and leap into some precious metals investments, it's highly important to choose a broker or dealer who will help you make the transaction. Besides the fact that you don't want the broker to make you, uh, broker, a good broker is a critical part of your investing arsenal. Good brokers can save you money and make sure that your strategy is implemented. Bad brokers can lose you money and drive you crazy.

Starting with Some General Points on Dealers and Brokers

In the world of securities, you need an individual or a firm (the broker) to help you buy, sell, and/or manage securities (or assets or other vehicles) for your portfolio. Here is a simple breakdown for who you need for what securities:

>> If you're into buying physical precious metal coins, bullion, numismatic coins, and so on, let me get this out of the way first. I provide tips for using these dealers later in this chapter. To understand bullion coins and bars, go to Chapter 9. For numismatic coins and collectibles, go to Chapter 10.

>> If you're looking into buying mining stocks, exchange-traded funds (ETFs), or options on these securities, you need a stock brokerage account, covered later in this chapter. Choosing a mining stock is covered in Chapter 7, and ETFs are covered in Chapter 8. Leveraged and inverse ETFs are the subject of Chapter 11.

>> If you're considering precious metals mutual funds, they're typically purchased directly through the mutual fund company offering it (see Chapter 8), although many mutual funds are now offered through stock brokerage accounts as a convenience for the investor.

>> If you want to get into trading futures (commodities) or options on these speculative vehicles, you need a futures brokerage account. If you're considering a managed futures account, that is also done through futures brokers. I give details on these types of accounts later in this chapter. Chapter 12 has the scoop on futures; flip to Chapter 13 for more on options.

>> If you're considering a precious metals retirement (IRA) account, you can do it through a full-service precious metals dealer (or through a financial institution that they deal with), and you can find details in Chapter 17 on taxes and retirement accounts.

TIP

A *stock brokerage account* is generally an easy account to understand because buying stocks is a familiar activity and a major part of the financial landscape. I cover stock brokerage accounts in my book *Stock Investing For Dummies* (Wiley) as well as later in this chapter. However, it can be a little confusing when it comes to an account in the world of futures and commodities. The words *futures* and *commodities* are used interchangeably, but they're distinctly different things. Before you try to decide on a broker, you should first decide what you'll get involved with. If you're going to speculate in the world of futures, then get familiar with the market before you open an account.

Both stock and futures accounts have a lot of commonality (margin, order types, and so on), but for the sake of accuracy and orderliness, I put them in different segments because enough differences exist.

Working with Gold and Silver Dealers

My clients and I have used precious metals dealers over the years, and I think that giving you some "golden rules" here (along with a "silver" rule or two) will help you make good dealer choices and successful purchases.

Sticking to major bullion coins

The major physical bullion coins are the American Gold Eagles, Canadian Maple Leafs, and the South African Krugerrand. They also come in silver such as the American Silver Eagle (Chapter 9 has the details on these coins). My preference for beginners is to stick to American Gold Eagles and Silver Eagles, with Canadian Maple Leafs also good for your bullion coin purchases. These coins are a deep and fluid market, and millions are bought and sold worldwide every week.

WARNING

When I say stick to bullion purchases for beginners, I mean it! Coin dealers will commonly upsell newbies to numismatic coins (partly due to the higher price markups), but it's very easy to overpay with numismatic coins due to a variety of factors that can be confusing (see Chapter 10 for an introduction to numismatic coins). You can price-shop for bullion coins, and it's easier to get a reasonable deal.

Investigating a dealer's reputation and reviews

REMEMBER

The quality of the dealer can be nearly as important as the quality of the coin itself. Make sure you find out how long the dealer has been in business, check out independent reviews, and get referrals from trusted associates and industry associations. Many precious metals newsletters and websites (see Appendix A) conduct comparison consumer reviews, so read up as much as you can. Lastly, you can inquire with other investors at various forums and groups on precious metals. These forums and groups are listed in Appendix A.

Getting at least three price quotes

Try to narrow your search to at least three dealers, and call them up to inquire with the same purchase. Say that you want to purchase a roll of American Silver Eagles. Use that as your order and get three price quotes from those dealers. Ask each about their percentage premiums over the spot price. Keep in mind that buying bullion coins is a straight commodity purchase, so getting the lowest price can be the best price. All things being equal, there's no advantage to paying more per ounce of metal.

Understanding ancillary charges

In terms of the bullion purchase itself, you'll pay a premium percentage cost above the spot price of the metal itself. If gold, for example, is $2,000 per ounce spot price and the dealer has a 2 percent markup for your bullion coin purchase, then your cost will be $2,040 (not including shipping, and so on). For bullion coins, the premium shouldn't exceed 5 percent.

Also, ask for all the charges involved in your purchase. Shipping and insurance are common add-ons. Many dealers offer decreased or even free shipping for larger orders. Most reputable dealers already have this information at their website.

Deciding whether to get physical metals online or visit a local dealer

TIP

Although you may get better prices from an online dealer, don't automatically disregard a local dealer you can visit. If you're selling coins and need cash quickly, a local dealer can be a good place to get your money that day. Also, a local dealer can give you the ability to see your purchase up close, and if the price is competitive with online dealers, you can get a good deal when there are no added charges such as insurance and shipping.

Picking apart a buy back policy

When you're buying bullion, you should find out at the point of purchase about selling it back. Most dealers obviously sell and buy precious metals. Find out about their prices and procedures for buying your metals. Many dealers typically buy bullion coins at either spot price or spot price plus a minor premium, such as 1 percent or 0.5 percent. Say that you're selling your Gold Eagle bullion coin for $2,000, and the dealer has a buyback of spot price + 1 percent. You'd get $2,020. Of course, if you mail in your coin, you need to pay shipping and insurance.

When you sell a coin that needs to be shipped, the dealer will assure the price for the day you call or email on the sales price, but because gold and silver prices fluctuate every day, he may guarantee the price only if he receives your coin by a specific date. Again, every dealer is different, so ask in advance or read the buying instructions at his website.

TIP

Be sure to use the tracking features by your shipper (such as the USPS, UPS, or FedEx) to make sure the dealer receives your item.

WARNING

At the time of writing, more states are charging sales tax on physical gold and silver purchases because they're seeking more revenue due to the struggling economy (caused by the pandemic and government lockdown). I'm in New Jersey, which started its sales tax on gold and silver as of 2020 (ugh!). Check with your state to find out whether this tax applies to your purchase (the dealer will tell you, too).

Getting the Scoop on Stock Brokerage Accounts

For most people investing in gold- and silver-related stocks and/or ETFs as well as call and put options on them, they'll use a standard stock brokerage account. A stock brokerage account should actually be the cornerstone of the long-term investor's wealth-building program because of the wide array of investments, techniques, and strategies available. The following sections discuss types of stockbrokers, types of stock brokerage accounts, and the steps of opening an account.

Beginning with types of stockbrokers

A long time ago, there was one category of stockbroker. That category was called . . . stockbroker! Then things changed during the 1980s. For investors like you and me, there came to be two basic categories:

>> **The full-service broker:** For investors who wanted more attention and service from their broker, a full-service broker was the choice. The commission was high, but many investors felt the price was justified due to personalized service and more guidance in the realm of choosing investments and setting financial objectives. If you think you need more attention and assistance and don't mind the extra cost, the full-service broker is for you.

>> **The discount broker:** With deregulation in the early 1980s, this paved the way for greater competition in the stock brokerage industry. With trailblazers like Charles Schwab, the discount broker was born and soon became a new and growing force in the world of stocks (and futures).

Appendix A lists a number of stockbrokers for you to choose from.

Assessing account types

As you get into stock investing, you'll find three basic types of accounts: cash, margin (or margin and options), and discretionary. Retirement accounts (such as individual retirement accounts, or IRAs, specifically for precious metals) are covered in Chapter 17.

>> **Cash account:** This is the simplest and easiest account to open. In a cash account, you pay everything in cash with no credit involved. This one is appropriate for small investors or for conservative investors. As you shop around, you'll find stockbrokers who take accounts with initial minimum investments of $2,000 or less.

>> **Margin account:** A margin account basically means that you have borrowing privileges in your account. In other words, you have the ability to use securities in your account as collateral and use the loan proceeds to purchase other securities in your account.

>> **Discretionary account:** Another type of account is a discretionary account, where you give trading privileges to others to trade your account. Of course, you have to do some serious due diligence before you do this, but you're better off doing your own research through the resources mentioned throughout this book.

Opening a stock brokerage account

Opening a stock brokerage account isn't difficult, but just to be sure, here's a step-by-step rundown:

1. Do the research.

TIP

Plenty of sources evaluate brokers. You can head to the library and look up *Forbes* magazine and *Barron's* that do regular reviews and comparisons of brokers. Websites such as www.investopedia.com and www.sec.gov also provide guidance on choosing a broker. Check out Appendix A for even more resources.

2. Ask questions.

For example: What are the commissions? What is the minimum investment? The sources in Step 1 can help with your inquiry.

3. Choose the type of account.

TIP

A cash account (see the previous section) is easy to get, but you're better off getting the margin and options account open so that you have more choices (such as buying/selling calls and puts).

4. Get the paperwork.

Either call the broker or visit his website. You can download and mail the forms (after you fill them out, of course). Many brokers let you fill out the forms at their site, but for those who still use a fax machine, you can fax the application if you prefer.

5. Fund your account.

Either mail in a check for the initial investment amount or transfer money electronically from your bank account.

6. Make a truckload of money!

Well, let's hope so.

Once you've got all that, you're ready for business. Keep in mind that just about all the broker websites have complete details on how to do an order, and so on (see the next section for more on orders). Of course, you can call the broker's customer service at his ubiquitous 800 number.

Distinguishing Types of Orders

When you're getting into stocks, ETFs, or options (or with futures, later in this chapter), how you invest can be just as important as what you invest in. Of course, the "what" is gold and silver (and securities related to them) but "how" you do it is important, too, as you find out in the following sections.

Stock brokerage services

In today's market and with today's technology, brokerage service is no longer merely a way to buy and sell securities. The stockbroker (even a discount one) has features and bells and whistles that can make for a more profitable investing experience.

The basic orders

REMEMBER

When you make that buy or sell transaction, you need to be familiar with what type of order. Doing the order through the broker's website is your best bet:

>> **Market order:** A market order is the instruction to the broker to purchase (or sell) that security immediately. You can use this one with stockbrokers and futures brokers.

>> **Buy limit order:** The order to purchase a security at a specified price (or better).

>> **Sell limit order:** The order to sell a security at a specified price (or better).

>> **Stop-loss order:** An order to sell a security you purchased previously at a specified price below the market price only in the event the security is dropping in price. A stop-loss order has the purpose of minimizing the downside risk.

Trailing stops

In the previous section, I mention stop-loss orders. Now take it a step further with the trailing stop strategy. For those of you who read my book *Stock Investing For Dummies* (pat yourselves on the back), you know that I'm a big proponent of trailing stops. I don't use them in every circumstance, but I consider them an important risk-management tool in the investors' arsenal.

What is the trailing stop? I'm glad you asked. It's an active strategy of implementing stop-loss orders. The stop-loss order is an order to help you reduce or remove the downside risk to holding a stock. A trailing stop means that you keep adjusting the stop-loss order to protect more and more of your investment as it increases in value.

Here's an example: Presume that you have 100 shares of Silver Mother Lode Mining Company (SML) at $30 a share. Let's say you put on a 10 percent stop-loss order and make it GTC (good till canceled). In that case, the stop-loss would be at $27 ($3 is 10 percent of $30) and would stay on indefinitely (based on how long that particular broker decides a GTC order time frame would be). Note that if SML's stock price falls, the worst that would happen is that it could hit $27 and be sold immediately and you wouldn't have to see SML go to $26 or lower.

What happens when SML does what you hope it does and goes up? Say SML goes to $40. This is great. So what happens with the stop-loss order? At this point, you should cancel that stop-loss at $27 and replace it with one at, say, $36. That would make it again 10 percent (10 percent of $40 is $4; $40 less $4 is $36), and again it would be a GTC order. At this point, you're protecting the original $30 per share plus a profit of $6. Again, the upside would have no limitation while you're limiting the downside. To protect 100 percent of your original investment plus a nice chunk of profit is a good deal.

Broker email alert services

Do you know that you can program your account at the broker's website as if it were a computer? Sounds almost futuristic, but it's really cool. Here's a brief rundown of what you can do:

>> **Price alerts:** If a stock you have (or one you're interested in) hits a price you specify, the broker will send you an email to let you know.

>> **News alerts:** When something happens such as major market-moving news, an email will alert you.

>> **Trade preprogramming:** You can go to the website and put in orders to buy or sell a stock, ETF, or option when certain conditions are met (for example, when that security hits a price or when another event occurs). You'll receive an email to let you know it happened.

>> **Trade triggers:** You can set up orders to occur when primary or secondary events occur, for example, "Buy or sell security B when security A does something (such as reach a 52-week high)."

The things you can do are limited only by your imagination. The point is that these added services give you more control over your securities in today's marketplace. These are just more tools in your wealth-building arsenal.

TIP

If your broker doesn't yet have these services, it's okay. There are some great websites that can give many of these features. A good example is MarketWatch (www.marketwatch.com).

Stock brokerage commissions and fees

The obvious charge for your trading comes in the form of commissions. But fortunately, in the year 2020, many discount stock brokerage firms slashed their commissions to less than $5 a trade for online stock, ETF, and option trades. Some brokers removed their fees altogether for regular trades so that your only costs are minimal SEC charges (typically less than $1 per trade).

If, however, you're buying over-the-counter stocks (such as junior minors), there are higher fees. In the summer of 2020, I bought a few hundred shares of a junior mining stock (covered in Chapter 7), and the total commission was $6.95 (which included the SEC charge), which is still lower than in prior years.

Margin in a stock brokerage account

Using margin in your account can increase the positive or increase the negative. After you've been approved for margin trading, you'll be allowed to borrow against marginable securities. A marginable security is basically almost any stock that isn't an over-the-counter stock or a small stock on Nasdaq. Most stocks listed on the New York Stock Exchange, for example, are marginable.

REMEMBER

With margin, you can, say, put $2,000 in an account and be able to buy up to $4,000 in stock. The minimum amount to set up a margin account depends on the broker (it could be for $5,000 or more). When you initially put that $2,000 in the account, you'll see (at the broker's website, for example) that you have cash of $2,000 and buying power of $4,000. (The broker lends you the difference.) With listed or marginable stock, the borrowing ratio is 50 percent. The ratio could be different depending on the security. (You can borrow up to 90 percent of the market value of Treasury bonds, for example.) Keep in mind that you'll pay margin interest on anything you borrow through your account.

The use of margin can magnify gains or, if you're not careful, losses. Say that you decide to start with $3,000, and the stock you're going to buy is 100 shares of the Yukon Gold and Silver Mining Company (YGSM) at $60 a share for a total of

$6,000. In this case, you'd use the full limit of 50 percent to make the purchase. (The 50 percent is the limit, and you don't have to go that high; it can certainly be less.) Say that YGSM goes up to $75 per share, making the total stock value $7,500. How did you do? That $15 gain amounted to a 25 percent gain ($15 is 25 percent of $60, the original stock price), but because you used only $3,000 of your own money, your actual percentage gain is 50 percent. At that point, you could choose to sell the stock and pay off the margin (don't forget margin interest and commissions). It's nice if it happens — but what if you're wrong?

Let's say that YGSM's stock price drops to $40 (yikes!). Now what? The account is now worth $4,000, but $3,000 is the margin loan from the broker; the loan ratio has fallen to 25 percent (your equity portion of the $4,000 account value is only $1,000, or 25 percent of the total amount). This is a problem, and you'll get a margin call to get that ratio back to 50 percent within one trading day. You'd either have to kick in another $2,000 or deposit more marginable securities in the account to restore the ratio to 50 percent (or better). If you don't, then the broker can liquidate positions in the account to restore the ratio. This is in keeping with the agreement you have with the broker, which says that you must maintain your margin ratio at the required level (or better).

To stay out of trouble with margin, here are some reminders:

>> With margin, you'll be charged interest. The longer the borrowing period, the more you'll pay.

>> Margin can magnify losses as well as gains.

>> Some stocks are eligible for margin trading and some aren't. Check with your broker for more details.

>> The money that you receive from selling stocks that were initially bought on margin will first go into liquidating any margin loans outstanding before you have any funds to withdraw or reinvest.

>> Different brokers have different requirements regarding margin, so again, check with the broker about terms and conditions.

>> Novice investors are best advised to use little or no margin to avoid the risks and volatility that can occur. Wait until you accumulate more funds and, more important, more experience and expertise.

Margin interest can be tax-deductible as investment interest, so discuss it with your tax advisor (more on taxes in Chapter 17).

Introducing Types of Futures Brokers

If you're going to go the high-powered route and speculate with futures and options on futures, now you're talking about a futures brokerage (or commodities brokerage) account.

WARNING

I always strive to make a clear distinction between "investing" and "speculating," and make no mistake about it, futures and futures options are 100 percent speculative (just a hair below gambling and a hair above blindfolded bungee jumping). I see no problem with folks doing futures, but the caution is to do so only with a relatively modest amount (say, less than 5 percent of your investable financial assets) in case of potential losses. Futures done right can build wealth, but futures losses are a more common occurrence with the general public.

I find it okay to price-shop brokerage accounts for stock investing, but I don't feel the same way about futures. It's important to have a professional broker who is experienced with the ebb and flow of this market. You want someone who has integrity and can guide you with implementing your trades according to your strategy. In terms of how they relate to you, consider the two types of futures brokerage accounts, full-service and discount:

>> **Full-service futures broker:** In a nutshell, you'll pay more for a full-service broker, but you'll get more services. In futures, a broker with experience, expertise, and resources can be valuable. The broker involved works with you to help you choose strategy and implement transactions. He offers advice and research on the various markets. The full-service futures broker also provides feedback on developments that can affect futures in general and the positions in your account in particular, such as the day's news and events.

>> **Discount futures broker:** The discount brokerage firm will basically place your orders for you with no guidance or advice. You get fewer services so that you end up paying less in fees and commissions. Ultimately, you do your own research and due diligence. A discount broker is a good choice for confident, experienced individuals who just want an inexpensive way to trade.

REMEMBER

Both types of brokers usually offer good websites with content and links that can help you be more informed with your speculating. As a financial planner who does all of his own hands-on investing, I'm very comfortable with a discount stockbroker, but I prefer a full-service futures broker. I believe that beginners and intermediate-level investors and speculators are better off with an experienced, full-service broker because of all the reasons and risks mentioned in this chapter as well as in Chapter 12. And hey, if you get really good at it, you can always move on to a discount broker. The next section provides details on choosing a futures broker.

Let me put another wrinkle in this topic about the different types of brokers. Whether the broker is full service or discount, you should know something about what type of brokerage firm it is from an industry and regulatory perspective:

>> **Futures commission merchant (FCM):** A FCM is an organization that provides the principal order clearing services for the futures industry. In other words, it's the main organization through which the buy and sell orders of futures contracts (and options on them) are made. FCMs are members of the individual futures exchanges, such as those operated by the CME Group (www. cmegroup.com). You can see a complete listing of FCMs at the website of the Commodity Futures Trading Commission (CFTC; www.cftc.gov).

>> **Introducing broker (IB):** Unless you're working with the retail division at an FCM, you're likely to work with an IB. The IB can be a full-service or a discount brokerage firm that works through the FCM. The transactions done by the IB are cleared through the FCM. The IB may or may not be a recognizable name, but it provides the service you seek (either full-service or discount). Although IBs can be large firms, they tend to be smaller firms, which means the service can be more personalized.

Selecting a Futures Broker

Unless you get a referral to a broker from someone you trust, such as a close friend or your tax or legal advisor, you'll end up doing some research to find a broker for your futures business. There are several places to start:

>> **Commodities Futures Trading Commission (CFTC):** The CFTC has consumer information on futures and futures brokers. You can visit it at www.cftc.gov.

TIP

>> **National Futures Association (NFA):** I highly recommend that investors visit the NFA's website at www.nfa.futures.org for several reasons. It provides information and guidance on choosing brokers. In addition, you can find out whether the brokers in question have any complaints or problems against them. If you've been victimized, you can file a complaint. Even though it's a private entity, the NFA does work as a regulatory body that can discipline wayward brokers. In addition, the NFA has educational resources and links for the investing public.

>> **Futures Industry Association (FIA):** The FIA is the trade group for futures brokers. It offers a wealth of information at its website (www.futuresindustry. org), including an extensive directory of brokers, futures information services, and links to futures-related companies, programs, and educational resources.

REMEMBER

When you're selecting a broker, you're basically choosing someone for your financial team in the same way you choose a tax advisor or insurance broker. It will hopefully be a long-term relationship. You obviously need someone you're comfortable with. Let me share with you what I look for when I'm meeting people I hope to do business with. I look for people who have ICE in their veins. What is ICE?

>> **Integrity:** They must have integrity, or why bother working with them?

>> **Competence:** If they're true professionals, then they should know what they're doing.

>> **Enthusiasm:** Do they enjoy what they're doing? If they don't, how will they get good at it? If they're not enthusiastic about their work, there's a good chance they won't be doing this line of work in due course.

So it's time to interview a potential futures broker. After you get past "What's your name?" and "How 'bout those Mets!" you start getting into that uncomfortable silence. Have no fear! This guide is here to help you ask the questions that should merit some answers:

>> **How many years of experience do you have working futures?** You want three or more years (but not 87).

>> **Do you have an area of futures that you specialize in?** Some brokers specialize in metals; for others, it's currencies or grains. Make sure they have proficient knowledge in your desired markets.

>> **Does your approach embrace fundamental analysis, technical analysis, or a mix of both?** You should know something about their knowledge of these areas and what they favor as an approach. (See Chapter 15 for an introduction to technical analysis.)

>> **What size account are you comfortable working with?** Only speculate with an amount that won't hurt you if you "lost it all."

>> **What are your firm's requirements for margin? Can you give me some examples of how margin would work with my account?** Ask them to provide guidance on how margin works before you actually do it.

>> **What are the commissions and fees, and what services are provided?** You want to know all the fees and trading costs involved.

>> **What is your track record (provided they have done discretionary trading for clients)?** You want to know that they are competent and have been successful in their approach.

> **» How are disputes or concerns handled at this firm?** Hopefully, you won't have conflicts with the broker, but it's good to know what to do if there is a potential conflict, such as an unauthorized trade or trades that you believe are too frequent.

After going through several brokers and firms, I finally found my broker Charlie. He's been my futures broker since 2003, and I list him and his firm in Appendix A. He treated me well, and it paid off for him because I sent him dozens of clients. In my book, he has ICE in his veins (kind of catchy, isn't it?). That's probably a good lesson for anyone in business. If you treat people well, they'll not only stick with you but also send you business.

Dealing with Futures Accounts

I personally like options on futures versus futures directly. Yes, you should find out as much as possible about futures (you can start with Chapter 12), but options on futures offer much of the same potential but with less risk. When I buy an option on a futures contract and the futures contract goes down the next day, I don't worry about a margin call. And if it's a cloudy day, I stay home and play Parcheesi. The sections that follow give you a good look at using a futures brokerage account.

Seeing how margin works in a futures account

Margin in a futures account is a tad more complicated than margin in a stock brokerage account (covered earlier in this chapter). Well, a big tad indeed.

For the futures broker, margin is a performance bond. In the area of futures, the volatility in market prices from day to day can be great. Because you put down money roughly equal to 10 percent (sometimes more) of the futures contract, it's possible that the futures contract market price goes against you.

The margin in a futures account acts as a good-faith deposit to cover swings in the market value of the contract. If the market price change is significant and adverse, you may be required to put more money in the account (the margin call) to maintain the necessary margin. Keep in mind that in futures, the margin you put down isn't a down payment on a futures contract. A futures contract isn't an asset you own; it's a liability, especially if the market moves against you. The margin is a good-faith amount sitting in your account just in case you're wrong about the performance of the futures contract market price.

Say you are bullish on silver and decide to go long on a silver futures contract. Say that silver is at $24 per ounce. How much margin would you pay? The notional value of the silver futures contract is $120,000 (5,000 ounces × $24). You may need to put up $12,000 as initial margin, and the broker may also have you put up another $1,200 as maintenance margin for a total amount of $13,200 ($12,000 plus $1,200). The maintenance amount is tied to the volatility of silver (in this case). Because you are long on the contract, if the price goes down, the futures broker may contact you for more money in your account (the "margin call").

WARNING

Keep in mind that if you go short on a contract, you also have margin requirements, and if the underlying asset goes up in value (in other words, it goes against you because you are short), that would trigger a margin call. Speak to your futures broker to explain the process in more detail before you do because it can be risky.

The margin is effectively an estimate of your possible loss in the next trading session (the next day) escrowed in advance. Because no one knows in advance which way the market could move, both the buyer and the seller post the margin.

TIP

Because the rules for margin can differ from broker to broker, work through some what-if scenarios with your chosen broker given the market you're looking to trade.

Watching out for problems in your futures account

WARNING

Churning is a problem you need to watch out for. Churning is when a broker performs a high level of activity (buying and selling) in the account for the (unspoken) purpose of generating commission income. Sometimes it doesn't seem evident in a commodities account because it can be quite normal to see a lot of trading transactions in a relatively short period of time. You must be most wary of churning, especially when you've given the broker discretionary trading authority in that account.

A new client came to me after closing out an account with a dubious firm located in Florida. He started the account with $60,000 and got out four months later with $57,000. Getting out with a net loss of $3,000 isn't the end of the world, but that's not the story. The real eye-opener came when Charlie (my broker) analyzed the account's activity. The statements indicated more than $17,000 of commissions during that brief four-month period! Gee! Maybe if my new client was so concerned with making a killing, he should have gotten a job there instead.

In addition to churning, the most often cited complaints have been high commissions and poor service. Because there are so many brokers, you can shop around. When you find a broker with whom you're comfortable, it's time for the fun stuff: filling out forms.

Opening a futures account

Here are the steps in finally opening your futures account:

1. **Read the forms and ask questions (as I recommend in the earlier section "Opening a stock brokerage account").**

2. **Put in the usual information: name, address, and so on.**

3. **Decide on the initial investment.**

4. **Understand what risks you'll tolerate.**

5. **Read the disclosure agreements about risk.**

6. **Submit the application and your funds and wait for the green light to start trading.**

7. **When you're ready, read (or reread) Chapter 12 on futures.**

After you've done your due diligence, you can open a futures account. When you see the paperwork and supporting documentation, you'll think that they cut down an entire redwood tree just for the forms (makes me regret not going long on those lumber futures). Anyway, after the usual stuff about your name, address, Social Security number, and so forth, you'll see questions and forms covering the topic of risk.

Commodities regulations try to make sure that small investors are made fully aware of the risks associated with futures and options on futures. You'll see for our purposes that there are really two different categories of investors in the world of futures (again, it's really speculating): the retail investor and the accredited investor.

>> **Retail investor:** The retail investor is the little guy or the small speculator (technically called the nonaccredited investor). If you have a regular job or you run a small business and your income is less than $200,000, then you're a retail investor. This category covers most folks. This is the category that the authorities (such as the CFTC) attempt to give some protection through documents that need to be filled out when you open your futures account. You'll be required to sign risk disclosure documents so that you're made aware of potential risks.

>> **Accredited investor:** The accredited investor is a different animal. It may not necessarily mean that you're particularly proficient at futures, but it does indicate that you can sustain losses without undue impact on your financial situation. An accredited investor is generally defined as one with total financial assets of $1 million or more (not including the value of your residence) and/or income exceeding $200,000 per year.

Checking out futures account commissions and fees

REMEMBER

The costs of transacting futures is a major issue. Asking your potential broker about how much he charges in commissions is necessary and obvious. Choosing on price alone isn't always the wisest thing because you want to make sure that you're getting value.

Here's an example. My futures broker Charlie's commissions aren't the cheapest and they're not the most expensive; the commission price is in the middle of the pack. I could certainly find cheaper commissions elsewhere. Heck! Just go on the internet, and you can see bare-bones commissions. However, you can't confuse price with cost. I may pay $50 for a trade and someone else may pay only $10 because it's an internet trade. Yet, more times than not, I'll save money over that internet trade. Why? In my case, Charlie "shops the price" as he places the order with the folks on the exchange floor. He'll end up buying the trade at a good price and save me $100 or more on the total trade. This isn't easy to do with a cookie-cutter approach at a futures website because the internet approach may lock in a price without negotiating.

Here are more points about commissions and fees:

>> **Round-turn commissions:** A round-turn commission covers both the buy and sell sides of the trade. This is typical when you purchase an option on futures.

>> **Half-turn commissions:** A half-turn commission covers only the buy or sell side of the trade. This is typical when you purchase futures directly (versus options on futures).

>> **Negotiable commissions:** Push for lower rates, especially if you are (or will be) an active trader.

    As of early 2020, average commissions per half-turn are in the range of $30 to $70. If you're in the upper part of the range, negotiate.

If you're using a full-service broker whose guidance has lost you money, consider negotiating for lower rates, or if they really do a bad job, move your business elsewhere.

If you're using a full-service broker and he's helping you make money, then don't be that concerned about the commission. Good guidance is hard to find, so why ruin a good thing?

TECHNICAL STUFF

All in all, commission rates are a better deal now in the internet age versus what they were 10 or 20 years ago. During the 1990s, many futures brokers charged $120 to $150 or more.

Note that whatever person actually helps you in the trade, that person won't be getting 100 percent of the commission amount. It does get divvied up by several parties. If that person is an introducing broker, then he or she must pay roughly $10 to $15 from that commission to the organization clearing the trade, the FCM. (See the earlier section "Introducing Types of Futures Brokers" for more about IBs and FCMs.)

Making futures orders

In the world of futures, you can implement many different orders, and I'll try to list as many as space can accommodate, but the most common trade orders that individuals will come across are market orders, limit orders, and stop orders, so I'll cover them first. Before those transactional orders (and others), I mention time condition orders.

REMEMBER

When speaking to your broker to put in an order, he'll take your instructions and repeat the order back to you before submitting it. Note that even though it's a verbal order, it's effectively a contractual transaction. The odds are that the conversation will be recorded just in case there's a question or a dispute regarding the verbal order.

Time condition orders

This is a simple order that works in conjunction with the transactional orders. The time order is your order to make the transactional order either a day order or a good-till-canceled, or GTC, order. In other words, you'll tell the broker that your order is in effect either for the day or indefinitely:

>> In a day order, you may say, "Buy a December silver futures contract at the price of $X or better, and this order is good for the day." This order will be filled only if silver hits $X (or a better price) during that day's trading session. If it doesn't hit $X by the end of the trading day, then the order won't be executed and will expire and be cleared off the slate. That's a day order.

>> A GTC in that same situation may be "Buy a December silver futures contract at the price of $X or better, and this order is good till canceled." With a GTC order, if that December silver futures contract doesn't hit the price target that day, then the order will stay on during the days to come until it gets filled. The GTC order won't stay there forever. Either it's filled or the client cancels it, or it may expire based on a time frame designated by the broker. Depending on the broker, the GTC order can remain active (open order) for 30 days, 60 days, 90 days, or another time frame (check with your broker).

REMEMBER

That wasn't so bad. Keep in mind that if you're not sure whether you're placing the order properly, don't be shy; tell the broker what you're trying to accomplish and ask for assistance in understanding and implementing the order. It's your money, and you're paying for service.

Market orders

This is the most common transactional order. In a market order, the broker tries to fill your order as soon as you submit it. You could voice a market order as "For my account #1234, buy two gold April futures contracts at the market."

TIP

The market order is a simple and common order, and I use it frequently. Understand that a market order won't always get you the best price because in the order you're basically saying you'll accept the market's price instead of waiting for a better price. For me, if I'm getting into a transaction worth thousands of dollars, I won't sweat $50 either way because if I dig in my heels to wait for a $50 savings, I may miss out on the order altogether.

Limit orders

In a limit order, the client requests that the trade be done at a specific price (or better). A limit order may be, "Buy one silver July futures contract at $75 or better good for the day." It may be filled at $75, or you may get it at a better price like $74.50 or $74. But it won't be filled at a price above your specified price. Limit orders are good to use during weak or quiet markets because it will be easier to obtain your price. A limit order can be a day order or a GTC order.

Stop orders: Buy and sell stops

A stop order is an order that turns into a market order the moment the market price of that futures contract hits a specified price. More accurately, stop orders can be buy stop orders or sell stop orders:

>> The buy stop is placed above the market price and becomes a market order when the futures contract trades at or above the specified stop price.

>> The sell stop is placed below the market price and becomes a market order when the futures contract trades at or below the specified stop price.

Cancellation orders (CXL orders)

Also called a straight cancel order, this order instructs the broker to cancel an order previously entered. That was simple!

Cancel former orders (CFO orders)

This order basically does the work of two orders. It cancels a prior open order and then replaces it with a new order.

Market on close orders (MOC orders)

This order instructs the broker to fill the order during the closing of market trading (during the last 30 seconds). The order must be filled at a price that is within the closing range. Whew! I wouldn't want to be a broker missing this order by seven seconds with a temperamental client.

Opening-only orders

This order gets implemented during the opening of trading that day. As with the MOC order, the order is transacted within a range of prices as the market opens.

One cancels the other order (OCO order)

This is technically two orders entered simultaneously but with a condition. The condition is that if one order is filled, then it automatically cancels the other order. Order one may be the desired order to be filled, but if market conditions make it impossible to fill, then order two would be filled. The filling of either order means that the other order isn't filled. Say that fast three times. Made ya try! Well, this order is akin to "If it's sunny today, we're going to the monster truck rally and going to get rowdy, but if it's cloudy, we'll stay home and play Parcheesi."

Even more orders

For the sake of completeness, I list other orders here. Speak to your broker about their applicability to you and your account:

>> Market-if-touched orders (MIT order)

>> Fill-or-kill orders (FOK orders)

>> Disregard tape orders (DRT orders)

>> Wire orders

Most brokers list the various orders that they can transact with complete descriptions (or a glossary) and examples in their literature or on their website.

Considering managed futures accounts

Managed futures accounts have been around since the late 1970s. A managed futures account is a futures account that's managed by a professional money manager registered with the CFTC and officially called a commodity trading advisor (CTA).

The CTA is a regulated professional who meets the educational requirements of the National Futures Association (NFA), a self-regulatory industry watchdog organization. (It operates similarly to the National Association of Securities Dealers [NASD].) Most CTAs use a proprietary trading system or some other formal method through which they make their trading decisions. CTAs could go long or short on futures contracts.

A managed futures account has the following advantages:

>> Diversification: For investors with money in stocks and bonds, commodities add a new dimension to their portfolio.

>> Professional management: You don't have to choose the individual futures to include; the CTA makes the day-to-day decisions.

>> Protection against political crises and natural disasters.

>> A hedge against inflation (such as rising food and energy costs).

An important aspect of commodities is that they do perform quite differently from stocks and bonds, so they add value to your overall portfolio. Many studies over the past quarter century have shown that commodities as a general investing class have performed very well during periods of political and economic stress. Commodities performed very well during the economic and political turmoil of the late 1970s and again during the 2000–2010 decade (in the wake of 9/11), hurricanes, and rising inflation. For 2020–2022, rising inflation will bode well for many commodities (especially gold and silver). In times such as those, diversified managed accounts tended to perform very well.

If you're in (or considering getting into) a managed account, ask the CTA about the approaches used to maximize profit and minimize risk. Here are the most common approaches used by CTAs:

>> **Going long:** Making a bet that something will go up in price.

>> **Going short:** Making a bet that something will go down in price.

>> **Spreads:** A hedging approach where both a long and short position are held. More about spreads is in Chapter 13.

You don't have to blindly accept anything the CTA says. You can review its track record and methodology:

>> **Drawdowns:** This is important information regarding the CTA's track record in the event that there was a decline in the equity (or account value) of a managed account. A drawdown represents the maximum downward move of the account value from the peak to the trough or valley. It's like a worst-case scenario taken from the CTA's recent activity. It's not meant to make you think that the same dip in account value is going to happen to you, but it is meant to indicate that losses can happen. It can also indicate how long losses can be recouped as the market rebounds. Past performance is included in the disclosure documents as required by the NFA.

The disclosure documents also indicate how the performance did over an extended period of time and show annualized percentage gains and losses to make it easy for prospective clients to compare with other CTAs and with acceptable market averages.

>> **Dispersion:** Dispersion is the distance of CTAs' monthly and annual performance using a mean or average level, which is a common way to evaluate how well they've done.

>> **Fees and account minimums:** A managed account by a CTA isn't like a mutual fund or hedge fund. The client has the ability to review the account and see what trades are made. CTAs don't make money from commissions because that would be a conflict of interest. The account's trades are cleared through an FCM (covered earlier in this chapter). CTAs typically make money as a percentage of the account's performance. Minimum account sizes can vary, but they've been as low as $25,000, although most CTAs require $50,000 or more.

TIP

Managed futures accounts aren't for everyone. Small investors are better off looking elsewhere (such as the stock market). But for those with large portfolios who want commodities in the mix, managed accounts are a viable choice. They must be doing something right; managed futures have more than $150 billion under their guidance. As inflation heats up and more of the world's population needs more of the basics of life, commodities will continue to be an attractive alternative. To find out more about CTAs, head to the NFA's website at www.nfa.futures.org.

IN THIS CHAPTER

» **Understanding taxable activity**

» **Computing gains and losses**

» **Checking out tax-deductible activity**

» **Being aware of special tax rules for precious metals**

» **Staying in the loop with tax resources**

» **Getting physical gold and silver into your retirement account**

Chapter **17**
Tax and Retirement Considerations

Complicated. Expensive. Annoying. Unfair. Of course, taxes have their negative side, too. This is life, and we deal with it. And look, if you're paying taxes, that means you're making money, so there is a bright side. The other side of tax obligations is, of course, tax benefits. In this chapter, I explore both as they apply to the world of precious metals and related investments.

REMEMBER

Keep in mind that tax laws change quickly, too quickly. If this chapter is to be relevant and accurate (as relevant and as accurate as can be given relentlessly changing tax laws), then it will be necessary not to get too specific. So you should check and double-check with your tax advisor.

Assessing Taxable Activity in Different Accounts

First things first. Before I discuss any tax liability from any investment transactions, you first need to find out whether there's any liability, to begin with. Keep in mind that your investment and speculative activity will generally take place in one of two types of accounts: a regular account with regular activity and a tax-sheltered account, such as an individual retirement account (IRA) or other retirement account (such as a 401[k] plan). I cover both of these accounts in the sections that follow.

REMEMBER

As a U.S. citizen, you report your annual taxes using Form 1040. Investment income, such as dividends and interest, are reported on Schedule B. Capital gains and losses (covered later in this chapter) are reported on Schedule D. Deductible investment expenses (also covered later in this chapter) are taken on Schedule A. These schedules cover most of the reporting that most individuals are required to do. As always, check with your tax advisor if you have other transactions and issues in your particular situation.

REMEMBER

You should be aware of whom you're paying tax to. In this chapter, although the major concern is paying your federal taxes, you'll probably also have to deal with state and local taxes. Again, check with your tax advisor if you have questions on handling these specific taxes.

Regular investment accounts

The regular investment account is one almost everyone has. There are no special rules except to pay tax on the following transactions:

>> **Dividends:** Dividends are payouts by a company to its shareholders. In a regular account, dividends are taxable.

>> **Interest:** Interest is paid by debtors to creditors. You can receive interest from holding bank accounts, corporate bonds, and U.S. Treasury securities (such as treasury bills and savings bonds). Municipal bonds are generally tax-free, but find out about your own state's tax laws.

>> **Capital gains:** A capital gain is any gain you generate when you sell a security or asset. For example, if you bought something for $10 and you sell it for $14, then your taxable capital gain is $4. Note that for regular investors, you pay the capital gains tax on gains that are realized.

Those are the basic taxable transactions you need to deal with. If your regular account is with a stock brokerage firm, it will provide you with a year-end 1099 form, and you should keep all statements. In addition, brokerage firms usually let their customers download trading data from their websites, which makes it easy to calculate gains and losses.

Table 17-1 shows you the investment vehicles of gold and silver assets covered in this book and the potential gains you may have. This table gives you a snapshot of what to watch out for and what could potentially be taxable with precious metals. Check the special rules for gold and silver collectibles later in this chapter.

TABLE 17-1 **Precious Metals Assets and Gains**

Asset	Typical Types of Gains*	Found in Chapter	Comments
Junior mining stocks	Capital gains	3	The broker sends a 1099
Major mining stocks	Capital gains and maybe some dividends	7	The broker sends a 1099
Mutual funds	Capital gains and maybe dividends and interest	8	The fund will send you a 1099
Physical bullion exchange-traded funds (ETFs)	Capital gains and maybe some dividends	8	Taxed as collectible**
All other gold- and silver-related ETFs	Capital gains and maybe some dividends	8, 11	The broker sends a 1099
Bullion coins and bars	Capital gains	9	Taxed as collectible**
Numismatic coins	Capital gains	10	Taxed as collectible**
Futures	Capital gains	12	The broker sends a 1099
Options on stocks and ETFs	Capital gains	13	The broker sends a 1099
Options on futures	Capital gains	13	The broker sends a 1099

*In this table, I mention only taxable gains (such as capital gains). Of course, there are capital losses, and they are generally deductible. For more information, see the section on capital gains and losses later in this chapter.

**Some types of precious metals investments are classified as "collectibles" and, therefore, get different tax treatment (see the later section "Surveying Special Tax Considerations"). The treatment is actually odd and unfair, but it's something to be aware of when the time comes to sell your precious metals investments.

Note: Gold and silver bullion coins approved and designated for IRAs are not considered collectible for tax purposes. Because tax laws change from time to time, consult with your tax advisor.

One of the ways around the current taxation of your gains in a regular investment account is to be aware of the benefits in the second basic type of account: the individual retirement account. Read on.

Individual retirement accounts

Although there are different types of retirement accounts, I'll just comment about precious metals–related investments (such as stocks, ETFs, and mutual funds) inside a typical individual retirement account (IRA). The most common types are Roth IRAs and traditional IRAs. In addition, many firms allow employees (past or present) to roll over the proceeds from a 401(k) plan to an IRA (called a "rollover IRA," of course!). For simplicity, I just refer to each of these various accounts as an IRA.

REMEMBER

The biggest benefit of the IRA is that any gains generated in the account are shielded from current taxes. Except for physical bullion, most forms of precious metals investments (especially paper ones such as stocks and ETFs) can be inside an IRA. Inside the IRA, any dividends and interest can be reinvested and are sheltered from current taxes. A major criteria in the IRA is that you don't withdraw any money until retirement (you can start in the tax year when you turn 59½ years old), although there are some allowable exceptions.

Because capital gains are the primary reason for getting into precious metals, buying and selling for gain can take place inside the IRA with no tax consequence. You won't have to worry about taxes until you start removing money from the account.

TIP

By the way, if you want to find a way to place gold and silver bullion into an IRA, get more details later in this chapter. An IRA is also a way to remove the pesky unfair tax treatment of gold and silver bullion as collectibles.

Understanding Capital Gains and Losses

The most common way to profit from precious metals–related investments is through capital gains (see the earlier section "Regular investment accounts"). The most basic point about capital gains is that they're taxable (an exception regarding retirement accounts is discussed earlier in this chapter), and the tax rate is different based on how long you hold the asset. Capital losses are generally tax-deductible.

To keep it straight, there are two basic time frames for capital gains tax rates. There are short-term gains (one year or less) and long-term gains (more than one year):

» Short-term capital gains are taxed as ordinary income, which is the same basic tax rate as income that you earn at your job or business. Ordinary income tax rates are considered the highest individual taxes, and because the United States has a progressive tax system, the more income you earn, the higher the taxes you pay. Higher taxes refers to paying more in taxes as well as higher tax rates (as in, you've made more money that bumps you into a higher tax bracket). So if you're not careful, short-term capital gains taxes end up being a double whammy. Check with your tax advisor if you have questions.

» Long-term capital gains are taxed at a lower, more favorable rate. Long-term means that you held an asset or security for more than a year. For 2020, the highest long-term capital gains tax rate is capped at 20 percent.

Technically, a capital gains loss isn't deductible in the same sense as when you pay a tax-deductible expense. A loss is deductible in the sense that you can apply it (offset it) against other income. In other words, if you have income from your job of $30,000 and you have a loss from the sale of stock of $2,000, then your gross income for federal tax purposes would be $28,000.

Generally, any capital losses you have must first offset capital gains before they can be used against other income on your Form 1040 individual tax return. After that, you can use up to a maximum of only $3,000 of capital losses per tax return per year. Any amount above that is treated as a "carry-forward" loss that can be taken in future years.

TIP

For more information about gains and losses, check out IRS Publication 544, "Sales and Other Dispositions of Assets," at www.irs.gov/pub/irs-pdf/p544.pdf.

Looking at Tax-Deductible Activity

After touching on the ugly side of taxes (paying them), you can then see the beauty of reducing their payment (tax deductions). No need to go nuts here and list all the possible deductions, but there are many.

As a general rule, the IRS allows deductibility of investment expenses as long as they're ordinary and necessary expenses paid or incurred to either produce or collect income or manage property held for producing income. The expenses must be directly related to the income or income-producing property, and the income must be taxable to you. For most investors, the following deductions generally fit that criteria and can be reported on Schedule A:

- » Attorney or accounting fees
- » Investment counsel and advice (which includes advisory services)
- » Fees to collect income
- » Safe deposit box rental fees
- » Investment interest

By the way, commissions you pay when you're buying and selling securities aren't deducted directly. Instead, they become part of the cost basis of the sale. For example, if you buy a security for $3,000 and the commission is $20, the actual cost basis (when you figure your gain/loss at the sale later on) is $3,020. If you sold that same security later on and sold it for $4,000 (with another commission of $20), then the sale amount would be $3,980. The gain would then be $960 ($3,980 sale amount less the cost of $3,020).

TIP

Keep in mind that the IRS disallows tax deductibility of some items such as travel expenses to a stockholders' meeting or the cost of an investment-related seminar. IRS Publication 550, "Investing Income and Expenses (Including Capital Gains and Losses)" goes into greater detail; visit www.irs.gov/pub/irs-pdf/p550.pdf.

Surveying Special Tax Considerations

For precious metals, you'll probably bump into some tax concerns that are especially related to your pursuits. In the sections that follow, I describe a couple of these concerns that you should consider.

Gold and silver as collectibles

Gold and silver are considered capital assets (unless you're a dealer, in which case they're effectively merchandise, and the income is ordinary business income). So far, so good. However, they're considered in the same class as collectibles such as stamps or art. Why does this matter?

Collectibles are taxed at the maximum 28 percent federal rate, even if you hold them for more than a year. The rule applies to both bullion (see Chapter 9) and numismatic coins and bars (see Chapter 10). If you hold the physical metal for less than a year, then the gain would be taxed as ordinary income up to the maximum federal rate. That is astonishing and disappointing, but that is the law. This rule also applies to bullion-specific ETFs such as Gold (symbol: GLD) and Silver (symbol: SLV) ETFs and other ETFs that specifically hold bullion gold and silver. (Find out more about ETFs in Chapter 8.)

REMEMBER

The tax rates hit you when the gains are realized. If you hold these properties and they have appreciated, there's no tax consequence until the actual sale.

Fortunately, the rule generally doesn't affect other precious metals such as mining stocks (see Chapter 7), options (see Chapter 13), futures (see Chapter 12), and metals-related mutual funds (see Chapter 8). Hopefully, future tax laws will correct this unfairness.

Tax rules for traders

If you're the occasional trader or speculator, the odds are that the regular tax rules would apply (not that the regular rules are so good to begin with, but read on). But what if you're an active trader?

If you're actively trading futures contracts or options on futures contracts, check with your tax advisor about how to proceed. You may qualify as a professional trader conducting a business. It could mean more tax deductions for you (hey, sounds good), but your trading then takes on a different characteristic. It's now a business activity, and the trading you do gets treated much differently. Welcome to the world of mark-to-market accounting.

WARNING

Mark-to-market (MTM) is an accounting procedure by which assets are *marked,* or recorded, at their current market value, which may be higher or lower than their purchase price or book value. Part of the benefit of MTM accounting is that you don't have the same tax constraints as investors. Investors, for example, have a capital loss limit of $3,000 but not with MTM because they're considered a trader doing business and not an investor doing personal transactions. MTM accounting can be complicated, and you definitely need professional tax assistance with it.

Tax Resources to Keep You Up-to-Date

Yeah . . . it's all pretty heady stuff. You may end up needing to make a fortune with your precious metals just to have the money to pay your taxes. Fortunately, it's not that bad. And besides, there are countries with steeper tax rates (like Canada and France), so you may want to consider moving to lower-tax places (such as Ireland and the Ukraine). But you can do just fine here in the good ol' USA by doing a little homework. The old adage fits: The more you know about taxes, the more money you end up keeping. Keep informed and hopefully keep more money by checking out the resources I discuss in the next sections.

The IRS (of course!)

What better source on taxes than the IRS itself? You pay them the big bucks, so you may as well get the free assistance you paid for. You can get the following publications from the IRS either by calling 1-800-TAX-FORM (800-829-3676) or by downloading them at www.irs.gov. The following publications go hand in hand with investing in precious metals:

>> **Publication 17, "Your Federal Income Tax":** If you file Form 1040 (who doesn't?), then this extensive guide will be very helpful. See www.irs.gov/pub/irs-pdf/p17.pdf.

>> **Publication 550, "Investment Income and Expenses (Including Capital Gains and Losses)":** This publication is tied directly to this chapter, so cozy up with it tonight. Visit www.irs.gov/pub/irs-pdf/p550.pdf.

>> **Publications 590-A, "Contributions to Individual Retirement Arrangements (IRAs)" and 590-B, "Distributions from Individual Retirement Arrangements (IRAs)":** This publication, split into two parts, covers IRAs in depth and is worth a peek. Check out www.irs.gov/pub/irs-pdf/p590a.pdf and www.irs.gov/pub/irs-pdf/p590b.pdf.

>> **Publication 544, "Sales and Other Dispositions of Assets":** This publication goes into greater detail about capital gains and losses (investments and otherwise). See www.irs.gov/pub/irs-pdf/p544.pdf.

TIP

If you have any tax questions and need to speak with someone, call the IRS during business hours at 1-800-TAX-1040 (800-829-1040). They usually have extended hours during the tax season.

Helpful tax websites

You can check out the following websites for additional tax help:

>> TaxMama (www.taxmama.com)

>> National Association of Enrolled Agents (www.naea.org)

>> Fairmark.com (www.fairmark.com)

>> GreenTraderTax (www.greentradertax.com)

>> A list of top tax blogs can be found at https://blog.feedspot.com/tax_blogs/

An ounce of prevention . . .

Perhaps the best recommendation I can give you is the last thing I want to express. Plan your future taxes. You heard that right. The best way to minimize the tax bite is to start tax planning before the year is up. Most taxpayers start figuring out their taxes after the tax year is done. In other words, millions of taxpayers try to figure out how to lower their tax bills (or increase their tax refunds) for the tax year 2020 in the year 2021. With 2020 over with, you can't change a darn thing — you can't change history! You can report only what happened and spend time finding deductions and credits for what you already did. Too late!

The best way to prepare your taxes (for, say, 2021) is to start long before 2021 ends. Keep in mind that when you do your taxable transactions, the timing is within your power. You can control when you transact, which means you have the power to defer, and you have the power to accelerate transactions (like paying tax-deductible expenses). In the world of taxes, timing means a lot. Selling securities is a perfect example: If you sold your losing positions in December and sold your winning positions the following month (in January, which is part of the subsequent tax year), you defer taxes on your winning positions until the next tax year. Keep good records of your transactions and have a tax planning session with your tax professional long before the tax year ends. That way you'll have a profitable jump on your taxes when you can do something about them.

To help you better anticipate your taxes in the year you are currently in, go to www.irs.gov and get a copy of Form 1040-ES (Estimated Tax for Individuals). It gives you the upcoming year's new amounts for tax rates and the like.

Adding Physical Precious Metals to an IRA

If you think that paper assets (stocks, bonds, mutual funds, and so on) are the only things that can sit inside an IRA (Roth or traditional), think again. Actual physical bullion assets (gold, silver, and/or platinum) can now be part of your retirement strategies under the tax-advantaged umbrella of your IRA. You get the scoop on what's allowed and how to add it in the following sections.

Precious metals allowed for IRAs

The following coins are examples of the types of coins that are allowed to be placed in an IRA:

>> American gold, silver, and platinum Eagle Bullion Coins.

>> Canadian gold, silver, and platinum Maple Leaf Bullion Coins.

>> Gold, silver, platinum, and palladium bars and rounds manufactured by a NYMEX- or COMEX-approved refiner/assayer and meeting minimum fineness requirements. Can be 1,000 oz or 1,000 oz bullion bars.

>> Other coins that *specifically* meet the IRS requirements for inclusion.

Here are some types of precious metals investments that are *not* allowed to be placed in an IRA:

>> Krugerrands (gold bullion coins minted by South Africa)

>> Old U.S. Gold numismatic or collectible coins

>> U.S. 90 percent silver coins (1964 and before)

The IRS laws covering precious metals IRAs can change from time to time, so check on the latest information with the tax resources listed earlier in this chapter.

For a detailed post on taxation and precious metals investments (both in and out of an IRA), check out https://bullionexchanges.com/learn/taxation-precious-metals-irs-reporting.

Companies where you can establish an account

Get the full details through organizations that have met IRS regulations that govern retirement accounts. As of June 2020, the following organizations have been approved for precious metals IRAs:

» Lear Capital (www.learcapital.com)

» Regal Assets (www.regalassetsbullion.com)

» Patriot Gold Group (www.patriotgoldgroup.com/)

» Rosland Capital (www.roslandcapital.com)

» Goldco (www.goldcopreciousmetals.com)

» Cornerstone Bullion (www.cornerstonebullion.com)

» Advantage Gold IRA (www.advantagegoldira.com)

» American Bullion (www.americanbulliononline.com)

» Gold IRA (www.goldira.com)

» Noble Gold IRA (www.noblegoldira.com)

The first organization you should contact is the bullion/coin dealer where you plan to buy your gold and silver to find out which of the preceding companies it works with. When you know that, contact them directly and find out about the paperwork and fees involved.

The actual ordering of the approved coins and bars will occur through the dealers, and they'll work with the IRA firms for logistics such as where the bullion is to be shipped for approved storage. The approved storage is an important part of the arrangement because, without it, you couldn't have the precious metals IRA at all.

REMEMBER

When setting up a precious metals IRA, you'll actually deal with three separate entities:

» The bullion dealer that sells the physical metal

» The third-party administrator (TPA) for documentation purposes

» The bullion vault where the physical metal is stored

TIP

Doing your homework about precious metals IRAs is my advice (and everyone's advice). Find out about fees and related costs. Here are a few sites that provide consumer research for this type of account:

>> Gold IRA Guide (www.goldiraguide.com) has some great tips, guidance, and a batch of questions for you (and the company) to get answers on.

>> Retirement Living's gold IRA reviews (www.retirementliving.com/best-gold-ira-accounts)

>> See that earlier precious metals IRA company list? All of them have consumer tips about precious metals IRAs in general and about how their *competitors* aren't doing a good job. Read at least three to four of their guides to narrow your choices.

5

The Part of Tens

Check out ten reasons to have gold and silver as investment assets.

Discover ten ways you can add gold and silver to your portfolio.

Understand ten (or so) rules for metals traders. I wish I had these important points when I started out!

Chapter **18**

Ten Reasons to Have Gold and Silver

I f after reading so many chapters on the greatness and goodness of gold and silver in this, the age of uncertainty, you still aren't sure about adding some gold and silver positions in your portfolio, then I may as well take another crack and give you ten high-powered reasons you should add them soon.

Gold and silver have endured all the tumult and chaos of history. They have survived humanity itself. The smartest money people throughout history always had them. Sometimes more, sometimes less, but the wealthy possessed them. Here are ten reasons you should possess them today.

REMEMBER

One benefit to mention is counterparty risk, which is a crucial benefit of gold and silver, but one that is rarely mentioned. It's a risk that maybe only one out of ten financial pros mention or think of. It is so important that I devote Chapter 2 to it so you can understand it more fully than a single entry in this chapter.

Gold and Silver Provide Diversification

Virtually every financial advisor and financial planner recite the word "diversification" in their sleep and in almost every meeting with their clients. Gold and silver belong in a diversified portfolio. But I am one of the few financial planners (I am a certified financial planner or CFP) who regularly mentions gold and silver to my clients and my students (and now to you, my reader).

That's right. Most financial professionals exclude gold and silver as they discuss diversification. Their diversification is principally among paper assets (such as stocks, bonds, exchange-traded funds, and mutual funds), and the only hard assets they typically include are real estate and personal property (cars, collectibles, and so on).

Of course, this isn't true all the time. I'm sure that at the height of major economic crises, a plurality of financial professionals do mention gold and silver, but all things being equal, they usually leave them out. I don't always emphasize gold and silver, and good and bad times do change often, so of course, your portfolio should adapt. But no matter how good or bad times get, possessing some gold and silver will always make sense to some degree.

REMEMBER

When times are bad, gold and silver excel as players in your portfolio. But when times are good, gold and silver make sense as hedges or as a form of insurance because bad times can return in sometimes unexpected ways. Using these eternal metals as a form of insurance (at a minimum) is a powerful reason to keep some because paper assets can become problematic before you know it. Why? Check out the next section.

Gold and Silver Allow for Privacy

In this day and age, when privacy is at risk given how easy it can be to get details in public records or splattered on the internet, your assets and other holdings are a public display of your potential wealth. There are plenty of folks out there that you should be wary of; whether it is thieves or snoopy relatives, there are plenty of reasons to guard your privacy. This is where gold and silver can shine.

If your neighbor lived in a mansion and you lived in a very modest home, you could easily and privately store a fortune's worth of gold, for example, in a drawer, and no one would be wise to you. The world at large doesn't easily detect the purchase of gold and silver, and when the day comes to sell them, you would only need to report the gains on your taxes. But so many nosy folks would have difficulty finding out about your shiny stash of precious metals.

Gold and Silver Are Portable Wealth

If you need to leave your home or your area — or your country — you can take gold and silver with you. Part of the value and appeal of having physical, precious metal in your hand is that you can take it with you. It's portable wealth, and the wealthy throughout history knew it full well.

When a country changes political parties or entire political systems (either through votes or violent means), it means that a segment of the populace has a reason to flee. Heck, in some parts of the world, political regimes seem to change with the seasons. A person's ability to be mobile was part of survival. In today's unstable world, mobility becomes a plus again. You can carry thousands of dollars of value with a few gold coins very easily. Of course, silver is valuable, but a sizable amount is very heavy and not as portable. But both can come in handy because gold can pay for large transactions, and silver can pay for the smaller ones.

Now another person can chime in with, "Paul, there are many things that are portable wealth — copper is a great example!" But copper is about $3 a pound as I write this chapter. Even $100 worth of copper is just too heavy and unwieldy to even carry across the street, never mind another part of the country or the world.

WARNING

Yet another person will say, "Physical cash is very portable, and you can easily put a debit card or a checkbook in your pocket." Hopefully, folks will have both cash and precious metals, but remember another drawback of both physical and digital cash. Physical cash is portable, but it does deteriorate physically over time, and its value can decline over time due to inflation. Digital cash is great in the age of internet technology, but what happens during a blackout? Even in dark times, you have metal in hand!

Gold and Silver Ease Retirement Concerns

For 2020–2030, retirement concerns will reach important levels. Due to the dangerous gyrations of markets and underfunding due to shortfalls in payroll taxes coupled with rising pension and retiree costs, millions of retirees will face difficulty. These difficulties stretch from corporate and municipal funding shortfalls to Social Security shortfalls.

Given that, the government (both the federal and also the state and local authorities) open the spigots of spending to address this deficit. Ultimately, this will cause inflationary pressures and other unforeseen problems. What should retirees do given this dilemma? Buy gold? Gold will retain its value and help boost wealth when the retirement funding crisis hits. Flip to Chapter 17 for more information on how gold and silver can play a role in retirement.

Gold Is a Safe Haven Asset

This reason is more attached to gold than to silver. Gold is, by and large, a monetary metal and a "store of value." It has earned from the mainstream financial media world the well-earned reputation as a "safe haven" asset, meaning that when storm clouds are pelting the economy and the financial landscape, nimble investors flee to gold for a measure of safety that often eludes many other conventional assets (such as stocks and bonds).

Note: Silver has many of the features of gold, but it doesn't tend to share "safe haven asset" status due to its dual nature as both a monetary metal and an industrial commodity.

As I wrote earlier this year in the sixth edition of *Stock Investing For Dummies*, in a chapter titled "Ten Investing Pitfalls and Challenges for 2020–2030," you see multiple major risks dotting the global landscape and facing all of us in one way or another.

Gold's strength stands up very well to most of those potential systemic risks. Gold has been a safe haven asset since humanity first started using it thousands of years ago. It survived numerous and endless wars, chaos, and economic crises, and its unique nature will most likely carry it through the next batch of worries. Of course, if we're talking about humongous meteors coming our way or if our planet careens toward the sun . . . uh, don't sweat the economy.

The Value of Gold and Silver Is Never Zero

Well, before humanity came along, I'm sure gold or silver didn't seem to be better than any other rock, but as soon as civilization got started and people needed to barter and trade, folks tried all sorts of materials for barter, such as rice or beans. But because of gold's unique properties that made it ideal as money, it quickly gained acceptance across many cultures and societies. This acceptance only strengthened over time. Why?

Yes, humanity invented paper currencies, but paper currencies were subject to the political whims of government corruption time and time again. When you give politicians and central bank bureaucrats the power to create "money" out of thin air, how soon do you think abuse and greed set in and money is over created?

WARNING

This "flaw" in man-made paper currencies leads to overproduction of currencies and the inevitable collapse of the currency itself. This is why the most common collapse in human history has been a currency collapse. Literally thousands of currencies have collapsed since (and during!) ancient times. I can confidently predict that most (all?) of today's currencies will collapse, especially given historic and massive problems tied to the crises unleashed during the COVID-19 pandemic of 2020 and the fallout from it.

But as sure as night follows day, gold will outlive today's currencies. When a currency collapses, it reaches the value of *zero*. However, gold (and silver, too) will most likely always have value, so the attraction and attachment to gold will continue. Got gold?

Gold Retains Its Value in Bear Markets

When stocks get hit hard and their prices decline substantially (20 percent or more), then it's called a bear market. You'll find as you analyze past bear markets that gold (more so than silver) tends to be strong, generally does well, and retains its value during this type of economic and market condition. Bear markets also tend to be times that are referred to as *deflationary*, where prices of consumer goods and services are generally flat or declining. In these moments, currencies tend to hold their value.

But the record is clear that gold holds its value very well. Gold actually did well during high-profile deflationary periods such as the Great Depression during the 1930s and in the aftermath of the 2008 financial crisis.

Gold and Silver Have Enduring Demand

As the world population keeps growing, demand for many things will keep growing. Given that, gold and silver will keep growing as demand for both (for different reasons) keeps growing.

When the world population surpassed 7 billion (circa 2010, give or take a month), gold was in the general range of $1,000 to $1,200. As the world population is near or at 8 billion people (give or take a city block), gold is around $2,000. Silver had an average price around $15 (or so) back then, and in the summer of 2020, silver was around $27 per ounce.

The point is simple: More people on the globe means more overall economic demand. Couple this dynamic with the fact that currency production (dollar, euro, yen) is growing even faster than the population means an environment conducive to rising gold and silver prices.

Gold and Silver Make Good Inflation Hedges

When most people think of inflation, they think that it means that the general prices of goods and services have gone up. Actually, when the price of goods and services go up, that isn't a problem of inflation; it's a *symptom*. Yes, it may be called "price" inflation, but it's a symptom of "currency" inflation, and that is the *problem*. The prices of goods and services don't just go up for no reason as if the weather changed that day. Those price increases are caused by *something*.

REMEMBER

Goods and services go up for two basic reasons: "supply and demand" and over-production of the currency that filters down to consumer markets. Price inflation is the condition where "too many dollars" are chasing a finite basket of goods and services. So really true inflation isn't about goods and services being more expensive; it's about the currency being too plentiful and too cheap!

Gold and silver do well in an inflationary environment because precious metals aren't subject to being overproduced in a nanosecond the way currencies are quickly overproduced. The Federal Reserve (the central bank of the United States), for example, was able to create trillions of dollars during the global COVID-19 pandemic of 2020 with a few mouse clicks.

Gold and silver can see their supply increase only through the hard and slow task of mining. New gold and new silver are added to aboveground supplies at the annual rate of only 2 percent (give or take a hundredth of a percent). So when dollars (or yen or euros or whatever currency) are overproduced, gold is overproduced at a much (and I mean *much*) lower rate. A currency (to retain value) has, by dint of creation, to be scarce to keep its value. Given this, gold and silver tend to be fantastic inflation hedges and very important in a portfolio when the risk of inflation grows. As I write this, the risk of inflation is indeed growing.

Gold Guards against Financial Bubbles

As I write this in the summer of 2020, there are bubbles everywhere, waiting to pop — and collapse. In the spring of 2020, to reinflate the economy, the U.S. Federal Reserve pumped trillions into both the economy and the financial system. This was in response to the desperate need for resuscitation after the government lockdown during the COVID-19 pandemic reached virtually every corner of the economy.

The Federal Reserve, in an unprecedented and far-reaching effort, was producing currency in an unbridled fashion, attempting to rescue as many asset classes as possible. The newly minted digital currency went to stocks, mortgages, junk bonds, and many other venues on the financial landscape.

The net effect is reinflated financial bubbles greater than at any time in modern history. The problem with bubbles is that they don't keep going up endlessly. Factors such as demand and supply (which are indeed evident in both the economy and in financial markets) do, in fact, puncture bubbles, which ultimately collapse, ending in tremendous and pervasive financial pain for those on the losing end of failing and falling investments.

But as you know by now, gold, especially physical gold, is virtually impossible to inflate. It takes tremendous effort to extract even a single ounce of the shiny metal from the ground.

Keep in mind that gold is a better guard against bubble possibilities than silver. I go into greater detail about gold in Chapter 5 and silver in Chapter 6.

Chapter **19**

Ten Ways to Add Gold and Silver to Your Portfolio

I recall seeing the movie *My Cousin Vinny,* and in a scene in a diner, they read the menu for breakfast, and the choice was, uh, "breakfast." Very funny . . . unless you're looking for greater choices, right?

It was not that long ago when choosing gold (and/or silver) for your portfolio was a similar dead-end singular choice. To look around and find out that the choice was, uh, "gold" was too stifling and limited. But it's different today. Here we are in the modern age, the "golden age," with choices on a "silver platter." The choices for gold and silver investors and speculators today are truly varied (fabulous dahling!). No one should say, "I don't know how to get it into my situation" or "but I have a 401(k) plan so forget about precious metals!"

By the way, in this chapter, you'll see some gold- and silver-related considerations for your portfolio that are new and different. I cite chapters for reference, but be sure also to check out the resources in Appendix A. Let's go!

Major Gold and Silver Stocks

For standard, relatively conservative investors, you can add some major gold and silver mining stocks that are available on the New York Stock Exchange (NYSE). I think a few quality shares in your regular brokerage account or your retirement account are a good consideration, especially when you're in the midst of an extended bull market (as I believe we are during 2020–2022 or longer).

REMEMBER

Make sure the stock is profitable with good fundamentals and a solid portfolio of mines with provable reserves (I include a listing of top mining stocks in Appendix B). Top that off with good reviews from industry analysts (many are listed in Appendix A), and you're good to go! Flip to Chapter 7 for an introduction to stocks.

Junior Gold and Silver Stocks

For those who are seeking more aggressive growth potential in your stock portfolio, junior mining stocks are good speculative choices. They tend to be low-priced stocks, so buying a few hundred shares isn't that expensive. If the share price is less than $10 per share (and often less than $5 a share), then the risk from a financial point of view isn't that great. In other words, if you have 100 shares of a $3 stock, the worst that happens is that you may lose most or all of that $300 risk capital.

Unless you're eating hot dogs and ramen noodles every night, it's not a life-changing amount. But what if the stock does strike gold (literally!) and it's in the middle of a historic bull market? Then it could be a life-changing windfall. Imagine how many cases of hot dogs and ramen noodles you could get (all cash, of course)!

For more details, check out Chapter 7. Also, take a look at the resources in Appendix A to make some wise speculations, and maybe have lobster some night.

Mutual Funds

For those who want exposure to precious metals but don't want to keep watching it, then consider mutual funds — an investment that has been popular and in use for a very long time. There are all types of mutual funds, but for our purposes, we seek a sector (or industry) fund that specializes in precious metals.

Typically, it would have a portfolio of mining stocks. Like a mutual fund, the investment managers actively buy, sell, and hold a portfolio of various mining stocks. The managers choose the stocks using their selection criteria. Essentially, you choose the industry, and the managers of the fund choose all the individual securities. If the industry is doing well, then your mutual fund will do well, too.

In the late 1970s, for example, the most prominent gold mining mutual at the time earned more than 1,000 percent gain during that gold bull market that lasted from 1976 to January 1980 (when gold and silver had their highs), but the fund was among the biggest losers in the subsequent years. So the lesson is clear: Choose your sector fund when that particular sector is doing well — in a bull market!

For 2020, gold- and silver-related mutual funds were among the big gainers. If the bull market continues in 2021 and beyond, the gains can continue, too. Find out more about mutual funds in Chapter 8.

Physical Metal ETFs

After physical bullion coins (see the following section), the next safest way to get gold and silver into your portfolio is through physical metal exchange-traded funds, or ETFs (which are covered in Chapter 8 and extensively listed in Appendix B). A physical metal ETF is the safest (all things being equal) vehicle you can add to your stock portfolio (whether it's a regular stock brokerage account or a retirement account). It's not leveraged or speculative, so it can be a conservative way to add exposure conveniently with a few mouse clicks.

Bullion Coins

It's easier than ever to buy physical gold and silver, and investors should consider some of both in their portfolio for the 2020–2025 time frame (give or take a month). Besides all the practical and financial reasons cited throughout this book, these coins are also beautiful works of art that would definitely grace your vault. Find out more about bullion coins in Chapter 9.

Numismatic Coins

Getting some quality (and I mean quality) gold and silver numismatic coins can be a great long-term investment (holding five years or longer). Long term because it takes time to appreciate enough to offset what can be a large part of the initial purchase, which is the dealer markup. Of course, this is an issue only if you plan on selling back to dealers down the road when you're ready to cash your coin(s) in.

When I say "quality," I mean that your selection is a top grade (brilliant uncirculated or Mint State 60 or better) and that the other numismatic aspects of it (coin series, scarcity, professionally certified grade, and so on) are also excellent. Numismatic coins are beautiful and can easily grow in value, especially when a bull market in precious metals is sandwiched nicely between when you bought it and when you're selling it. For more details, check out Chapter 10.

Leveraged ETFs

For those who want to speculate with gold and silver but are too skittish to get into aggressive vehicles such as futures (see Chapter 12) and don't want to settle for merely matching gold and silver's gains, leveraged ETFs are a happy medium.

Because leveraged ETFs are regularly rotating positions offering some combination of futures, options, and other derivatives right inside the portfolio, I like them because they don't have the risk of expiring, which is the primary risk with options.

TIP

A good approach (to minimize risk) is to stagger your purchases of a leveraged ETF. Perhaps buy 50 shares in the beginning and buy some more shares in a week or so to take advantage of a pullback.

Chapter 11 has the full scoop on leveraged ETFs. Appendix B also has an extensive list of leveraged ETFs in the sections on gold and silver ETFs.

Junk Silver

Junk silver is a reference to silver coins (usually dimes, quarters, and halves dated 1964 or earlier) that have been in circulation and have no collectible or numismatic value. The coins are bought essentially due to their silver content and are actually a convenient way to put silver in your physical portfolio. These coins do have currency value, and you could use them to buy goods and services — but *don't!* They are much more valuable as bullion, and their value grows as the price of silver increases.

Besides simply finding them in your change much the same way you find other coins more valuable than their mere face value (such as Lincoln wheat cents dated 1909–1958), you can actually buy a quantity with most gold and silver bullion dealers. See Appendix A for a list of dealers.

Junk silver is based on silver content and no other consideration, so do price-shop this one. Ask for price quotes from multiple dealers, including any shipping and insurance charges, for the lowest cost.

Gold and Silver Cryptocurrencies

Cryptocurrencies (such as Bitcoin) hit the general investing public's consciousness during 2017–2018, and they quickly became attractive alternatives on the financial landscape. They were "the new kids on the block," and after some rollercoaster times during 2018–2019, they seem to have found a sound footing as an alternative for those dabbling with currencies.

During 2020, there are at least five new cryptocurrencies available with a nice twist — backed by precious metals. Now, I'm not a cryptocurrency guy, as I'm more comfortable with the other vehicles I've written about in this book and my other *For Dummies* books, but if you're already comfortable with cryptocurrencies, I think that those that are backed up by gold and silver offer some strength and advantages that aren't present in the conventional cryptocurrencies.

Gold- (or silver-) backed cryptocurrencies have the dual benefit of being today's digital means of transactions while being supported by metals with a 5,000-per-year track record, so yeah, I'd take this route if I was enamored with cryptocurrencies.

My suggestion is simple. If you're seriously considering gold- or silver-backed cryptocurrencies, then read the book *Cryptocurrency Investing For Dummies* (authored by my friend Kiana Danial and published by Wiley), and take a deep dive in the resources in Appendix A for this intriguing way to participate in gold and silver.

Buying through Goldmoney and OWNx

Now, this isn't a new twist on gold and silver as if it were a stock or ETF or other vehicle; it's simply a neat way to buy, sell, and accumulate purchases in gold and silver. These are buying services, and it lets you easily set up a purchase plan to buy a set amount of gold or silver on a schedule that you choose. What's that? You want to buy $50 of silver per week or $100 of gold per month? Not difficult at all.

The transactions are done through a website account, and every week you can see how much of either (or both) metals you accumulated. If you need to sell a portion or all of your metal holdings, you can do it in a few clicks (or taps). Silver is purchased in ounce units, and the minimum for gold is 1 gram.

TIP

To find out more, go to their websites:

» Goldmoney (www.goldmoney.com)

» OWNx (www.ownx.com)

Be sure to find out about their fees and service charges and see whether they make sense for you.

Chapter **20**

Ten (Or So) Tips for Gold and Silver Speculators and Traders

As I write this book, I believe (given the research and data available to me) that we entered the greatest gold and silver bull market in my lifetime in 2020. As of early August 2020, gold is above $2,000 per ounce, and silver is about $28 per ounce. Both assets beat most asset classes handily during the first eight months of 2020. There's no reason that I can think of that both can't be at significantly higher price levels for 2021–2022.

For investors, the considerations are physical gold and silver, mining stocks, and exchange-traded funds (ETFs), and all of these have performed well so far. But how about those who want staggering, life-changing gains that can be possible in a historic bull market? Yes, I'm talking about speculators and traders. The gains can be great, and as long as you understand (with discipline) how to deal with the volatility and risk for loss, you'll be good to go.

I'll cheer you on as well, and you can accomplish some amazing wealth goals with gold and silver going forward, but I do want you to focus on some "golden rules" to enhance your chances of success. I've used the golden rules in this chapter for my clients and students over many years, and they should serve you well. Although I'm applying them to the world of gold and silver, many of these can serve as guidelines with other assets and investment vehicles in the world of speculating and trading. Go get 'em! (For an introduction to the differences among investing, trading, and speculating, head to Chapter 3.)

Focus on a Specialty

During 2020, I focused on silver, and the financial rewards have been great. I've seen speculators and traders playing many vehicles, and it tends to be "hit or miss." Even though some aspects of trading tend to be in a variety of venues (such as technical and fundamental analysis), I do subscribe to the idea of developing expertise and knowledge in a specific market or asset versus being a "jack (or jill) of all trades."

REMEMBER

In this book, the focus is obviously gold and/or silver. My focus in recent months has been silver. Focus is important because your success will be a laser, not a shotgun. Get intimately familiar with an asset, specific market, or investment vehicle. Find out "how it ticks" and what drives it both up and down. This focus is part of the foundational success leading to your financial rewards.

Do Research and More Research

Once you choose what you'll focus on (as I suggest in the previous section), get all the information you can about it. Get the data. Find out what the experts are saying in that specific category. What are the popular industry blogs reporting with news and views? What are company CEOs and fund managers saying? How about market statistics? What is going on with demand and supply? Are there market drivers or other factors that can influence price in the industry? How about other markets that affect the market you're in?

TIP

Fortunately, for gold and silver, most of the important resources are mentioned throughout this book and listed in Appendix A. You're welcome!

Be a Contrarian

Long, long ago, the billionaire J. Paul Getty was quoted as saying, "Buy when everyone else is selling and hold until everyone else is buying. That's not just a catchy slogan. It's the very essence of successful investing." My guess is that he was actually talking about trading and speculating, but I'll take it!

During gold and silver's most recent bear market (2011–2019), both metals were unloved by the general market. No one had a positive remark about either in the mainstream financial media. But the contrarian "looks under the hood" and sees whether the ingredients are there for the next bull market. After all, bull markets start in moments of pessimism and despair. If no one wants this asset or vehicle, that means that prices are very low. It means that demand and supply favor the discerning buyer.

The same point is true when everyone loves a specific asset or vehicle. If everyone wants it, then how much more upside is there really? The contrarian understands that bear markets start at the height of jubilation and optimism. Markets get overbought and conditions then favor the discerning seller.

As I write this, gold and silver are in the early stages of a major bull market. As it gets mature and even your neighbor or the Uber driver starts giving you advice on gold and silver, start planning your exit!

Limit Your Grubstake

Before you get enamored and plan on betting the farm on gold or silver or whatever is being loved in the media, become disciplined about how much you plan on using for your speculative and trading pursuits. Very, very often I have seen how people got burned when they bet too much of their money on a jubilant choice.

REMEMBER

Limit how much you'll deploy, and keep in mind that the bulk of your financial assets should be in quality investments, cash (savings accounts), hard assets (your residence), and strategies that give you proven gains, such as paying off debt.

Stagger Your Entry

A common approach (unfortunately) is that as soon as someone opens his account for the purpose of speculating/trading, he deploys the full amount of the funds immediately. If he started with, say, $10,000 on Monday morning, the entire amount has been used for positions by that afternoon. Then, when opportunities arise the next day or later that week, he has no funds to use.

Keep in mind that you and I can't foresee every short-term twist and turn. It has happened very often to me, even when I invested conservatively, that what I bought went down right after I acquired it.

A good approach to consider is to limit your entry point to, say, only 25 percent of your tradable funds. Wait a week or two, and deploy the next 25 percent if you see a buying opportunity. Again, wait a week or two, and deploy another 25 percent. Keep the remaining 25 percent of your funds for buying opportunities that arise.

Use the Right Speculative Vehicles

The "how" in speculating and trading can be just as important as the "what." This is especially important for the beginner and intermediate traders and speculators.

For example, you may all set to speculate with futures (the "what"), but if you don't know how dangerous they can be, then I suggest call and put options on futures (the "how"). Futures can be very volatile and risky, and you can possibly have a greater loss than the amount you used; therefore, limit your risk by using options.

What's that? You want to speculate on gold and silver by getting in call and put options on, say, gold and/or silver ETFs (the "what")? Sure, but I usually tell beginners (and beginning-intermediates) to use long-dated options. Many folks use options that typically expire in nine months or less. I prefer (especially for beginners) options such as LEAPs (long-term equity anticipation options), which is the "how."

Why? LEAPs typically expire in a year or longer, frequently much longer. As I write this in August 2020, I can find call and put options on many gold- and silver-related vehicles such as stocks and ETFs that expire in June 2022 (I found them on the Chicago Board Options Exchange at www.cboe.com). That is nearly two years of time value — cool!

All things being equal, buying an option expiring in, say, two years, is much less risky than an option expiring in three or six or nine months. But I bet you knew that. For more details on options, see Chapter 13. Futures are covered in Chapter 12.

Have Multiple Positions

When possible, have multiple positions on so that you have flexibility given market conditions, both current and expected. If, for example, you're bullish on gold and the call option you bought on it is profitable, you'll be asking yourself, "Gee, should I hold on or sell it?" Of course, there may be other factors at play, such as whether you need the money, see other opportunities, and so forth.

If you're bullish on gold, and if you have the cash, then consider multiple positions such as two or more call options (for example). That way, you're not in an "all or nothing" position. You have more flexibility. You can sell a portion of your position so you can have some cash "on the sidelines" that's ready for deployment on new opportunities.

REMEMBER

Of course, don't go ape and have 100 options on. But be diversified and have some cash on the side if possible so that you can take advantage of opportunities when the market ebbs and flows.

Use Technical Indicators

When you're investing (and I mean investing, not trading or speculating), you could probably do fundamental analysis all by itself and do very well because real investing is a long-term pursuit (measured in years and maybe decades). Some speculating can indeed be long term, but most speculating is short term (typically measured in months). Trading is almost exclusively short term (measured in days or weeks — and sometimes hours!).

TIP

Given that, serious short-term speculators and experienced traders will generally rely on technical analysis. Moving averages, charts, and volume data become very important. I personally don't trade that much, but I've done plenty of short-term and long-term speculating, so I take seriously data that helps see "oversold" and "overbought" conditions such as the relative strength index (RSI). For more details, head over to Chapter 15.

Do Some Hedging

When you see that your positions are doing extremely well, consider hedging. Hedging is basically a bet against your primary position or expectations; it's essentially a form of insurance if the market unexpectedly turns against you. Keep in mind that markets turning against you are typically unexpected turns!

Say that you have 20 call options you purchased recently on silver, for example, and that they are currently very profitable. Silver was on a tear, and at the moment, you're not sure whether it will continue or correct (pulling back or declining temporarily but still in a long-term bull market). Experienced folks start to hedge, even if only on a limited basis. Perhaps they'll write some covered calls or buy some short-term protective puts (see Chapter 13). Learn about hedging to protect positions.

By the way, if those calls are very profitable, consider the point in the next section.

Take a Profit

When you're investing, time is on your side, which is why "long term" is a vital component. Well-chosen investments (stocks, ETFs, mutual funds, and hard assets) will zigzag upward over time. Time helps you make money.

But shorter-term vehicles such as futures and options have a limited shelf life. Futures and options can be great for speculative wealth building, but they're no good at all for preserving that wealth. Given that, don't be hesitant with profit-taking to some extent.

If, for example, you have a profitable call option on silver futures and it's deep in the money (ITM) and expiring in the near future, cash it in ASAP. Take the profit before it declines significantly or evaporates outright. Fortunes can change rapidly with your futures and options positions, so take profits knowing that you can always add other positions just as readily.

Use Brokerage Orders

TIP

I'm adding an 11th item. Please utilize the various types of orders that are available with your brokerage account. I regularly use limit orders, stop-loss orders, and trailing stops in both my investing and (especially) in my speculating. These orders are very powerful and useful tools that can help you optimize gains and minimize losses. Find out more about them in Chapter 16 (covering brokers and their services).

6 Appendixes

Appendix A

Resources for Gold and Silver Investors

Getting and staying informed are ongoing priorities for gold and silver investors. The lists in this appendix represent some of the best information resources available.

Websites and Blogs

The first place investors and speculators should go is the websites and blogs that specialize in gold and silver. The more you know about the market, the better your decisions.

Gold Eagle
www.gold-eagle.com

Gold Seek
www.goldseek.com

Gold Silver blog
www.goldsilver.com

Jay Taylor
www.miningstocks.com

Kitco Blog
www.kitco.com

Kitco Silver
www.kitcosilver.com

Mine Web
www.mineweb.com

Precious Metals Investing Blog
www.preciousmetalsinvesting.com

Silver Doctors
www.silverdoctors.com

Sprott Media
www.sprottmedia.com

SRSROCCO Report
www.srsroccoreport.com

TF Metals Report
www.tfmetalsreport.com

321 Gold Blog
www.321gold.com

You can find more blogs by searching at the following sites:

Best of the Web's blog directory
www.blogs.Botw.org

Top 70 Gold Blogs, Websites & Influencers in 2020
https://blog.feedspot.com/gold_blogs

Top 25 Silver Blogs, Websites & Influencers in 2020
https://blog.feedspot.com/silver_blogs

Newsletters and Advisories

Here is a list of the top analysts and investors in gold and silver who also provide both free and paid information for site visitors and subscribers.

Bill Murphy
www.lemetropolecafe.com

David Morgan
www.themorganreport.com

Doug Casey
www.Internationalman.com

Egon von Greyerz
www.goldswitzerland.com

James West
www.midasletter.com

Jay Taylor
www.miningstocks.com

Jeff Clark
www.goldsilver.com

Martin Katusa
www.katusaresearch.com

Michael Maloney
www.goldsilver.com

Rick Rule
www.sprottmedia.com

Ted Butler
www.butlerresearch.com

Zeal LLC
www.zealllc.com

News and Commentary Sites for Gold and Silver Information

The following sites aren't gold/silver sites per se, but they do a great job with global economic news and views, and they frequently include gold and silver as a part of their overall reportage.

Benzinga
www.benzinga.com

Greg Hunter's USAWatchdog.com
www.usawatchdog.com

HoweStreet
www.howestreet.com

King World News
www.kingworldnews.com

Korelin Economics Report
www.kereport.com

Market Sanity
www.marketsanity.com

Mish's Global Economic Trend Analysis
www.mishtalk.com

Peak Prosperity
www.peakprosperity.com

SafeHaven
www.safehaven.com

Zero Hedge
www.zerohedge.com

Gold and Silver YouTube Channels

There are many great video commentaries, reports, and interviews about gold and silver, and YouTube has some great channels to keep you updated.

Arcadia Economics
www.youtube.com/user/ArcadiaEconomics

Gold Silver
www.youtube.com/user/whygoldandsilver

Palisade Radio
www.youtube.com/c/PalisadeRadio

Silver Bullion TV
www.youtube.com/c/SilverBullion

Silver Dragons
www.youtube.com/c/SilverDragons47

Books about Gold and Silver

Some of the best research available is in a convenient book (am I right?), and these books are perfect for those who want serious gold and silver info.

Guide to Investing in Gold & Silver: Protect Your Financial Future by Michael Maloney. Published by WealthCycle Press.

Michael Maloney is an eminent commentator on gold and silver, and this book deserves a spot on your bookshelf.

How to Invest in Gold & Silver: A Complete Guide with a Focus on Mining Stocks by Don Durrett. Published by Ten Books Publishing.

This book contains lots of great guidance on choosing mining stocks for the modern portfolio.

The Silver Manifesto by David Morgan and Chris Marchese. Published by PM Industries.

David Morgan is literally one of the top three silver experts in the world, and this book is excellent for beginners and intermediates.

Stack Silver Get Gold: How to Buy Gold and Silver Bullion without Getting Ripped Off! by Hunter Riley III. Published by B24 Group.

This book is a solid, practical guide on buying physical gold and silver.

Other Books of Interest to Gold and Silver Investors

Very often, gold and silver are counterplays to other markets and venues. The more you understand them, the better your precious metals moves.

The Coming Bond Market Collapse: How to Survive the Demise of the U.S. Debt Market by Michael G. Pento. Published by John Wiley & Sons, Inc.

The global bond market is a huge bubble that will send shock waves through stock markets and economies; Pento tells you why and what to do.

Crash Proof 2.0: How to Profit from the Economic Collapse by Peter D. Schiff with John Downes. Published by John Wiley & Sons, Inc.

A great "crash course" on the problems facing the modern economy and how to strategize with your portfolio.

The ETF Book: All You Need to Know About Exchange-Traded Funds by Richard A. Ferri. Published by John Wiley & Sons, Inc.

Considering the marketplace, exchange-traded funds (ETFs) are better choices than stocks for some investors, and this book does a good job of explaining them.

High-Level Investing For Dummies by Paul Mladjenovic. Published by John Wiley & Sons, Inc.

My shameless plug for another great book. Seriously, this book takes stock investing to the next level. I cover more strategies and resources on investing and speculating with stocks, ETFs, and options so you can find out what it takes to be with history's great investors and speculators.

The Money Bubble: What to do Before It Pops by James Turk and John Rubino. Published by DollarCollapse Press.

These are epic times as historic currency bubbles and crises unfold with serious consequences for stocks and other aspects of the financial picture. This book gives you great guidance for enhancing your financial safety.

Trade Associations and Industry Sources

Whenever you need industry news and views, demand-and-supply statistics, and other critical data, industry associations are a great source. Here are the major ones for gold and silver.

CPM Group
www.cpmgroup.com

Gold Anti-Trust Action Committee (GATA)
www.gata.org

Silver Institute
www.silverinstitute.org

World Gold Council
www.gold.org

Government Agencies

Whether you are looking for consumer guidance or want to understand the legal side of an industry, check out the relevant government agency that oversees it. Here are two critical ones.

Commodities Futures Trading Commission (CFTC; for futures)
www.CFTC.gov

Securities and Exchange Commission (SEC; for stocks and ETFs)
www.sec.gov

Gold and Silver ETFs

Although an extensive list of gold- and silver-related exchange-traded funds (ETFs) is in Appendix B, there are always new ETFs issued. If we're in a gold and silver bull market, the interest can drive the creation of new ETFs, and sites such as these will help you find and analyze them. (I discuss different types of ETFs in Chapters 8 and 11.)

ETF Daily News
www.etfdailynews.com

ETF Database
www.etfdb.com

ETF Trends
www.etftrends.com

ETFguide
http://etfguide.com

Gold and Silver Dealers

Before you start perusing the following list of bullion dealers, let me first insert info for the U.S. Mint in case you need questions answered about U.S.-issued gold/silver bullion coins (American Gold Eagles and American Silver Eagles) so you can know about the coins you're seeking to purchase.

United States Mint
Phone 1-800-USA-MINT
Consumer information
www.usmint.gov/news/consumer-alerts/consumer

Great! Now onto those dealers (see Chapter 9 for an introduction to bullion).

Ainslie Bullion
www.ainsliebullion.com.au/

Amagi Metals
Phone 1-800-578-4653
Website www.amagimetals.com

American Gold Exchange
Phone 1-800-613-9323
www.amergold.com

American Hartford Gold Group
Phone 1-800-462-0071
Websitewww.americanhartfordgold.com

Apmex
Phone 1-855-533-4131
Website www.apmex.com

BGASC.com
Phone 1-888-992-4272
Website www.bgasc.com

Blanchard Gold
Phone 1-888-568-4438
Website www.blanchardgold.com

Bullion Exchanges
Phone 212-354-1517
Website https://bullionexchanges.com

Bullion Trading LLC
Phone 212-997-2520
Website https://bulliontradingllc.com

CMI: Gold & Silver
Phone 1-855-217-5041
Website www.cmi-gold-silver.com

Gold Dealer
Phone 1-800-225-7531
Website www.golddealer.com

Goldco
Phone 1-855-233-2832
Website https://goldco.com

Golden State Mint
Phone 1-800-320-8260
Website www.goldenstatemint.com

Investment Rarities, Inc.
Phone 1-800-328-1860
Website www.investmentrarities.com

JM Bullion
Phone 1-800-276-6508
Website www.jmbullion.com

Kitco
Phone 1-877-775-4826
Website https://online.kitco.com

Money Metals Exchange
Phone 1-800-800-1865
Website www.moneymetals.com

Noble Gold Investments
Phone 1-877-646-5347
https://noblegoldinvestments.com

Patriot Gold Group
Phone 1-877-711-6522
Website www.patriotgoldgroup.com

Provident Metals
Phone 1-800-313-3315
Website www.providentmetals.com

Rosland Capital
Phone 1-800-685-0560
Website www.roslandcapital.com

SchiffGold
Phone 1-888-465-3160
Website https://schiffgold.com

Scottsdale Bullion & Coin
Phone 1-888-812-9892
Website www.sbcgold.com

SD Bullion
Phone 1-800-294-8732
Website https://sdbullion.com

Silver Gold Bull
Phone 1-877-628-5303
Website https://silvergoldbull.com

Silver.com
Phone 1-888-989-7223
Website www.silver.com

TexMetals.com
Phone 361-594-3624
Website www.texmetals.com

Buying Services

If you don't want to make a huge purchase in gold and silver and prefer a way to accumulate ownership in gold and silver especially geared to small investors, then you may want to check out the following sources.

GLINT
https://glintpay.com/en_us

Goldmoney
www.goldmoney.com

Own X
www.Ownx.com

Silver Token
www.silvertoken.com

Futures and Options Resources

When you're ready to speculate in gold and silver through futures and options, then these are some of the best places to start. I list industry groups (they have great educational resources) as well as an industry pro who has educated my students and clients on futures.

Chicago Board Options Exchange (CBOE)
www.cboe.com

CME Group (operates NYMEX/COMEX and CBOT)
www.cmegroup.com

Options Industry Council (OIC)
www.optionseducation.org

Charles Nedoss
www.lasallefuturesgroup.com
www.buyaput.com

Cryptocurrencies Related to Gold and Silver

In recent years, cryptocurrencies established themselves as viable choices along with traditional investment and speculative vehicles. The top gold-backed cryptocurrencies are

» Digix Gold Tokens (DGX)

» GoldMint (MNTP/GOLD)

» Xaurum (XAUR)

» PAX Gold (PAXG)

Here are sites that provide information and guidance for "crypto" beginners and for experienced folks.

Bitcoin Exchange Guide

www.bitcoinexchangeguide.com

Cointelligence

www.cointelligence.com

Cointelligence also has an extensive listing of gold-backed cryptocurrencies at www.cointelligence.com/content/gold-backed-cryptocurrency

Crypto Rating

www.Crypto-rating.com

Cryptocurrency Investing For Dummies by Kiana Danial (published by Wiley)

Note: While there are gold-backed cryptocurrencies, a stable, established silver-backed cryptocurrency is yet to emerge. But when it does, the preceding sources will likely be among the first to report on it.

Technical Analysis

Because so many want to participate in gold and silver as short-term plays, technical analysis becomes a necessary tool. Here are some of the better resources for this (see Chapter 15 for details).

Big Charts (provided by MarketWatch)
https://bigcharts.marketwatch.com

Chris Vermeulen
www.thetechnicaltraders.com

Clive Maund
www.clivemaund.com

Elliott Wave International
www.elliottwave.com

Robert McHugh, PhD
www.technicalindicatorindex.com

Slope of Hope
www.slopeofhope.com

Stock Technical Analysis
www.stockta.com

StockCharts.com
www.stockcharts.com

Brokers

When you're ready to buy securities such as stocks and ETFs, you'll do so in a brokerage account. Here are the top stock brokerage firms (see Chapter 16 for more information).

Ally Financial
Phone 1-855-880-2559
Website www.ally.com

Charles Schwab & Co.
Phone 1-800-435-4000
Website www.schwab.com

E*TRADE
Phone 1-800-387-2331
Website www.etrade.com

Edward D. Jones & Co.
Phone 314-515-3265
Website www.edwardjones.com

Fidelity Brokerage Services
Phone 1-800-343-3548
Website www.fidelity.com

Merrill Lynch
Phone 1-800-637-7455
Website www.ml.com

Morgan Stanley
Phone 1-888-454-3965
Website www.morganstanley.com

Muriel Siebert & Co.
Phone 1-800-872-0444
Website www.siebertnet.com

TD Ameritrade
Phone 1-800-669-3900
Website www.tdameritrade.com

Thinkorswim
Phone 1-866-839-1100
Website www.thinkorswim.com

Vanguard Brokerage Services
Phone 1-877-662-7447
Website https://investor.vanguard.com/home

Wall Street Access
Phone 1-800-709-5929
Website www.wsaccess.com

Wells Fargo Securities
Phone 1-866-224-5708
Website www.wellsfargoadvisors.com

Appendix B

Gold and Silver Investments

After reading all the great information and wisdom in the rest of this book, what better way to end than to provide a list of the major gold and silver investments (stocks and exchange-traded funds, or ETFs) for your consideration? Just do your homework before investing your first dollar.

The layout of each table is that the stock symbol is first and then the name. This appendix is limited mostly to major stocks and ETFs listed on the New York Stock Exchange (NYSE). To find junior mining stocks, you can do a search at www.nasdaq.com and www.otcbb.com. You can also use the resources in Appendix A to help you find and analyze these vehicles.

TIP

To find the top junior mining stocks, consider looking at the holdings of an ETF (or mutual fund) that has a portfolio of junior mining stocks. Some junior mining stock ETFs are in the listings later in this appendix.

REMEMBER

The following tables are provided as a start for your research, not a list of recommendations. Please do your due diligence and research your mining stock choices regarding their fundamental data, prospects, and so on before making any investment decision.

Major Gold Mining Stocks

The stocks in Table B-1 are on the New York Stock Exchange (NYSE).

Major Gold Mining Stocks on the NYSE

Symbol	Name
GOLD	Barrick Gold Corp Stock
GS	Goldman Sachs Group Inc Stock
NEM	Newmont Goldcorp Corp Stock
FCX	Freeport-McMoran Copper & Gold Inc Stock
HMY	Harmony Gold Mining Company Limited Stock
GFI	Gold Fields Ltd ADR Stock
KGC	Kinross Gold Corp Stock
AUY	Yamana Gold Inc Stock
SBSW	Sibanye Gold Ltd ADR Stock
SAND	Sandstorm Gold Ltd N Stock
VGZ	Vista Gold Corporation Stock
GORO	Gold Resource Corporation Stock
AUMN	Golden Minerals Company Stock
PZG	Paramount Gold Nevada Corp Stock
ASA	ASA Gold and Precious Metals Ltd Stock
SA	Seabridge Gold Inc Stock
AGI	Alamos Gold Inc Stock
EGO	Eldorado Gold Corp Stock
KL	Kirkland Lake Gold Ltd Stock
OR	Osisko Gold Ro Stock
EQX	Equinox Gold Corp Stock
USAS	Americas Gold and Silver Corp Stock

Major Silver Mining Stocks

The stocks in Table B-2 are on the New York Stock Exchange (NYSE).

TABLE B-2

Major Silver Mining Stocks on the NYSE

Symbol	Company Name
WPM	Wheaton Precious Metals Corp Stock
AG	First Majestic Silver Corp Stock
SBOW	SilverBow Resources Inc Stock
MAG	MAG Silver Corp Stock
GPL	Great Panther Silver Ltd Stock
ASM	Avino Silver & Gold Mines Ltd Stock
FSM	Fortuna Silver Mines Inc Stock
EXK	Endeavour Silver Corp Stock
SVM	Silvercorp Metals Inc Stock
SILV	SilverCrest Metals Inc Stock

Gold-Related ETFs

All of the ETFs in Table B-3 are located on the New York Stock Exchange (NYSE) unless otherwise noted (such as Nasdaq or OTC Markets).

TABLE B-3   **Gold-Related ETFs**

Symbol	Company Name
CEF	Sprott Physical Gold and Silver Trust
GDX	VanEck Vectors Gold Miners ETF
GDXJ	VanEck Vectors Junior Gold Miners ETF
GLD	SPDR Gold Shares ETF
DZZ	DB Gold Double Short ETN ETF
GLL	ProShares UltraShort Gold ETF
DGP	DB Gold Double Long ETN ETF
GLDM	SPDR Gold MiniShares ETF
BAR	GraniteShares Gold Trust ETF
GOAU	U.S. Global GO GOLD and Precious Metal Miners ETF
IAUF	iShares Gold Strategy ETF
AAAU	Perth Mint Physical Gold ETF
GBUG	Barclays Bank iPath Gold ETN ETF
DUST	Direxion Daily Gold Miners Index Bear 2X Shares ETF
GOEX	Global X Gold Explorers ETF
PGJ	Invesco Golden Dragon China ETF — Nasdaq
DGL	Invesco DB Gold Fund ETF
DGZ	DB Gold Short ETN ETF
NUGT	Direxion Daily Gold Miners Index Bull 2X Shares ETF
UBG	UBS ETRACS CMCI Gold Total Return ETN ETF
RING	iShares MSCI Global Gold Miners ETF — Nasdaq
JDST	Direxion Daily Junior Gold Miners Index Bear 2X Shares ETF
JNUG	Direxion Daily Junior Gold Miners Index Bull 2X Shares ETF
SGDJ	Sprott Junior Gold Miners ETF
GLDI	Credit Suisse X-Links Gold Shares Covered Call ETN ETF
OUNZ	VanEck Merk Gold Trust ETF
SGDM	Sprott Gold Miners ETF
DGLDF	VelocityShares 3x Inverse Gold ETN Linked to the S&P GSCI Gold Index ER ETF — OTC Markets
UGLDF	VelocityShares 3x Long Gold ETN Linked to the S&P GSCI Gold Index ER ETF — OTC Markets

Silver-Related ETFs

All of the ETFs in Table B-4 are located on the New York Stock Exchange (NYSE) unless otherwise noted (such as Nasdaq or OTC Markets).

TABLE B-4   **Silver-Related ETFs**

Symbol	Company Name
CEF	Sprott Physical Gold and Silver Trust
USV	UBS ETRACS CMCI Silver Total Return ETN ETF
SILJ	ETFMG Prime Junior Silver Miners ETF
SLVO	Credit Suisse X-Links Silver Shares Covered Call ETN ETF — Nasdaq
SIL	Global X Silver Miners ETF
SBUG	Barclays Bank iPath Silver ETN ETF
DBS	Invesco DB Silver Fund ETF
SLVP	iShares MSCI Global Silver and Metals Miners ETF
SIVR	Aberdeen Standard Physical Silver Shares ETF
PSLV	Sprott Physical Silver ETF
ZSL	ProShares UltraShort Silver ETF
AGQ	ProShares Ultra Silver ETF
SLV	iShares Silver Trust ETF
DSLVF	VelocityShares 3x Inverse Silver ETN Linked to the S&P GSCI Silver Index ER ETF — OTC Markets
USLVF	VelocityShares 3x Long Silver ETN Linked to the S&P GSCI Silver Index ER ETF — OTC Markets

Mutual Funds

For guidance on mutual funds, check out Chapter 8; major gold and silver mutual funds are listed there. To locate even more gold- and silver-related mutual fund choices, here are great resources to help you. Each source has a searchable database for locating funds.

>> Mutual Fund Directory (https://mutualfunddirectory.org/)

>> InvestorGuide.com (www.investorguide.com/mutual-fund-list.php)

>> MutualFunds.com (www.mutualfunds.com)

>> Investment Company Institute (www.ici.org)

Index

C

gold versus, 46
investing essentials, 70–71
investing for income, 27
portfolio, adding to, 266
risk management tools, 38
speculating on, 23
trading, 23
trading vehicles, choosing, 193
stop orders, 238–239
stop-loss orders
for leveraged ETFs, 136
as risk management tool, 38–39, 79
trailing stops, 226–227
straddle options combination, 179–180
straight cancel order, 239
strategy for trading, choosing, 193–196
strike price, 171
supply of precious metals, 49, 59
support, 208–209
symmetrical triangle chart pattern, 212
systemic financial risks, 30

T

taxes
for active traders, 249
capital gains and losses, 246–247
deductions, 247–248
IRAs, 246, 252–254
overview, 243–244
on physical gold and silver purchases, 223
planning for, 251
precious metals IRAs, 252–254
on regular investment accounts, 244–246
resources, 250–251
short term versus long term trading, 218
special considerations, 248–249
Taylor, Jay, 83
technical analysis
Bollinger bands, 217
channel lines, 207–208
chart patterns, 210–213

charts, types of, 209–210
crossovers, 216
defining, 202
divergence, 216
fundamental analysis versus, 202–205
futures, using with, 162–164
general discussion, 203–204
indicators, 215–217
MACD, 216
moving averages, 213–215
oscillators, 215
overview, 201–202
resistance and support, 208–209
resources, 290–291
RSI, 215–216
short term versus long term trading, 217–218
for speculating and trading, 275
technical analysis, 218
tools of, 205
trend lines, 207
trends, identifying, 205–209
Technical Stuff icon, 3
technology demand, for gold, 48
ten-day moving average, 214
theft, 19, 31, 107
thinly traded markets, 31
time condition orders, 237–238
time value of options, 171–172
Tip icon, 2
Tocqueville Gold Fund, 88
trade associations, 284
trade preprogramming, 227
trade triggers, 227
trading
contrarian approach, 136–138, 273
defined, 23
focusing on specialty, 272
futures, 158–161
futures trading coupled with options, 195–196
gold-to-silver ratio, 196–199
hedging, 275–276
investing versus, 190

About the Author

Paul Mladjenovic is a certified financial planner (CFP), national seminar leader, author, and consultant. Since 1981, he has specialized in investing, financial planning, and home business issues. During those nearly four decades, he has helped hundreds of thousands of students and readers build wealth through his nationwide seminars, workshops, conferences, and coaching program. Paul has been a CFP since June 1985 (more than 35 years).

Besides this book, Paul has written *Stock Investing For Dummies* (all six editions), *High-Level Investing For Dummies*, *Micro-Entrepreneurship For Dummies*, *Zero-Cost Marketing*, *Precious Metals Investing For Dummies*, and *The Job Hunter's Encyclopedia*. In 2019, he coauthored *Affiliate Marketing For Dummies*. His national (and online) seminars include "The $50 Wealth-Builder," "Ultra-Investing with Options," and the "Home Business Goldmine," among others. The full details on his (downloadable) financial and business start-up audio/video seminars can be found at www.RavingCapitalist.com. A page at this site (www.RavingCapitalist.com/goldsilver) provides resources and views to help readers navigate today's uncertain markets and gives them a venue for questions. His online courses can also be found at educational venues such as Udemy.com, Skillshare.com, Freeu.com, and MtAiryLearningTree.org.

Since 2000, Paul has built a reputation as an accurate economics and market forecaster. His long record includes accurate forecasts of the housing bubble, the energy crisis, the Great Recession, the rise of precious metals, and much more. He has been interviewed or referenced by numerous media sources, such as Comcast, CNN, MarketWatch, Bloomberg, OANN, Fox Business, Futures magazine, Kitco, GoldSeek.com, Investopedia, Minyanville.com, FinancialSense.com, PreciousMetalsInvesting.com, and other media venues.

You can view Paul's profile at www.linkedin.com/in/paulmladjenovic, follow him at www.twitter.com/paulmlad, and also check out the author's page at www.amazon.com/author/paulmladjenovic. Readers can email questions or inquiries directly to paul@mladjenovic.com or at the bio page at www.RavingCapitalist.com.

Dedication

I dedicate this with endless love to my wife, Fran, and my boys, Joshua and Adam. Your support and prayers helped me through this beyond words. You fill my heart and mind with joy and gratitude.

I also dedicate this to Slavko. You were a magnificent example of being an angel bringing joy to those around you in ways too numerous to count. God bless you, my beautiful brother. Please keep guiding your family and friends from Heaven!

Author's Acknowledgments

Wow! Another book in the pipeline — how thrilling! But a fantastic team made this happen, a group for whom I have tremendous admiration and gratitude. The diligent and professional team at Wiley did it again, and I am super appreciative! They are proof that quality books come from quality people. I wish each and every one of them health, joy, and a successful future, with all my mind and heart! I will always cheer them on!

And those wonderful folks include Michelle Hacker, my project manager, and the best in the business! She is a fantastic editor and manager who helped me through a tough and tight schedule, and she kept me sane during the crunch. Her professionalism, expertise, and calm demeanor are the reasons I always ask for her by name. God bless you, Michelle. Keep being you, and thank you for being magnificent! (And don't forget to get some gold and silver!)

I don't know why Georgette Beatty says yes when I ask for her, but I am always thrilled when she is on my team! She could easily work with better authors than a troglodyte like me, but I am grateful for her professionalism, expertise, and ability to take my junkyard-style prose and make it into the readable and enjoyable text and style that Dummies readers expect. Thank you, Georgette, and God bless you and your family! I will always cheer you on, too!

Jennette ElNaggar, you complement the team so well, and I appreciate your hard work making this book a worthy endeavor. I hope to work with you again, and I wish you continued success!

The technical editor, Ted Sudol, kept me on point with my content. His great analysis, constructive comments, and suggestions were superb, and this is why his site PreciousMetalsInvesting.com is so darn good! Thank you — keep being great!

With deep and joyful gratitude, I thank Tracy Boggier, my superb acquisitions editor. Thank you so much for being my champion at Wiley and shepherding yet another *For Dummies* guide for me to author, and I can't express enough appreciation for all that you do. *For Dummies* books are great, and they appear on your bookshelf only through the planning and professional efforts of publishing pros like Tracy.

I am grateful to Sheree Bykofsky, my longtime book agent and dear friend. This year marks my 20th year with you, and you have been magnificent through every minute. Thank you for your expertise, guidance, and hard work. God bless you and your family!

Fran, Lipa Zyenska, I thank you and my boys, Adam and Joshua, with all my heart for your support and for being my number one fans throughout the writing of this book. I am grateful to have you by my side always! I thank God for you, and I love you beyond words!

Lastly, I want to acknowledge you, the reader. Over the years, you've made the *For Dummies* series the popular and indispensable books they are today. Thank you, and I wish you continued success!

Publisher's Acknowledgments

Senior Acquisitions Editor: Tracy Boggier

Project Manager: Michelle Hacker

Development Editor: Georgette Beatty

Copy Editor: Jennette ElNaggar

Technical Editor: Ted Sudol, www.preciousmetalsinvesting.com

Production Editor: Mohammed Zafar Ali

Cover Image: © Inok/Getty Images

Leverage the power

Dummies is the global leader in the reference category and one of the most trusted and highly regarded brands in the world. No longer just focused on books, customers now have access to the dummies content they need in the format they want. Together we'll craft a solution that engages your customers, stands out from the competition, and helps you meet your goals.

Advertising & Sponsorships

Connect with an engaged audience on a powerful multimedia site, and position your message alongside expert how-to content. Dummies.com is a one-stop shop for free, online information and know-how curated by a team of experts.

- Targeted ads
- Video
- Email Marketing

- Microsites
- Sweepstakes sponsorship

20 MILLION PAGE VIEWS EVERY SINGLE MONTH

15 MILLION UNIQUE VISITORS PER MONTH

43% OF ALL VISITORS ACCESS THE SITE VIA THEIR MOBILE DEVICES

700,000 NEWSLETTER SUBSCRIPTIONS TO THE INBOXES OF

300,000 UNIQUE INDIVIDUALS EVERY WEEK

# of dummies

Custom Publishing

Reach a global audience in any language by creating a solution that will differentiate you from competitors, amplify your message, and encourage customers to make a buying decision.

- Apps
- Books
- eBooks
- Video
- Audio
- Webinars

Brand Licensing & Content

Leverage the strength of the world's most popular reference brand to reach new audiences and channels of distribution.

For more information, visit dummies.com/biz

PERSONAL ENRICHMENT

Staying Sharp	Facebook	Guitar	Investing	Beekeeping	Digital Photography
9781119187790	9781119179030	9781119293354	9781119293347	9781119310068	9781119235606
USA $26.00	USA $21.99	USA $24.99	USA $22.99	USA $22.99	USA $24.99
CAN $31.99	CAN $25.99	CAN $29.99	CAN $27.99	CAN $27.99	CAN $29.99
UK £19.99	UK £16.99	UK £17.99	UK £16.99	UK £16.99	UK £17.99

Meditation	Pregnancy	Samsung Galaxy S7	iPhone	Crocheting	Nutrition
9781119251163	9781119235491	9781119279952	9781119283133	9781119287117	9781119130246
USA $24.99	USA $26.99	USA $24.99	USA $24.99	USA $24.99	USA $22.99
CAN $29.99	CAN $31.99	CAN $29.99	CAN $29.99	CAN $29.99	CAN $27.99
UK £17.99	UK £19.99	UK £17.99	UK £17.99	UK £16.99	UK £16.99

PROFESSIONAL DEVELOPMENT

Windows 10	AutoCAD	Excel 2016	QuickBooks 2017	macOS Sierra	LinkedIn	Windows 10
9781119311041	9781119255796	9781119293439	9781119281467	9781119280651	9781119251132	9781119310563
USA $24.99	USA $39.99	USA $26.99	USA $26.99	USA $29.99	USA $24.99	USA $34.00
CAN $29.99	CAN $47.99	CAN $31.99	CAN $31.99	CAN $35.99	CAN $29.99	CAN $41.99
UK £17.99	UK £27.99	UK £19.99	UK £19.99	UK £21.99	UK £17.99	UK £24.99

SharePoint 2016	Fundamental Analysis	Networking	Office 2016	Office 365	Salesforce.com	Coding
9781119181705	9781119263593	9781119257769	9781119293477	9781119265313	9781119239314	9781119293323
USA $29.99	USA $26.99	USA $29.99	USA $26.99	USA $24.99	USA $29.99	USA $29.99
CAN $35.99	CAN $31.99	CAN $35.99	CAN $31.99	CAN $29.99	CAN $35.99	CAN $35.99
UK £21.99	UK £19.99	UK £21.99	UK £19.99	UK £17.99	UK £21.99	UK £21.99